SCAT

SCAT

CARL HIAASEN

THORNDIKE PRESS
A part of Gale, a Cengage Company

Copyright © 2009 by Carl Hiaasen.
Thorndike Press, a part of Gale, a Cengage Company.

Thorndike Press® Large Print Striving Reader Collection.
The text of this Large Print edition is unabridged.
Other aspects of the book may vary from the original edition.
Set in 16 pt. Plantin.

LIBRARY OF CONGRESS CIP DATA ON FILE.
CATALOGUING IN PUBLICATION FOR THIS BOOK
IS AVAILABLE FROM THE LIBRARY OF CONGRESS

ISBN-13: 978-1-4328-7550-3 (hardcover alk. paper)

Published in 2020 by arrangement with Random House Children's Books, a division of Penguin Random House, LLC

Printed in Mexico
Print Number: 01   Print Year: 2020

This is dedicated to the memory of
Dr. David Maehr, a gifted wildlife biologist
who helped me during the research for
this book. Dave spent many years
tracking and studying Florida's
endangered panthers. Because of
his efforts, and those of others who
followed, these magnificent cats still
roam wild in the swamps and prairies
of southern Florida.

ONE

The day before Mrs. Starch vanished, her third-period biology students trudged silently, as always, into the classroom. Their expressions reflected the usual mix of dread and melancholy, for Mrs. Starch was the most feared teacher at the Truman School.

When the bell rang, she unfolded stiffly, like a crane, and rose to her full height of nearly six feet. In one hand she twirled a sharpened Ticonderoga No. 2 pencil, a sure sign of trouble to come.

Nick glanced across the aisle at Marta Gonzalez. Her brown eyes were locked on Mrs. Starch, and her thin elbows were planted like fence posts, pinning her biology book open to Chapter 8. Nick had left his own textbook in his locker, and his palms were sweating.

"Good morning, people," said Mrs. Starch, in a tone so mild that it was chilling. "Who's prepared to tell me about the

Calvin cycle?"

Only one hand rose. It belonged to Graham, who always claimed to know the answers but never did. Mrs. Starch hadn't called on him since the first week of class.

"The Calvin cycle," she repeated. "Anybody?"

Marta looked as if she might throw up again. The last time that had happened, Mrs. Starch had barely waited until the floor was mopped before instructing Marta to write a paper listing five major muscles used in the act of regurgitation.

Nick and the other students had been blown away. What kind of teacher would punish a kid for puking?

"By now," Mrs. Starch was saying, "the photosynthetic process should be familiar to all of you."

Marta gulped hard, twice. She'd been having nightmares about Mrs. Starch, who wore her dyed blond hair piled to one side of her head, like a beach dune. Mrs. Starch's school wardrobe never varied: a polyester pants suit in one of four faded pastel colors, and drab brown flats. She painted heavy violet makeup on her eyelids, yet she made no effort to conceal an odd crimson mark on her chin. The mark was the shape of an anvil and the subject of wild speculation,

8

but nobody had gotten up the nerve to ask Mrs. Starch about it.

Marta's eyes flicked miserably toward Nick, then back to the teacher. Nick was fond of Marta, although he wasn't sure if he liked her enough to sacrifice himself to Mrs. Starch, who had begun to pace. She was scanning the class, selecting a victim.

A droplet of perspiration glided like a spider down Nick's neck. If he worked up the courage to raise his hand, Mrs. Starch would pounce swiftly. Right away she'd see that he had forgotten his biology book, a crime that would be forgiven only if Nick was able to explain and then diagram the Calvin cycle, which was unlikely. Nick was still struggling to figure out the Krebs cycle from Chapter 7.

"Plants, as we all know, are vital to human existence," said Mrs. Starch, on patrol. "And without the Calvin cycle, plants could not exist. Could not exist . . ."

Graham was waving his arm and squirming like a puppy. The rest of the class prayed that Mrs. Starch would call on him, but she acted as if he were invisible. Abruptly she spun to a halt at the front of Marta's row.

Marta sat rigidly in the second desk, behind a brainy girl named Libby who knew all about the Calvin cycle — all about *every-*

thing — but seldom made a peep.

"The chart on page 169," Mrs. Starch went on, "makes it all plain as day. It's an excellent illustration, and one that you are likely to encounter on a test. Quite likely . . ."

Marta lowered her head, a tactical mistake. The movement, slight as it was, caught Mrs. Starch's attention.

Nick sucked in a breath. His heart raced and his head buzzed, because he knew that it was now or never. Marta seemed to shrink under Mrs. Starch's icy gaze. Nick could see tears forming at the corners of Marta's eyes, and he hated himself for hesitating.

"Come on, people, snap out of your coma," Mrs. Starch chided, tapping the pencil on Libby's desk. "The Calvin cycle?"

The only reply was a ripping noise — Marta's trembling elbows, tearing holes in the pages of her book.

Mrs. Starch frowned. "I was hoping for a sea of hands," she said with a disappointed sigh. "But, once again, it seems I'll have to pick a volunteer. An unwilling volunteer . . ."

As the teacher pointed her pencil at the top of Marta's head, Nick raised his hand.

I'm toast, he thought. *She's gonna crush me like a bug.*

Lowering his eyes, he braced to hear Mrs.

Starch call his name.

"Oh, Duane?" she sang out.

Great, Nick thought. *She forgot who I am.*

But when he looked up, he saw the teacher aiming her pencil at another kid on the other side of the classroom. The mean old bird had totally faked him out, and Marta, too.

The other kid's name really *was* Duane, and Nick had known him since elementary school, when he was two years ahead of Nick and known as Duane the Dweeb. One summer, Duane the Dweeb grew five inches and gained thirty-one pounds, and from then on everybody called him Smoke, because that's what he wanted to be called. Some kids said it was because he was a pyro.

"So, Duane," Mrs. Starch said sweetly. "Have you finished Chapter 8?"

Rumpled and sleepy-looking, Smoke grunted and raised his eyes toward the teacher. Nick couldn't see his expression, but the slump of his shoulders suggested a profound lack of interest.

"Duane?"

"I guess I read it, yeah."

"You guess?" Using a thumb and two fingers, Mrs. Starch spun the yellow pencil into a blur, like a miniature airplane propeller. Under less stressful circumstances it

11

would have been entertaining.

"I read so much," Smoke said, "I forget which is which."

Several students struggled to smother giggles.

Marta reached across the aisle, nudged Nick, and mouthed the words "Thank you."

Nick felt his face redden.

"For raising your hand," Marta whispered.

Nick shrugged. "No big deal," he whispered back.

Mrs. Starch moved across the classroom and positioned herself beside Smoke's desk. "I see you brought your biology book today," she said. "That's progress, Duane."

"I guess."

"But you'll find that it's much easier to read when it's not upside down." Mrs. Starch rotated the textbook, using the eraser end of her No. 2 pencil.

Smoke nodded. "Yeah, that's better."

He tried to flip open the book, but Mrs. Starch pressed down firmly with the pencil, holding the cover closed.

"No peeking," she said. "Tell me how the Calvin cycle produces sugar from carbon dioxide, and why that's so important to photosynthesis."

"Gimme a minute." Smoke casually began to pick at a nasty-looking zit on his meaty,

12

fuzz-covered neck.

Mrs. Starch said, "We're all waiting," which was true. The other students, including Nick and Marta, were on the edge of their seats. They were aware that something major and possibly legendary was about to occur, though they had no clue that within forty-eight hours they would each be questioned by sheriff's deputies and asked to tell what they'd seen and heard.

Smoke wasn't as tall as Mrs. Starch, but he was built like a bull. His size and attitude intimidated all of his classmates and most of his teachers, though not Mrs. Starch. When Smoke tried to flick her pencil off his book, it didn't budge.

He leaned back, cracked his knuckles, and said, "What's the question again?"

Marta groaned under her breath. Nick gnawed his upper lip. The longer Smoke stalled, the worse it was going to be when Mrs. Starch lowered the boom.

"For the last time," she said coldly, "tell us about the Calvin cycle."

"Is that like a Harley?" Smoke asked, and the students erupted in laughter.

They grew quiet just as quickly, because Mrs. Starch was smiling — and Mrs. Starch *never* smiled.

Marta covered her face. "Has he got a

death wish, or what?" she said to Nick, who had a bad feeling about the whole scene.

"So, Duane, it turns out you're a comedian!" Mrs. Starch said. "And all this time we thought you were just another dull lump with no talent and no future."

"I guess," said Smoke, who had resumed probing his inflamed blemish.

"You do a lot of guessing, don't you?"

"So what?"

"Well, *I* am guessing that you haven't even glanced at Chapter 8," said Mrs. Starch. "Am I right?"

"Yeah."

"And I'm also guessing that you're more interested in playing with your acne than you are in learning the photosynthetic process."

Smoke's hand came off his neck and dropped to his side.

Looming over him, Mrs. Starch said, "A teacher's job is to identify and cultivate each student's strengths, and then encourage him or her to utilize those strengths in the pursuit of knowledge."

There wasn't a trace of anger in her voice, which Nick found creepy.

"So, Duane," she continued, "what I'd like you to do — since you're obviously fascinated by the subject — is to write a five-hundred-word essay about pimples."

The class cracked up again — Nick and Marta, too, in spite of themselves. This time the kids couldn't stop laughing.

Mrs. Starch waited before continuing. "You should start with some basic human biology — what causes glandular skin eruptions in adolescents? There's plenty of information on the Internet, Duane, so I'll expect at least three source citations. The second part of the paper should summarize the history of acne, both medically and in popular culture. And then the last section could deal with your own personal pimple, the one with which you seem so enchanted."

Smoke stared darkly at Mrs. Starch.

"And here's the best part, Duane," she said. "I want the essay to be funny, because you're a funny fellow. An extremely funny fellow."

"Not me."

"Oh, don't be modest. You had everybody in stitches just a moment ago." Mrs. Starch turned her back on Smoke and bobbed the pencil gaily in the air. "Come on, people, what do you say? Wouldn't it be amusing for Duane to write a humorous essay on pimples and then read it aloud to the whole class?"

Nobody was giggling anymore, and even

Graham had yanked down his hand. Smoke wasn't a popular kid, but it was impossible not to feel sorry for him. Mrs. Starch was being exceptionally brutal, even for Mrs. Starch.

Marta looked queasy again, and Nick was starting to feel the same way. Smoke was a loner and definitely freaky, but he never hassled anybody as long as he was given plenty of space.

"Nick?" Mrs. Starch said.

Nick sagged at his desk and thought: *I can't believe this.*

"Mr. Waters, are you with us today?"

"Yes, Mrs. Starch."

"Be honest — wouldn't you and your classmates enjoy hearing Duane read his pimple paper?"

Nick's chin dropped to his chest. If he answered yes, he'd risk making a mortal enemy of Smoke. If he answered no, Mrs. Starch would pick on him mercilessly for the rest of the school year.

He wished that he could make himself faint, or maybe swallow his own tongue. An ambulance ride would be better than this.

"Well?" Mrs. Starch prodded.

Nick tried to think of something to say that would free Smoke from doing the essay and at the same time not anger Mrs. Starch.

"Honestly, I'd rather learn about the Calvin cycle," he said, "than Duane's zits."

A few students snickered nervously.

"No offense," Nick added, with a lame nod to Smoke, who sat expressionless.

Mrs. Starch showed no mercy. She spun around and tapped Smoke on the crown of his head. "Five hundred words," she said, "by the end of the week."

Smoke scowled. "I don't think so."

"Excuse me?"

"It ain't fair."

"Really? Is it fair for you to come to my class so unprepared and hopelessly unfamiliar with the study material? To waste my time, and that of your fellow students — you think *that's* fair, Duane?"

Smoke brushed a shock of jet-black hair out of his eyes. "I 'pologize, 'kay? Now just let it go."

Mrs. Starch bent down slowly, peering like a heron about to spear a minnow. "Well, what happened to our class comedian?" she asked. "Are you all out of jokes?"

"I guess."

"That's too bad, because I expect five hundred hilarious words — double-spaced."

"No way," Smoke said.

Mrs. Starch positioned the tip of the

pencil so that it was even with the tip of his nose.

"Way," she said.

Nick looked anxiously at Marta, who had closed her biology book and laid her head upon the desk.

Smoke took a swat at the pencil, but Mrs. Starch jerked it away.

"Get outta my face," he said, "or else you'll be sorry."

"Is that a threat, Duane?" Mrs. Starch didn't sound too worried.

Smoke said, "Ain't a threat. It's a fact."

"No, here's a fact." Once more she leveled her pencil at his nose. "You *will* write a five-hundred-word essay about pimples and you *will* read it aloud to all of us, or you *will* fail this class and have to take it again next year. Do you understand?"

Smoke crossed his eyes as he stared down the yellow shaft of Mrs. Starch's No. 2 Ticonderoga.

"I guess," he said.

Then he calmly chomped the pencil in half, chewed up the graphite along with the splinters, and swallowed the whole mouthful with a husky gulp.

Mrs. Starch backed away, eyeing with alarm the moist stump of wood that remained in her fingers.

18

Nobody else in the room moved a muscle except for Smoke, who dropped his biology book into a camo-patterned backpack, stood up, and ambled out the door.

TWO

As they were walking home from the bus stop, Nick told Marta: "It's not over between those two. You just wait."

"I am *so* glad there's no class tomorrow," she said. "I can't deal with it — she's a witch and he's a total moron."

The science classes were taking an all-day field trip to the Black Vine Swamp, which was way out near the Big Cypress Preserve. Mrs. Starch herself had picked the location, describing it as "a festival of photosynthesis." The swamp was famous for exotic orchids and ancient cypress trees, but Nick was hoping to see a panther.

"We'll probably catch malaria from the mosquitoes," Marta said, "but it can't possibly be more painful than her stupid biology class."

Nick laughed. "We haven't had rain for two weeks. There won't be many mosquitoes."

"Spiders, then. Whatever." Marta waved and turned up the driveway of her house.

Nick lived three blocks away, in the same subdivision. His house was actually closer to the bus stop, but lately he'd been taking the long way home so that he could walk with Marta.

From the front step, she called back to him: "Hey, do you think he'll show up for the field trip?"

"Smoke?"

"Who else?"

Nick said, "I hope not."

"Me, too." Marta waved once more and disappeared through the doorway.

As soon as Nick got home, he hurried to the computer in the den and checked his e-mail. He was waiting to hear from his father, a captain in the National Guard who for the last seven months had been stationed in the Anbar province of Iraq.

Nick's dad e-mailed almost every morning, but Nick and his mother hadn't heard from him in three days. This had happened before, when his father was on a field mission with his unit. Nick tried not to let himself worry.

His mom was a guard at the Collier County Jail. She got off work at 4:30 in the afternoon and was usually home by 5:15 at

21

the latest. Nick stayed at the computer, researching an English paper and rechecking his e-mail every few minutes. By the time his mother came in the door, he'd still heard nothing from his father.

"How was your day?" his mom asked.

"Some kid ate Mrs. Starch's pencil. You wouldn't believe it," Nick said. "Gobbled it right out of her hand."

"Any particular reason?"

"He was mad, I guess. She made fun of a big ol' gnarly zit on his neck."

Nick's mother set her purse heavily on the kitchen counter. "Tell me again why we're spending all this money on a private school."

"Wasn't my idea," Nick reminded her. "Smaller classes?"

"That was one reason."

"And better teachers, you said."

"So we'd been told."

"And the low Freak Factor," Nick added.

"Right." His mother frowned. "And now you're telling me there's a boy in biology who thinks he's a termite."

"More like a beaver," Nick said. "But Mrs. Starch shouldn't have made fun of him. He's not a kid you want to mess with."

Nick's mother took a bottle of V8 juice from the refrigerator and emptied it into a small glass.

"What's the pencil-eater's name?" she asked.

"Duane Scrod. You don't know him."

"Spelled S-c-r-o-d?"

Nick said, "Yeah, that's right."

"Then it's Duane Scrod Jr. I know his father, Duane Sr."

"From the jail?"

Nick's mom nodded. "He did six months for burning down a Chevy dealership in Port Charlotte, all because his Tahoe blew a transmission on Alligator Alley."

No wonder the kid turned out the way he did, Nick thought. *His old man's a whack job.*

"What's for dinner?" Nick asked his mother.

"Spaghetti, spaghetti, or spaghetti."

"Guess I'll try the spaghetti."

"Excellent choice."

"Hey, did Dad e-mail you at work today?"

"No. How about you?"

"Not yet," Nick said.

His mother managed a smile. "Don't worry. He's probably away from base camp."

"I'll go look on the computer again —"

"Let's eat first, Nicky. Know what? I'm not really in the mood for pasta. Why don't we go out for some barbecue?"

"You sure, Mom?"

23

"Sure as can be," she said, finishing off the juice. "What time is it in Iraq right now?"

"Like one-thirty in the morning."

"Oh, then he's probably asleep."

"Yeah," Nick said. "I bet he's sleeping. I bet we'll hear from him tomorrow."

The headmaster, Dr. Dressler, was neat and cautious and mild-spoken. He was happiest when the Truman School ran smoothly and harmony was in the air. He was unhappiest when the students and faculty were buzzing and distracted.

"Tell me exactly what happened," he said to Mrs. Starch.

She held up the half-eaten pencil. "The young man has serious anger-control issues," she said.

Dr. Dressler examined the evidence. "And you're sure he didn't spit the rest out?"

"Oh, no, he swallowed it," Mrs. Starch reported. "Most definitely."

"Why didn't you send him to the nurse's station?"

"Because he stormed out of my classroom," she said, adding with disapproval, "sixteen minutes *before* the bell. Sixteen full minutes."

"The splinters could be harmful to his

24

internal organs —"

"I'm well aware of that, Dr. Dressler."

"The boy's parents should be notified as soon as possible."

"And informed, at the same time, of his disruptive and unacceptable actions."

"Of course," Dr. Dressler said uneasily.

Like everybody else at the Truman School, he tried to avoid Mrs. Starch whenever possible. Ever since taking the headmaster job, he'd heard strange stories. She lived alone, yet no one seemed to know whether she was divorced or she was a widow. According to one rumor, her house was filled with stuffed dead animals, such as skunks and raccoons. According to other gossip, she kept fifty-three snakes as pets, including a diamond-back rattler.

Officially, Mrs. Starch's private life was none of Dr. Dressler's business. As a teacher she was punctual, thorough, and hardworking. Students might be afraid of Mrs. Starch, but they also learned plenty from her. Truman classes always scored exceptionally well on the biology questions in the PSATs and SATs.

Still, Dr. Dressler couldn't help but wonder if any of the weird tales about Mrs. Starch were true. He found himself uncomfortable in her presence, probably because

25

Mrs. Starch was so large and imposing and spoke to him as if he were a half-witted nephew.

She said, "I'll be happy to phone Duane's parents myself."

"That's all right. You've got the field trip tomorrow —"

"We're all packed and ready to go, Dr. Dressler."

"Good. Very good." He smiled impassively. "But I'll contact the Scrods. It's my responsibility."

"Oh, I really don't mind," Mrs. Starch said, a bit too cheerily.

"Let me handle it, please."

Mrs. Starch rose to leave. Dr. Dressler carefully sealed the mangled remains of the pencil into a plastic baggie of the type used for sandwiches.

"The pencil was in my hand when he attacked it. He could easily have nipped off my fingers," Mrs. Starch said. "I assume disciplinary measures will be taken."

The Truman School had a detailed Code of Conduct for students, but offhand the headmaster couldn't think of a rule that applied to eating a teacher's pencil. He supposed that it fell under the category of "unruly behavior."

"What prompted Duane to do something

26

like this?" he asked Mrs. Starch.

"He became angry when I asked him to write a paper," she explained, "and the reason I asked him to write a paper was that he failed to do his class reading assignment. As a result, he was unable to discuss the study material when called upon."

"I see." Dr. Dressler opened a drawer and deposited the baggie containing the mangled pencil into it.

"By the way, will you be coming along on our field trip?" Mrs. Starch asked. "You can ride with me."

"I'm afraid I can't," the headmaster replied quickly. "I've got a . . . a meeting, a board meeting in the morning. Board of trustees."

And if there's not a meeting, Dr. Dressler thought, *I'll arrange one.* He was not an outdoor person, and his contact with nature was limited to glimpses of wildlife on Animal Planet while he flipped channels between cooking shows. Dr. Dressler was certain that any place called the Black Vine Swamp was no place he wanted to be.

"You don't know what you're missing," Mrs. Starch told him.

"I'm sure you're right."

After she left his office, Dr. Dressler phoned the Scrod household. A man an-

27

swered, growled something that Dr. Dressler couldn't understand, and hung up.

Perplexed, Dr. Dressler pulled out the file of Duane Scrod Jr. It showed that the boy had been held back two years in elementary school and later was expelled from a public middle school for fighting with his P.E. teacher. During that scuffle, the teacher lost three teeth and the tip of his right pinkie finger, which Duane had gnawed off and consumed.

Dr. Dressler thought: *There seems to be a pattern here.*

The mystery of how a person such as Duane Scrod Jr. got accepted into the Truman School was solved when Dr. Dressler came across a letter from the previous headmaster reflecting a large cash donation from Duane's wealthy grandmother, who was also paying his tuition.

Dr. Dressler concluded that it would be bad for the Truman School and its future endowments if young Duane became seriously ill from devouring Mrs. Starch's pencil. He put away the file and somewhat wearily headed for the parking lot, where he got into his car and — using his nifty new dashboard GPS — made his way to the address of Mr. Duane Scrod Sr.

The unpainted block house sat along an

unpaved road through some pine scrub on the outskirts of Naples. By the time Dr. Dressler arrived, the sun had set and the woods were humming with night insects. In the driveway sat numerous vehicles, none of them well maintained. There was a battered pickup truck, a motorcycle with crooked handlebars, a mud-splattered ATV on blocks, a dented minivan missing two doors, and an SUV upon which someone had painted, in bright orange letters: BOY-COTT SMITHERS CHEVY!!!!!

Although no lights were on inside the house, the front windows were open and Dr. Dressler could hear classical music, which he found encouraging. It was a Bach concerto.

The headmaster straightened his necktie and rang the bell. When no one responded, Dr. Dressler began to knock.

Eventually a lean, unshaven man appeared at the screen door. He wore hunting garb, a red trucker's cap, and no shoes.

"You from the guv'ment?" The man pointed aggressively at Dr. Dressler with a rusty pair of pliers. "If you're here about the taxes, don't be surprised if I pull off your lips and feed 'em to my bird. I got a macaw speaks three languages."

Dr. Dressler resisted the impulse to run

away. "I'm f-f-from the Truman School," he stammered. "Are you Duane's father?"

"I am," the man said. "How 'bout some ID?"

Nervously, Dr. Dressler drew a business card from the inner pocket of his suit jacket. Duane Scrod Sr. snatched the card and disappeared for several minutes. When he returned, a large bird with brilliant blue-and-gold plumage was perched on his left shoulder. With its crusty hooked beak, the macaw was shredding Dr. Dressler's card.

Duane Scrod Sr. opened the screen door and propped it ajar with one knee. "What did D.J. do now?" he asked.

"D.J.?"

"Duane Junior. I know he must've done something bad because (a) you're here and (b) he's not. You wanna come inside?"

Dr. Dressler shook his head and politely said no thanks. "Your son had what I would call a disagreement with one of his teachers today. A homework issue, from what I understand."

"And this is front-page news?" When Duane Scrod Sr. laughed, the macaw laughed, too. It was a perfect imitation, and Dr. Dressler was totally creeped out.

He realized that he'd made a mistake by visiting the house. Duane Jr. obviously

30

hadn't told his father what had happened in Mrs. Starch's class, and undoubtedly he had no intention of telling his father, even if he got sick as a dog from eating the pencil.

"I don't see why you drove all the way out here," Duane Scrod Sr. muttered. "Did my dear old rich ex-mother-in-law call up the school or somethin'? Light a spark under your butt?"

"No, Mr. Scrod. This was my idea." Dr. Dressler was itching to leave. "I just wanted to check on your son. Get his side of the story. Clarify our homework policy, you know, to avoid any further confusion about his responsibilities."

"Confusion?" Duane Scrod Sr. cackled, followed uncannily by his macaw. "D.J. ain't confused. D.J.'s just D.J."

"Well, his teacher and I were concerned," Dr. Dressler said, which was only half true. Mrs. Starch hadn't seemed concerned at all. "You should be aware that D.J. swallowed a pencil at school today. He might need to see a doctor."

Duane Scrod Sr. snorted. "The boy's got an iron stomach. When he was a little shrimp he used to eat rocks, oyster shells, lug nuts, even a piano wire. A pencil won't hurt him, that's for sure."

"Still, I'd feel better if I could speak with

31

him," the headmaster said.

"Well, like I said, he's not here. He didn't get home from school yet."

Dr. Dressler couldn't hide his concern. "But classes ended hours ago. It's already dark out, Mr. Scrod —"

"You got good eyes."

"Did D.J. call to say why he'd be late?"

"Just chill out, guy."

"Wasn't there soccer practice this afternoon?" the headmaster said. "Maybe he's still at the ball field."

Duane Scrod Sr. informed Dr. Dressler that Duane Jr. wasn't on the soccer team, the football team, the lacrosse team, or any other team at the Truman School.

"He keeps to himself," Duane Sr. explained. "Rides solo, you might say. His granny bought him a cell phone but I don't believe he's ever answered it."

Dr. Dressler felt a sickly wave of apprehension. He had a mental image of Duane Jr. lost in the woods and writhing in agony, his innards full of needle-sharp pencil splinters. This was followed by an equally unpleasant vision of Dr. Dressler himself being fired by the Truman board of trustees and then getting dragged into court by the Scrod family.

"Sometimes D.J. doesn't come through

32

the door until way late," Duane Sr. was saying. "I don't bother to wait up — he's a sizeable young man, and not many folks are dumb enough to mess with him."

Dr. Dressler took out another business card and wrote his home phone number on the back. "Would you mind calling me as soon as you or Mrs. Scrod hear from your son?"

"There's no Mrs. Scrod around here," said Duane Sr., "at the moment."

"Oh. I'm sorry."

"What for? We get by just fine, don't we, Nadine?"

The macaw made a purring noise and nibbled the frayed collar of Duane Scrod Sr.'s hunting jacket.

Dr. Dressler handed the card with his phone number to the man, who immediately gave it to the bird.

"Don't you worry about Junior," he said, letting the screen door bang shut. "He'll show up when he shows up. G'night, now."

Dr. Dressler hustled down the driveway toward his car, which out of habit he had locked. While groping for his keys, he heard an animal scurrying through the scrub, and he felt his heartbeat quicken.

The scent of pine needles made Dr. Dressler sneeze violently, and he was startled by a voice from inside the darkened house.

"Bless you!" Nadine squawked. *"À vos souhaits! Gesundheit!"*

THREE

The students, groggy and rumpled, gathered shortly after dawn in the school parking lot. Nick was sitting alone on a curb when Marta walked up.

"You okay?" she asked.

"Just tired is all." He'd been on the computer since 4 a.m., but no e-mails had arrived from his father in Iraq.

Marta sat down. "Where's Smoke?"

"Haven't seen him," Nick said.

"Good. Maybe he quit school — he's old enough to drive, he's gotta be old enough to drop out, right?"

"Don't get your hopes up."

Marta said, "I'm sorry, but he seriously scares me."

"Worse than her? No way," said Nick.

Mrs. Starch had arrived wide-awake and in high spirits. She wore wading boots, stiff canvas pants, a baggy long-sleeved shirt, and a frayed straw hat under an upturned veil of mosquito netting. Mrs. Starch always prepared for the worst.

"Slather up, people!" she barked. "Sunblock, bug juice, lip balm — it's a jungle out there!"

Nick and Marta got in line for the bus. "Maybe she'll get bit by a scorpion," Marta muttered.

"That would be awful," Nick whispered, "for the scorpion."

Mrs. Starch whistled sharply. "Did everybody in my classes remember to bring their journals?" She held a black writing notebook above her head. "Keep a list of everything you see — insects, mammals, birds, trees. This will count as a lab grade."

Graham, who was dressed like a pint-sized version of the Crocodile Hunter, raised his hand. Mrs. Starch ignored him, as always.

"We have three portable first-aid kits," she went on, "and each teacher will be carrying one. If you get into a situation where you need help, speak up right away. Remember: Stay with your hiking teams, do *not* wander off, and, most importantly, be respectful toward this very special place that we're exploring. Turn off your cell phones — if I or any of the other teachers hear one ringing, it will be confiscated."

Mrs. Starch put down the black notebook

and picked up a device that Nick recognized as a portable boat horn. They made loud, gassy honks and were a favorite toy of drunken idiots at Buccaneers football games. Nick's dad had season tickets.

"This will be our emergency signal," said Mrs. Starch, demonstrating the boat horn with a short, earsplitting beep. "If you hear that sound, immediately line up behind your teacher and proceed straight back to the bus. Any questions?"

Graham hopped up and down, waving one arm.

Mrs. Starch stared past him. "All right, people," she said, clapping. "Let's enjoy our day in the Black Vine Swamp!"

The bus was roomy and clean and air-conditioned, unlike the one they rode to school. Nick and Marta sat together toward the front, their backpacks stowed under their seats.

Marta nudged Nick and pointed out the window. Mrs. Starch was getting into her car, one of those teardrop-shaped hybrid models that ran on both electricity and gasoline. It had a "Save the Manatee" license plate.

"I guess she left her broomstick at home," Marta said.

Nick thought it was odd that Mrs. Starch

37

wasn't riding out to the swamp with everybody else. He wondered if, after what happened the day before, she might not want to be on the bus with Smoke.

But, to Nick and Marta's relief, Smoke was nowhere to be seen. The other science teachers, Mr. Neal and Miss Moffitt, moved up and down the aisle, collecting forms from each of the students. The forms, which were signed by the parents, said that it wasn't the school's fault if their kid got hurt on the field trip.

"I almost called in sick. I do *not* like swamps," Marta confided to Nick.

He said, "I hope we see a panther."

"Are you crazy?"

"Seriously — that would be so cool." Never in the recorded history of Florida had a panther harmed a human being. Now there were fewer than a hundred of the big cats left in the whole state.

"I got a video camera," Nick said, "just in case."

Marta said her mother wanted her to bring home a ghost orchid. "I said, 'Yeah, right, Mom. It's against the law.' And she goes, 'But I'll take good care of it!' And I'm like, 'You want me to go to jail, or what?' Gimme a break."

Nick could tell that Marta was in a better

38

mood because Mrs. Starch wasn't on the bus. The absence of Smoke was a bonus.

"How's your dad?" Marta asked, which caught Nick off guard.

"He's okay."

"When's he get back?"

"Twenty-two days." Nick hadn't told Marta or any other friends that his father had been sent to Iraq; the Naples newspaper had published the names of those serving in the war zone, and the list had been posted on the bulletin board outside the Truman gym.

"And after that he's home for good?" Marta asked.

"I sure hope."

Nick put on his iPod, and Marta put on hers. The ride took almost an hour because a truck full of tomatoes had flipped over on State Road 29, blocking traffic. A fire-engine crew was hosing the ketchup-colored muck off the pavement. Nick spotted a dead buck by the side of the road, and he figured that the tomato truck must have struck it in the early fog. He wondered if the deer had been running from a panther.

Eventually the bus made a slow turn onto a rutted dirt track that was very narrow. Twice the bus had to pull over to let flatbed trucks pass from the opposite direction.

Nick noticed that both trucks had red diamond-shaped logos on the doors and looked brand-new. They barely slowed at all, churning dust as they rumbled by the bus.

The wet prairies that usually glistened in the morning had turned brownish and crispy without rainfall. Ahead, Nick could see a rising tree line that marked the edge of the Black Vine Swamp.

He dug into his backpack for a tube of sunblock, and he smeared some on his arms and neck.

"Don't forget your nose," Marta said. "Here, let me do it."

"No, that's okay —"

"Hush." She snatched the tube, squirted a dollop of white goo into the palm of one hand, and then carefully coated every square inch of Nick's face, like she was painting on a mask. He was terrified that the other kids might see what she was doing.

"Now it's my turn," Marta announced, tugging off her iPod.

"What?"

She handed him the tube and shut her eyelids tightly. "Careful. That stuff burns if it drips in your eyeballs."

Nick felt trapped. He hunkered low in his seat.

40

Marta said, "My uncle gets basal cells all the time — that's a kind of skin cancer. They cut 'em off at the doctor's office."

Nick hastily smeared the sunblock cream on Marta's cheeks and forehead. "Okay," he said in a low voice, "you're good."

"Ears, too," she told him.

"Aw, come on."

"What's your problem, Nick? I'm sorry, but it runs in our family. Basal cells — you can ask my mom."

He couldn't say so, but touching her skin felt weird. Not bad, just weird. Afterward Marta checked herself out in the bus driver's rearview mirror to make sure that Nick hadn't missed any exposed places.

"Good job," she said. "That wasn't so awful, was it?"

For the rest of the trip, Nick pretended to be fascinated by the view out the window. Finally the bus jounced to a stop and the kids piled out.

Mrs. Starch was waiting. The mosquito veil wasn't quite long enough to cover her jutting chin, leaving her vivid anvil-shaped scar on display. Beneath the mesh she wore enormous purple sunglasses that made her look like a mutant dragonfly.

"Come on, people, get organized," she said, clapping again and starting to pace.

41

Each teacher had a team of fifteen students. The kids milled around anxiously while the names were called out. Nobody wanted to be on Mrs. Starch's team, because they knew that Mrs. Starch would make them work harder than the other teachers. The whole point of going on a field trip was to goof off.

Marta leaned close to Nick and said, "If she calls on me, I swear to God, I'll fake a heart attack."

But, by some small miracle, it was Mr. Neal who called out Marta's name — and then Nick's. They had been spared.

Mrs. Starch led the whole group down a winding boardwalk through the scrub and pineland hammock, into thicker woods. There, in the cool shade of ancient bald cypress trees, the boardwalk ended.

The teams split up in separate directions. Above the treetops, the sky shone bright and cloudless. Despite the drought, there was still enough water in the strand to make the hike a soggy challenge. The students had been advised to wear long pants to protect their legs, and to wear old sneakers that they could throw away after the trip. Only Graham had been foolish enough to show up in shorts, and soon his shins looked like they'd been clawed by a tomcat.

Mr. Neal's specialty was botany, and every so often he'd pause to point out a plant or a shrub of local interest. Mindful of Mrs. Starch's instructions, Nick and Marta would automatically pull their journals from their backpacks and take notes. By the time they stopped for the first rest break, their species list included pond apple trees, strangler figs, laurel oaks, wax myrtles, sabal palms, wild coffee, and resurrection ferns.

Animal life was more elusive. Mr. Neal spotted a barred owl high on a tree bough, and later a young red-bellied turtle basking on a mossy log. Graham shrieked at the sight of a ribbon snake that he somehow mistook for a poisonous cottonmouth. Marta and two other girls briefly got tangled in a tent-sized spiderweb, while a boy named Mickey Maris captured a green anole lizard that Mr. Neal made him release on the spot.

Nick, who was scouting for signs of panthers, came across fresh pig tracks, but not much else. Occasionally he could hear the other student teams as they moved at a distance throughout the swamp. Once he was certain that he'd picked up Mrs. Starch's voice yodeling, "We are now in bromeliad heaven!"

At noon Mr. Neal's group sat down for

43

lunch beneath a crooked cypress that he estimated was five hundred years old. The kids had brought their own sandwiches — Nick's was turkey and cheese, Marta's was peanut butter and Nutella. They shared a lime Gatorade that Nick's mother had packed in a padded cooler bag.

Addressing the team, Mr. Neal said, "Can anyone tell me why we're not getting bothered by mosquitoes?"

Graham's hand shot up. He looked flabbergasted when Mr. Neal called his name.

"Because . . . ," he began. "Because . . ."

"Yes, Graham?"

"Because of . . ."

"Go on."

"Of . . . of . . ." Graham shrugged in defeat. "I don't have a clue."

Mr. Neal pointed to another student. "Rachel?"

"Because the weather's been too dry for skeeters," Rachel said.

"A good theory," the teacher said, "but there's still plenty of water for the little buggers to lay their eggs in. Nick Waters, what's your guess?"

Nick wasn't paying attention; he was thinking about his father. Marta elbowed him and he looked up, flustered, and said, "What? I didn't hear the question."

"Why aren't we getting chewed up by mosquitoes?" Mr. Neal asked with a touch of impatience.

Marta decided to return Nick's favor from the day before in Mrs. Starch's class. She cut herself into the discussion and said, "Because mosquito fish are eating up all the baby mosquitoes?"

"Excellent!" Mr. Neal looked relieved that somebody got it right.

"Now I've got a question," Marta said. "Why do they call it the Black Vine Swamp when all the vines we've seen are green?"

Graham raised his hand to try again, and the other students groaned. Mr. Neal said, "I'm not sure I know the answer to that one — anybody got a theory?"

At that moment they heard a piercing cry rise from among the towering cypresses. It didn't sound like any noise that a person could make.

Mr. Neal was as startled as the hikers, although he tried not to show it. He raised a finger to his lips as a signal for everyone to stay quiet. A woodpecker hammering on a dead stump stopped abruptly and flitted away.

Some of the kids got spooked, but Nick was excited. He thought he knew what kind of animal they'd heard. He grabbed the

45

video camera from his backpack and, after groping to locate the Record button, aimed the lens toward the part of the woods from where the wild cry had come.

It was hard to make out details through the viewfinder because of the forest shadows, and because Nick's hands were shaking slightly. Marta had edged closer, peeking over his shoulder.

"You see that? See it?" She pointed at the screen of the viewfinder.

Something was running among the tree trunks — a large, tannish blur.

"Where'd it go?" Marta whispered. "What was it?"

"Just wait," Nick said, but there was no other movement.

Moments later, the students heard splashes, and then a heavy rustling that faded into silence.

Nobody made a peep until Mr. Neal spoke. "Probably just a fox or a wild hog — nothing to worry about," he said, not sounding too sure of himself.

Nick switched off the camera. "That was too big for a fox. I bet it was a panther."

Not all of the other kids shared his curiosity about the big cats, and some of them expressed dismay at the possibility of crossing one's path. Mickey Maris stood up and declared that they should all march back to the bus at once.

Mr. Neal said, "I doubt seriously if that was a panther."

"What about a bear?" Graham squeaked. "They got black bears out here — Mrs. Starch said so!"

While Mr. Neal tried to calm the students, Nick fiddled with the control menu on the video camera. He wanted to replay the tape at slow speed so that he might get a better look at the creature.

Marta tweaked his arm. "Hey, do you smell something?"

Nick looked up from the camera and took a sniff. "That's smoke," he said.

"Definitely."

Just then they heard two long blasts from Mrs. Starch's boat horn. Everybody began murmuring and clustered around Mr. Neal, who told them to follow him back toward the boardwalk as quickly as possible — but no running, he said, and no talking.

The students didn't have to be told twice. Hurriedly they zipped up their book bags and lined up behind the teacher, who led them briskly along the same wet, peat-filled slough that they had come in on. The smoky odor grew heavier, and in some places a gray haze was visible through the trees.

After assembling at the boardwalk, the three teams merged to form a long single line. At the very end of it was Mrs. Starch, who burped the air horn to make the students turn around and pay attention.

"Listen up, people!" she said. "A small wildfire has sprung up on the far edge of the swamp — pretty common for this time of the year. It'll probably burn out when it reaches the cypress muck, but there's no sense taking any chances. That's why we're cutting short our field trip and heading back to school. Straight back to school."

Marta groaned and leaned against Nick. "What if she makes us go to her class? I'm gonna be sick again, all over the place."

"Pray for a flat tire on the way home," Nick said.

He was disappointed because he'd hoped for another opportunity to see the panther, or whatever it was that had darted into the cypress shadows. However, a wildfire was nothing to fool with. If a strong wind kicked up, the blaze would race across the land faster than any human could possibly run.

"Please stay in line behind Mr. Neal and Miss Moffitt," Mrs. Starch said. "I'll be coming along in a minute — Libby dropped her medicine, so I'm going back to find it." She clapped so loudly that it sounded like a paper bag popping. "Now get your fannies in gear! Move!"

At the time, nobody questioned Mrs. Starch's decision to go back. Libby Marshall had frequent asthma attacks, and she always carried an inhaler. The haze from the fire would make it harder for her to breathe.

"Quickly and quietly," urged Miss Moffitt as the kids began streaming toward the bus.

Nick was walking behind Marta, who was behind Graham, who was behind Mickey Maris, who was behind Rachel, who was behind Hector, the star of the soccer team. The students were in such a rush that they were stepping on each other's heels. Nick lost one of his sneakers when he was overrun by the boy next in line, an algebra ace named Gene, who stepped around him and kept going.

When Nick knelt to retrieve his shoe, he glanced back down the curving boardwalk just in time to see Mrs. Starch, in her straw hat and dragonfly glasses, marching alone into the smoky swamp.

He had no idea that she wouldn't be coming out.

FOUR

The camera battery went dead, so Nick and Marta couldn't view the videotape on the bus. By the time the kids got back to the school, it was so late that Mr. Neal and Miss Moffitt let them finish the day doing homework in the cafeteria.

Marta had an appointment with her orthodontist, so Nick walked home from the bus stop alone, his sneakers squishing. He kicked them off at the front door and ran to the den to check his e-mail.

Nothing.

Nick's father belonged to the 53rd Infantry Brigade of the Florida Army National Guard, which called itself the Gator Brigade and had its own Web site. Whenever a soldier got killed in action, a memorial page was posted. Nick held his breath and clicked on the tab.

A photograph appeared of a reservist who'd died when a roadside bomb exploded while he was on foot patrol near Baghdad. It wasn't Nick's dad, but Nick read the tribute closely.

The soldier was thirty years old, with a wife and two small children in Tampa. The picture showed the man dressed in his crisply pressed army uniform in front of an American flag. He looked so strong and confident that it was almost impossible to believe he was dead.

Nick swallowed to keep himself from crying. He closed out the National Guard Web site and switched over to YouTube so that he could watch some funny videos. Nick considered it his number one job to keep up his mother's spirits; he didn't want her coming in the door and catching him with tears in his eyes.

By the time she got home from work, he felt better. He'd recharged the camera battery, and he was getting ready to look at the tape from the Black Vine Swamp.

"How was the field trip?" his mom asked.

Nick told her about the wildfire.

"Thank God nobody was hurt," she said. "How did it start?"

Nick shrugged. "Who knows? It's the dry season — fires pop up all the time."

"Well, you definitely had a more exciting day than I did."

She removed some plastic containers from the refrigerator and announced that she was fixing a Greek salad for dinner because she was too tired to cook.

"One cool thing happened: I think I saw a panther in the woods," Nick said. "It's on the video — you want to check it out?"

His mom sat on the sofa. Nick plugged the camera into the wall and connected it to the television set. "You'll have to watch close. It's kind of blurry," he said, "and real short."

When he pressed the Play button, the cypress strand came into view. The picture, though wobbly and somewhat out of focus, was easier to see on a TV screen than on the camera's small viewfinder.

"There it is!" Nick exclaimed when the tannish form crossed between the tree trunks.

After a few moments of stillness, the screen went blank.

"That's it?" his mother asked.

Nick touched the Rewind button. "Let's watch again."

From beginning to end, the tape lasted only fifteen seconds. Nick paused it when the animal came into view.

His mom said, "Honey, that's one funky-looking panther."

The animal was moving at an angle away from the camera, so its head wasn't fully visible. The torso didn't look long and streamlined like a panther's; the creature was more blocky and upright.

"Maybe a wild hog," his mother said.

"Wrong color. We heard a cry, and it sounded like a big cat, I swear." Nick played the tape in slow motion, rewound it, and played it again.

Where's the tail? he thought glumly. *Panthers have long, black-tipped tails.*

"Freeze it right there!" His mother popped up from the sofa. "Okay, now zoom in. *Zoom!*"

"I can't zoom in Play mode. It's not like Photoshop."

"Then just look!" She went up to the TV and pointed to a dark band around the animal's midsection. "Can you see that?"

Nick could see it just fine. "I don't believe this," he said.

His mom smiled. "You've been ponged, Nicky."

"You mean punked."

"Whatever," she said. "Your 'panther' is wearing a belt!"

Dr. Dressler stayed longer than usual after school let out. Miss Moffitt and Mr. Neal

53

were in his office, giving an account of what had happened during the field trip. Dr. Dressler was shaken by what he was hearing.

"So the last time either of you saw Mrs. Starch, she was actually going back into the swamp," he said, "with a wildfire burning?"

"To get Libby Marshall's asthma inhaler," Mr. Neal said.

Dr. Dressler was trying not to appear freaked-out, but in his entire twelve-year career as a private school administrator, he'd never lost a teacher before.

"But why didn't you wait for her to return?" he asked.

"Because of the fire," Mr. Neal said. He turned for moral support to Miss Moffitt, who nodded.

"Mrs. Starch told us not to wait," Miss Moffitt explained. "She said to move the kids out of there as fast as we could, and she'd meet us back at school. She had her own car."

"Yes, yes, you told me." Dr. Dressler drummed his fingers on his desk. The explanation made total sense; the safety of the students was always the first priority. Of course Mrs. Starch would have ordered the bus to leave the area as soon as possible.

Mr. Neal cautioned against jumping to conclusions. "Maybe she drove straight home instead of coming here. Or maybe she stopped at the grocery. Did you try her cell phone?"

"About ten times," Dr. Dressler said. "No answer."

He doubted if the Truman School had an official procedure for reporting a teacher missing. Most likely he'd have to notify the police.

He said, "Maybe someone should take a drive to her house, just to make sure she's not there."

Neither Miss Moffitt nor Mr. Neal seemed eager to volunteer. All the faculty members had heard the peculiar stories about Mrs. Starch — the deadly snake collection, the taxidermied critters, and so on.

"Would you happen to know if she has relatives living around here?" Dr. Dressler inquired. "Somebody we could contact, to see if they've heard from her?"

Neither Mr. Neal nor Miss Moffitt could recall Mrs. Starch mentioning any family connections.

"I heard that her husband moved to Brazil ten years ago," Miss Moffitt said.

"I heard he disappeared," Mr. Neal said, "without a trace."

Dr. Dressler struggled to contain his exasperation. "There's got to be *somebody* — a sister or brother or cousin twice removed." He made a mental note to look through Mrs. Starch's employment file and find out whom she'd listed as next of kin.

The meeting was interrupted by the telephone. It was a lieutenant from the county fire department, returning an earlier call from Dr. Dressler.

Mr. Neal and Miss Moffitt heard only the headmaster's side of the conversation, which was mostly "I see" and "I understand" and "Really?" His face was gray when he hung up the phone.

"The firefighters didn't find Mrs. Starch," he said, "but her car was still parked on the dirt road near the boardwalk, where she'd left it."

"A blue Prius?" Mr. Neal asked.

Dr. Dressler nodded tightly.

Miss Moffitt slumped. "Oh my, no."

"The fire was already out when the crews got there," the headmaster said, "which is good news."

Mr. Neal said, "They're still out there looking for her, right?"

Dr. Dressler explained that the Black Vine Swamp was so dense and jungly that the floodlights from the fire trucks were useless.

"The searchers will return at sunrise," he said.

Miss Moffitt stared glumly out the window. "This is terrible. We should've never let her go back there alone."

"You had no choice. It was more important to move the students out safely," Dr. Dressler said. "Both of you go home and get some rest. I'll be in touch if I hear any news."

Once Mr. Neal and Miss Moffitt had left, the headmaster phoned the county sheriff's office and said he wanted to report a missing teacher. The dispatcher said a deputy would come to the school and take all the information.

While he was waiting, Dr. Dressler opened a legal pad and uncapped a silver fountain pen, which had been a gift from the Class of 2003. He knew he had to write something about the wildfire and Mrs. Starch to read at the morning assembly.

He couldn't imagine what he could possibly say that would settle the questions everyone at the Truman School would be asking, or that would stop a dozen wild rumors from racing through the halls.

Miss Moffitt was right. This was a terrible thing.

Libby Marshall was so wired after the field trip that her parents didn't think they'd ever get her to sleep. She couldn't stop talking about Mrs. Starch, wondering why she hadn't shown up at school with the asthma inhaler.

"I hope she's okay," Libby told her father. "What if she got caught in the fire? What if she's hurt?"

Libby's mother said, "I'm sure she's all right, sweetie. I bet she'll have your medicine waiting for you in class tomorrow."

Her dad wasn't so certain. Jason Marshall was a detective for the Collier County sheriff's office. He got concerned when Libby told him about the wildfire, and about the teacher who went back alone to retrieve Libby's inhaler. It seemed strange that Mrs. Starch hadn't even phoned.

While Libby was brushing her teeth, Jason Marshall went to the kitchen and quietly called a friend who was a firefighter. The firefighter said that the blaze near the Big Cypress was no longer burning, but he confirmed that the crews had found an automobile registered to a woman named Bunny Starch, who was missing and believed lost in the swamp.

Libby's father didn't want to upset Libby even more, so he didn't tell her what he'd learned. She'd find out soon enough — probably the minute she got to school the next day.

Finally, around ten-thirty, Libby finally drifted off. Within half an hour her mother was out like a light, too. Bonnie Marshall owned a popular breakfast shop on Marco Island, and every morning she got up before dawn to make the long drive.

Now it was Jason Marshall who couldn't fall asleep. He sat up in bed with a book open on his lap, but he wasn't reading. His thoughts were on Libby's teacher.

Any half-intelligent person could survive a night in the Big Cypress. All you had to do was hunker down someplace dry and be still. Except for the bugs, nothing would bother you — at least no wild animals would.

The worst thing was to panic and go thrashing off into the wilderness, which was a good way to get bitten by a water moccasin or gored by a wild pig or chased by a bear. Jason Marshall hoped that Libby's biology teacher had the common sense to remain calm and wait for help to arrive.

It was well past midnight when Jason

Marshall's eyelids grew heavy and he turned off the light. The next thing he knew, Bonnie was shaking him by the shoulders because their dog was barking furiously in the living room. The clock on the nightstand said 2:20 a.m.

"Sam's going nuts," Bonnie told him. "You better go check on him."

Sam was a black Labrador retriever. He was five years old and extremely mellow — he seldom barked at anything, even stray cats. Jason Marshall opened the drawer of the nightstand and took out his police revolver, which had a combination lock on the trigger.

He pulled on his jeans and hurried to the living room, where Sam stood rigidly at the front door. The dog was growling, and the hair on his ruff bristled.

"Easy, boy," Jason Marshall said, and popped the trigger lock off the pistol. The detective felt his heart hammering in his rib cage; he'd never seen Sam so intense.

"Who's there?" he said through the door.

No reply. Sam cocked his big black head and whined.

"Who is it?" Jason Marshall demanded again.

He heard nothing on the other side. Quietly he unbolted the door, Sam gazing up at him expectantly.

"Sit," Jason Marshall said, and the dog sat.

The detective's gun was in his right hand. He placed his left hand on the door, flung it open, raised the revolver, and stepped outside.

Nobody was there. Sam followed Jason Marshall across the open porch and down the front steps. There the dog halted, lifted his quivering wet nose, and sniffed the night air.

Nothing moved in the front yard, which was illuminated by a pale crescent moon. The crickets were chirping and the geckos were trilling, and everything seemed perfectly peaceful.

"What'd you hear, boy?" Jason Marshall asked Sam, who began following an invisible trail down the walkway, toward the gate.

Maybe it was a raccoon, thought the detective, *or a possum.*

Whatever the intruder was, Sam seemed satisfied that he'd done his job and scared it away. Wagging his tail, he casually strolled off to relieve himself in Bonnie Marshall's prized vegetable garden.

Jason Marshall tucked the revolver into his waistband and walked around the house to check the backyard. The dog quickly

61

caught up and loped ahead playfully. When they returned to the front of the house, Sam bounded up the steps and began nosing intently around the porch.

Bonnie Marshall peeked out the door. Libby, in her robe and fuzzy slippers, stood behind her.

"Everything's fine. Dog must've heard a raccoon," Jason Marshall said. "Back to bed, scooter."

"But Sam never barks," Libby said sleepily, "and I totally heard him barking."

"Well, maybe it was a whole herd of raccoons," her mother said. "Now he's his sleepy old self again, so let's hit the sack. Momma's gotta be up early tomorrow."

"Dad, how come you've got your gun out?"

Jason Marshall glanced down at the grip of the pistol sticking up from his jeans. "In case there was a prowler," he said to Libby, "but there wasn't. Now go back to bed, sugar —"

"Hey, who gave Sam a new toy?" she asked.

Jason Marshall turned and saw the Labrador sitting proudly in the doorway, holding something shiny in his mouth. His tail whipped back and forth like a hairy windshield wiper.

"Put it down, Sam. Down!" Bonnie Marshall said.

The dog happily ignored her.

She said, "Jason, you'd better get that thing away from him before he swallows it."

Sam was famous for eating items other than food. Jason Marshall grabbed Sam's collar and tugged him inside the house. Then he began the slimy chore of prying the dog's jaws apart with his fingers, which wasn't easy.

"C'mon, be a good boy," Jason Marshall implored. "Drop it, Sam."

The dog decided he was in the mood for a chase and started dashing in crazy circles around the room. Every time the Marshalls had him cornered, he'd squirt through their legs and take off running again.

"I give up," Bonnie Marshall said finally. "Good night, all."

Libby kicked off her slippers. "Me, too," she sighed, and headed for her room.

Jason Marshall sat down in an armchair to wait. With nobody pursuing him, Sam soon got bored with the game. He lay down panting on the rug and dropped his mystery toy at Jason Marshall's feet.

Libby's father sat forward, staring in surprise. He picked up the small plastic tube, wiped off the dog slobber, and looked at the initials written with a green Sharpie on the cap.

There was no mistake.

It was his daughter's asthma inhaler, the one that she'd lost in the Black Vine Swamp.

FIVE

The Truman School had once been known as the Trapwick Academy, named after the man who had founded it eighteen years earlier. Vincent Z. Trapwick was a rich Rhode Island banker who'd moved to southwest Florida and gotten even richer.

Vincent Trapwick didn't want his three snotty, pampered children attending school with ordinary kids, so he started his own private school and kept out just about everyone who didn't have the same skin color, religion, and political point of view as Vincent Trapwick.

As a result, the Trapwick Academy had a ridiculously small enrollment and lost money by the bucketful, although Vincent Trapwick didn't seem to care. When he died, he left two hundred thousand dollars to the school, which was a generous amount but hardly enough to keep it running forever.

So the board of trustees gradually loosened up the admissions policy and began reaching out to the community, recruiting all kinds of students. For the first time, scholarships were offered to bright kids and athletes whose families couldn't afford the expensive tuition. Enrollment grew steadily, and so did the Trapwick Academy's reputation.

Things were rolling along smoothly until Vincent Trapwick's own kids — now graduated and grown to adulthood — started getting into trouble. The eldest, Vincent Jr., was caught embezzling millions of dollars from his late father's bank to support wild gambling junkets to Monaco. The middle one, Sandra Sue, on three occasions drank too much beer and drove her golf cart off the Naples Pier. The youngest, Iggy, was arrested for ripping off Social Security checks from old folks living in the chain of shabby nursing homes that he owned.

The name Trapwick kept popping up in the newspapers, and not in a way that was flattering to the Trapwick Academy. Ironically, the same spoiled children for whom the school was created had grown up to become its most embarrassing advertisements.

In an emergency meeting — held late one

66

night after Iggy Trapwick had been stopped at the Sarasota airport while wearing a diaper stuffed with cash — the board of trustees voted unanimously to change the academy's name. They chose to call it the Truman School, after President Harry S. Truman (who'd been dead for a long time and therefore was unlikely to cause any public relations problems).

To save money, the board voted not to replace the entire granite statue of Vincent Z. Trapwick that stood in front of the school auditorium. Instead, a local sculptor was hired to chisel off Vincent Trapwick's face and reshape the remaining nub of stone into the studious features of the thirty-third president of the United States.

The sculptor did the best he could, working on a tight schedule with a low budget. The statue's new face was distinguished enough, but as small as a kitten's.

Unfortunately, the finished piece did not bear a striking resemblance to Harry S. Truman. The body was all wrong, and nothing could be done about it. Vincent Z. Trapwick had weighed two hundred fifty-one pounds, while President Truman had weighed only one hundred seventy-five. As a result, most people viewing the school's statue for the first time had no idea who it

67

was supposed to be.

When Nick and Marta stepped off the bus, three sheriff's deputies were standing by the odd granite figure, guessing aloud at its identity.

"What's going on?" Marta said to Nick.

"Don't ask me. Maybe it's Just-Say-No Day."

Once a year, the Truman School brought in police officers, doctors, and counselors to speak to the students about drug and alcohol abuse. However, the three deputies acted like they were on a call. They carried clipboards and had their portable radios turned on.

"Something's up," said Marta.

Nick agreed. "Maybe there was another break-in."

Over the Christmas holidays, burglars had stolen several laptops from the school's computer lab. The culprits were two teen-aged brothers from Fort Myers who were later caught speeding through a red light, the missing laptops stacked in the bed of their father's pickup truck. The kids had confessed that they intended to pawn the computers and use the money to buy video games.

Marta nudged Nick and told him to ask the deputies why they were there. Probably because his dad was a military officer, Nick had no problem dealing with authority figures (except for Mrs. Starch).

As he approached one of the deputies, he heard her joking that the Harry Truman statue looked like "a bowling pin in an overcoat."

"Excuse me," Nick interrupted politely. "Did something happen here at the school this morning?"

Caught by surprise, the deputy suddenly got serious. "We can't talk about it. Your principal will make an announcement."

"The headmaster, you mean," Nick said.

"Same difference."

The first bell rang, and students started pouring into the auditorium. Marta and Nick found an empty row in the back, near the door. Usually the morning assembly was incredibly boring — a good opportunity to finish your homework or to return your text messages.

After the daily blessing, which seemed to drag on forever, Dr. Dressler approached the podium and said he had a short statement to read. He unfolded a sheet of paper and began:

"As some of you know, yesterday's field trip to the Black Vine Swamp was ended early because a small wildfire broke out in

69

the area."

Nick snapped shut his algebra book and sat up. Marta turned off her cell phone.

"All Truman students were evacuated promptly and returned to campus safely," Dr. Dressler went on. "However, one of our biology teachers — Mrs. Starch — went back down the hiking path to retrieve a student's medicine. She didn't return to the school and hasn't been seen, so we have reason to believe she might have gotten lost and had to spend the night in the swamp."

A murmur rippled through the auditorium. Marta pinched Nick and said, "Oh . . . my . . . God."

Nick's mind was racing. He hadn't yet told Marta what he and his mother had seen on the videotape: that the animal he'd thought was a panther was actually a human being, scrambling through the cypresses.

Now Nick couldn't help but wonder if that mysterious figure wearing the dark belt — the person who'd probably made that creepy animal cry — was involved with Mrs. Starch's disappearance.

What if it was Smoke? he thought. *What if the kid went crazy and did something awful?*

Nick pried Marta's fingers from his arm.

"The authorities were out there at day-

70

break to continue searching for Mrs. Starch," Dr. Dressler continued from the stage. "Fortunately, the fire went out and the weather last night was mild, so there's no reason to believe she's in any danger. The search teams are experienced and very thorough, and I'm confident of a positive outcome."

Nick whispered, "I don't see Smoke anywhere."

Marta looked up and down the rows of heads in the auditorium. "He's probably just late," she said. "He's always late for assembly."

"Yeah."

"This is so freaky, Nick." Marta puffed her cheeks and let the air hiss out. "I mean, I can't stand the woman, but still, to think of her lost in that swamp . . ."

At the podium, Dr. Dressler turned the paper over and continued reading: "You probably noticed some law enforcement officers on campus this morning. Please don't be alarmed or make any rash assumptions. It's routine procedure in such cases. Students in Mrs. Starch's classes, and the others who went on the field trip, may be called aside to chat with the deputies today. I would encourage you to be as helpful as you can be."

Marta said, "I better call my mom."

"What for?" Nick asked.

"In case there's gonna be something on TV about this. She'll wig out."

Dr. Dressler concluded his prepared statement and moved on to less exciting announcements about an upcoming soccer tournament, a change in the lunch menu (no chili for a week, due to a spoiled shipment of ground beef), and a new rule in the dress code that banned "all styles of open-toed sandals" on campus.

The students weren't listening; they were buzzing about Mrs. Starch. The mood in the auditorium was one of restless curiosity, not worry. Thanks to the headmaster's reassuring speech, most of the kids believed that the searchers would soon locate the missing teacher. Once Mrs. Starch was found, the Black Vine Swamp episode would only add to her colorful legend.

After assembly, Nick and Marta stood by the Harry Truman statue and waited for the bell. Libby Marshall rushed over, highly agitated.

"Dr. Dressler was wrong — Mrs. Starch isn't lost! She got out of the Glades last night!" Libby blurted. "I've gotta tell him so he can put it on the intercom."

"You saw her? Where?" Marta asked.

Libby shook her head. "I didn't see her, but she stopped by my house and left *this* on the porch!" Libby displayed her asthma inhaler like a trophy. "Sam found it. He's our dog."

Nick said, "Did anyone actually see her?"

"No, but Sam heard her on the front steps and started barking like crazy. And who else could it be? She's the one who went back to find my inhaler."

Although Nick didn't like Mrs. Starch any more than the other students did, he'd been hoping that she wasn't hurt, or worse. Libby's news was encouraging.

"I wonder why she didn't knock," he said.

" 'Cause it was late," Libby said impatiently, "and the lights were off. She probably didn't want to wake up anybody."

That made sense to Nick and Marta.

"Now I've gotta go find Droopy Dressler," said Libby, "and straighten him out." She hurried off.

The bell rang, and Marta picked up her backpack. "I gotta admit, I'm glad that mean old hag made it out of the swamp okay."

"Me, too," Nick said.

"I don't know why we should care what happens to her."

"Because she was doing a brave thing, go-

73

ing back for Libby's medicine with a wildfire coming."

Marta shrugged. "Yeah. Even witches have their good days."

Dr. Dressler was hopeful but perplexed.

After the assembly, he'd received a call from the fire lieutenant, who reported that Bunny Starch's blue Prius was gone at daybreak when the crews had returned to the Black Vine Swamp. The lieutenant surmised that, sometime during the night, Mrs. Starch had found her way back to her car.

That theory was bolstered by the information from Libby Marshall, who'd burst into Dr. Dressler's office and blurted the story of her asthma inhaler so breathlessly that he feared she might need to use it.

The facts strongly suggested that Mrs. Starch was alive and had safely exited the wilderness. How else would Libby's lost medicine have been delivered to her front porch?

What nagged at Dr. Dressler was this: Nobody had seen or spoken to the biology teacher.

She hadn't shown up for classes that morning, which, given the circumstances, was excusable — yet she hadn't even called to say she'd be absent. That was a violation of the Truman faculty attendance policy, and nobody was a bigger stickler for school rules than Mrs. Starch.

In eighteen years she'd missed only one day of teaching, when she accidentally rolled her car while swerving to avoid a rabbit on the way to school. She'd borrowed the ambulance driver's radio to call in sick, and the next day she had returned to Truman with a plaster cast on one arm, a patch over one eye, and two metal pins in her collarbone.

After Libby left his office, Dr. Dressler immediately tried calling Mrs. Starch's cell phone . . . and calling and calling and calling. Then he phoned her house — no answer there, either. It was baffling.

Dr. Dressler reluctantly agreed that the sheriff's deputies should go ahead and interview the students. Technically, at least, Bunny Starch was still a missing person.

After speaking with Libby, Nick and Marta expected Mrs. Starch to be waiting with a pencil twirling in biology class. They were surprised to see Miss Moffitt sitting at Mrs. Starch's desk, and even more surprised when a sheriff's deputy poked his head in the doorway and asked for Duane Scrod Jr.

Miss Moffitt said, "Duane's absent today."

"All right." The deputy scanned his clipboard. "How about Graham Carson?"

Graham eagerly raised his hand, and the deputy motioned for him to come along. Graham was beaming self-importantly as he marched from the room.

"I don't get it," Marta murmured to Nick. "What's with the cops? Don't they know the old bird is okay?"

Nick was mystified as well. If Mrs. Starch was safe, why were the deputies hanging around and asking questions?

Another uniformed officer entered the classroom and called Marta's name. Her eyes widened and she looked fretfully at Nick.

He said, "No big deal. Just tell 'em what you know."

After a few minutes Marta returned and, looking annoyed, plopped down at her desk. "I told him Mrs. Starch was all right, but he just kept on asking me more stuff."

"Like what?" Nick said.

"No talking, please!" It was Miss Moffitt. Sternly she pointed at the blackboard, upon which she had chalked the words "Reread Chapter 8."

Libby Marshall was called out next, and Nick assumed that she'd be the final interview. Once Libby told them that Mrs. Starch had delivered the asthma inhaler last night, the deputies would realize there was nothing to investigate.

But Libby came back to class red-faced and fuming. Nick wondered what in the world was going on.

One by one, the remainder of Mrs. Starch's biology students were summoned. Sometimes the interviews were short, and sometimes they lasted awhile. There were so many interruptions from kids coming and going that it was difficult to concentrate on the Calvin cycle, or any other topic in the biology book.

Nick was the last to be called. He was led to an empty classroom by the same female deputy to whom he'd spoken near the Truman statue. The deputy told Nick to sit down (which he did) and relax (which was impossible).

"Let's go over what happened on the field trip yesterday," she said. Balanced on her lap was a clipboard holding a blank report form, upon which she'd printed Nick's full name. "When Mrs. Starch turned back to look for the young lady's asthma inhaler, you're sure she was alone?"

"Yes, I saw her walking down the boardwalk all by herself," Nick said.

The deputy scribbled on the paper.

Nick quickly added, "She must be all right, because she brought back Libby's asthma inhaler last night. Did you know about that?"

The deputy nodded and kept writing.

"Then I don't get the point of all this," Nick said.

"Let's go back to the day before the field trip," said the deputy. "I want to ask you about something that happened in class between Mrs. Starch and a boy named Duane Scrod."

Nick felt the muscles in his neck stiffen. "She pointed a pencil at him, and he bit it in half."

"Didn't he also threaten her?"

"What do you mean?"

The deputy said, "Some of your class-mates remember Duane saying something like, 'You're gonna be sorry.' And then Mrs. Starch saying, 'Is that a threat?' Do you recall such a conversation?"

Nick recalled it quite clearly. He also recalled worrying that Smoke might be seri-ous. Nick felt uneasy telling this to the deputy, because he couldn't be sure *what* Duane Scrod had meant.

But Nick's father had taught him to always be truthful, no matter how hard it might be.

"Mrs. Starch told Duane to write five hundred words about pimples," Nick began. "That's no joke."

The deputy obviously had heard about the essay from the other students, because she displayed no reaction.

Nick went on: "Then Duane said something like, 'You'll be sorry,' whatever. He was mad — kids say all kinds of stupid stuff when they're mad."

The deputy took a few more notes. "Does Duane have a nickname?" she asked, as if she didn't already know.

"Smoke," Nick said.

"Why do they call him that?"

"Because that's what he wants to be called."

The deputy glanced up. "Some of the other students said it's because he's a pyromaniac — because he likes to mess with fire."

"I don't know. We don't hang together," Nick said.

"But you've heard that rumor, right?"

Nick could sense that the deputy wanted him to say that Duane was a nut case. "I thought you wanted me to stick to what I saw and what I know," he said. "I didn't think you were interested in rumors."

The deputy raised her eyebrows. "Sometimes rumors turn out to be true, Nick."

"Can I go back to class now?"

She said, "That wildfire at the Black Vine Swamp wasn't really a wildfire. It was arson."

"What?"

"The investigators called it a 'controlled burn.' Whoever set the fire also dug a trench line on the other side so it would burn itself out. They knew what they were doing," the deputy said.

Nick was dumbfounded.

The deputy tapped her pen lightly on the clipboard. "Do you think Duane would ever try such a thing, to get back at Mrs. Starch for what happened in class? Light a brush fire to freak her out and spoil the field trip?"

"I have no idea," Nick said honestly.

In his mind he was replaying the glimpse of that tannish blur in the cypress trees, the panther that turned out to be a human. Maybe it was Smoke.

Nick kept this thought to himself. He needed to go home and look at the videotape of the swamp prowler again.

The deputy went on: "Duane was pretty angry about that essay assignment, wasn't he?"

"Sure," said Nick, thinking: *Who wouldn't*

be angry? Mrs. Starch had totally humili-
ated the guy.

"Were you aware that Duane got in
trouble once for burning down a construction trailer out near Immokalee? He was
only ten years old when it happened," the
deputy said. "Another time, they caught him
torching a billboard on the interstate, using
mops dipped in gasoline. Three in the
morning, a state trooper busted him."

"Are you serious?" Nick was stunned.
Those weren't typical dumb-kid pranks;
they were crimes.

"Are you afraid of Duane?" the deputy
asked.

"Not really. He doesn't hassle anyone."

"Was Mrs. Starch afraid of him?"

Nick had to chuckle at that one. The
deputy asked what was so funny.

He said, "If you met Mrs. Starch, you'd
think it was pretty funny, too."

The deputy scribbled another few lines,
then capped her pen. "Nick, do you have
any idea where we might find Duane?"

Nick firmly shook his head. "Nope. That's
the truth."

The deputy rose. "Thanks for your help."

"I really don't know the guy at all," Nick
insisted.

"That's the thing. Nobody seems to know

81

him, do they?" She opened the door and motioned for Nick to leave.

SIX

After classes let out, the deputies stopped by the headmaster's office and said they were done with all the interviews except for two.

"Well, I haven't heard from Mrs. Starch yet," Dr. Dressler told them, "and Duane Scrod is absent from school."

The female deputy said a detective would follow up on the case, if necessary. "It'll be hard to prove the young man lit the fire," she said, "but sometimes they'll come right out and admit it when you ask 'em. Pyros are funny that way."

Dr. Dressler sat upright. "Whoa — back up a second. You think *Duane* started that wildfire?"

"Didn't anybody tell you?" the female deputy said.

The headmaster shook his head numbly.

"The kid has a history of doing this stuff," the other deputy added.

When she told Dr. Dressler about the other fires, he couldn't conceal his shock. "I had absolutely no idea," he said gravely. "Let me give you the boy's address."

"We already got it, thanks. From his juvenile jacket."

Dr. Dressler had heard nothing back from Duane Scrod Sr. regarding his son's whereabouts, which wasn't surprising. Perhaps the deputies would have better luck getting information from the man with the loud-mouthed parrot, or whatever the heck kind of bird it was.

The headmaster wondered why the school files contained no record of Duane Jr.'s past arsons. He assumed that Duane's rich grandmother had pulled some strings to conceal those incidents from the Truman admissions committee.

It was disturbing for Dr. Dressler to think that any student might be capable of setting a dangerous blaze to get revenge against a teacher whom he didn't like.

But, as the deputy had said, proving guilt would be difficult, if not impossible. The fire department's investigators hadn't found anything incriminating at the scene, not even a burned match. The arsonist had done a good job of covering his tracks.

As soon as the officers left, Dr. Dressler

tried calling Mrs. Starch, and again there was no answer at home or on her cell phone.

Dr. Dressler's secretary popped her head in the doorway. "The Carsons are here," she said.

The headmaster grunted dejectedly. At least once a week, George and Gilda Carson came in to talk about their son Graham, who they were convinced was a genius and should be advanced by at least one and possibly two grade levels.

Dr. Dressler knew for a fact that Graham Carson was a rather average student who would benefit from an algebra tutor and possibly a little extra help in French. He was a nice enough kid, just a bit overeager — and much more tolerable than his pushy, self-important parents.

"I can't deal with the Carsons. Not today," Dr. Dressler told his secretary.

"But they're waiting in the hall."

"Tell them I've got strep throat. Or my cat's having dental surgery. Make up *something!*" the exasperated headmaster said, and crept out the back door of his office.

Even with his map tracker, Dr. Dressler had trouble finding Mrs. Starch's home. The address listed in her employment file was 777 West Buzzard Boulevard, which did not appear on the GPS data disk.

So the headmaster located East Buzzard Boulevard and went west until the pavement stopped and the roadbed turned to dirt. He drove for another two miles until he reached a dead end, where a solitary tin mailbox poked up from the saw palmettos.

The number on the mailbox was 777, but there was no name.

Dr. Dressler got out of his car and scanned the scrub and woods for signs of a building. He found a scruffy narrow path that looked more like a wagon trail than a driveway, and cautiously he trekked along the winding course until it led to a clearing.

And there, shuttered and sagging, stood a three-story wooden house. Weeds crawled up the walls, and shades had been drawn behind all the windows.

As he'd be the first to admit, Dr. Dressler was not a particularly brave soul. He was uncomfortable in such a scraggly, untamed place, far from the comforting clatter and clang of civilization.

Staring with trepidation at the old house, the headmaster couldn't push out of his mind the dark rumors that he'd heard about Bunny Starch. The same impulse to flee that Dr. Dressler had fought during his visit to the Scrod residence tugged at him even more urgently now.

But again he resisted his fears — Mrs. Starch might be ornery and odd, but she was a loyal and valued member of the Truman School family. It's my duty, Dr. Dressler told himself, to make sure she's all right.

He would have felt better about the mission — *much* better — if Mrs. Starch's blue Prius had been parked beside the house. It wasn't.

Dr. Dressler called her name, but there was no reply. His pulse was fluttering as he approached the front steps.

"Mrs. Starch? Are you home?"

Nothing.

"Mrs. Starch? It's me, Dr. Dressler."

He put one foot on the porch, then froze.

A rat was perched on a rocking chair. It was staring at him.

Not a little white rat, either, but a chubby brown one. Its mouth was open in a slight sneer, revealing long, yellowed front teeth.

Dr. Dressler wasn't fond of rodents, large or small. They ate garbage and carried terrible diseases and nested in attics and produced hordes of filthy baby rodents. . . .

"Scat!" he said, clapping his hands. "Go away!"

The rat didn't move, which was distressing.

Maybe it's got rabies, Dr. Dressler thought anxiously. *Maybe it's going to leap for my throat!*

"Shoo! Get lost!" he cried.

The rat didn't blink, didn't even twitch. Dr. Dressler thought this was very suspicious.

He got an idea. He took the car keys from his pocket and tossed them at the rat. The keys clunked the vermin on the head and knocked it off the rocker onto the planks of the porch, where it lay motionless.

Motionless and stiff as a board.

"You've gotta be kidding," Dr. Dressler muttered.

The rat wasn't alive. It had been stuffed, like a deer or a trout on a trophy wall.

When the headmaster picked it up by the tail, he noticed something fastened around its neck: a tiny leather collar with a brass nameplate.

Dr. Dressler peered at the name engraved on the stuffed rat's collar: CHELSEA EVERED.

The headmaster shuddered slightly. Chelsea Evered had been a star student at the Truman School a few years earlier — straight A's, swim team, tennis team, early acceptance to Rollins College.

But Dr. Dressler remembered something

else about the girl: she had once asked for — and received — a transfer out of Mrs. Starch's honors biology class.

Judging by the name on the rat, Mrs. Starch had never forgiven Chelsea Evered for that.

Dr. Dressler carefully placed the taxidermied rodent back on the rocking chair and, after getting up his nerve, knocked on the door. He was greatly relieved when there was no response.

Hurrying down the steps, he glanced back at the gloomy, lifeless house and wondered if the headmasters of other private schools ever had to cope with teachers as weird as Bunny Starch.

A long striped snake scooted across Dr. Dressler's path, and he broke into a heated jog. He was sweaty and out of breath by the time he reached the car. He jumped inside and locked the doors.

That's when something about Mrs. Starch's mailbox caught his eye, something he hadn't noticed when he arrived.

The little red flag was raised.

Which meant that she was sending out mail, which meant that she really *had* found her way home from the Black Vine Swamp . . . and that she was alive and well.

Which was good news — the best possible

news, in fact!

Yet why, wondered Dr. Dressler, hadn't she returned his many voice messages? Why wasn't she picking up her phone?

The headmaster unlocked his car door and furtively got out. After looking around to make sure he was alone — and, standing on the edge of those woods, he was *very* alone — he opened Mrs. Starch's mailbox.

Only one letter was inside. Dr. Dressler was startled to see his own name on the envelope, addressed to the Truman School.

The headmaster knew he should wait for the postal service to properly deliver Mrs. Starch's letter, but curiosity got the better of him. He snatched the envelope from the box.

Not wishing to encounter the mailman and have to explain why he was taking the letter, Dr. Dressler drove straight back to campus.

There, in the privacy of his office, he opened it and began to read:

Dear Dr. Dressler,

It is with great regret that I must request an indefinite leave of absence from my position at the Truman School, due to a sudden family emergency.

I'm sorry for any inconvenience that

90

this may cause my students and fellow faculty members. Be assured that I will return to my teaching duties as soon as my personal situation is settled.

Thank you for your patience and understanding, and for respecting my privacy on this matter.

Most sincerely,
B. Starch

The letter had been typed on Mrs. Starch's personalized stationery. The headmaster reread it twice before folding it back into the envelope.

Mrs. Starch's file already lay open on his desk. Dr. Dressler leafed through every page — her job application, her pension records, her insurance forms.

Wherever Mrs. Starch had been asked to list her next of kin, she had printed the word "none."

Dr. Dressler wearily rubbed his forehead, thinking: *How can there be a family emergency if she has no family?*

Nick brought Marta home to show her the swamp video on the television screen. It was the first time she'd been inside his house.

"That your dad?" She pointed to a framed

photograph on the coffee table.

"Yeah, that's him," Nick said.

"Is that a sailfish he's got? It's huge."

"A hundred and ten pounds." Talking about his father made Nick want to go online and check for an e-mail, but he decided to wait until he was alone.

He said, "C'mon, let's look at the tape."

When he paused the part where the tan blur appeared, Marta sprang off the sofa. "I see it! I see the belt!"

"Like the kind cowboys used to wear," Nick said, "to carry their bullets."

"But is it *him?* I can't tell." She scrunched her eyes, examining the image on the TV screen.

Nick couldn't remember if Smoke ever wore an ammo belt to hold up his pants. Marta said the Truman dress code probably didn't allow it.

"When are you gonna tell the police about this video?" she asked. "Or *are* you gonna tell 'em?"

All day, Mrs. Starch's students had been talking about their interviews with the sheriff's deputies, and about the news that Smoke was being investigated in connection with the Black Vine Swamp fire.

Nick told Marta that he didn't know what to do about the tape. "You can't see the guy's face — there's no way to be sure who it is."

"Betcha five bucks it's him," she said. "I bet he snuck out there and lit that fire to get back at Mrs. Starch."

Nick had to agree that Smoke was a likely suspect, considering his previous crimes.

"Where does he live, anyway?" Nick asked Marta.

"I don't know — and I don't *want* to know," she said. "Probably in a cave somewhere."

As soon as Marta was gone, Nick hurried to the den and checked the computer. Nothing from his dad, not a word.

Nick could no longer pretend that this was a normal interruption in communication. Never since his arrival in Iraq had Capt. Gregory Waters gone so long without e-mailing home. Nick felt sick and anxious — something must have happened. There could be no other explanation.

He really didn't want to be alone with such horrible thoughts, so he dashed out the door and ran until he caught up with Marta.

She heard his footsteps coming and turned around, surprised. "Hey, what's up?" she asked with a smile.

Nick slowed down and started walking

beside her — shoving his hands in his pockets, trying to act casual. He said, "I gotta go up to the Circle K and get some milk and stuff."

"But that's, like, two miles."

"No big deal. I promised my mom." It wasn't a particularly clever story, but it was the best Nick could come up with.

"Want me to go with you?" Marta asked.

" 'Kay."

Secretly Nick was elated that Marta had offered to walk with him. He hoped she would start chattering, as she often did when she was in a good mood. Nick desperately needed something to distract him from worrying about his dad.

Sure enough, Marta launched into a speech about her English essay. Jane Austen was the topic, and although Nick couldn't have been less interested, he let himself be dragged along in conversation. His imagination was much better off in the British countryside than in the Anbar province of Iraq.

To reach the convenience store, Nick and Marta had to cross Green Heron Parkway, a four-lane street that connected to the interstate. The road had been open only a few months, but already it was one of the busiest in the county.

Finally the light turned red and the traffic came to a stop. Nick was halfway across the intersection when he spotted a blue Prius like the one Mrs. Starch drove. It was three or four cars back in line, and Nick shielded his eyes from the sun so that he might see the driver. The glare was blinding.

"Are you crazy?" Marta shouted back at him. "You're gonna get flattened like a pancake."

Nick hurried across the road. The light turned green and the traffic began to roll.

As the Prius motored away, Nick caught a glimpse of the driver — definitely *not* a woman. Nick couldn't see the guy's face, but he had wide shoulders and a dark knit hat tugged down over his ears.

Wrong car, Nick thought.

Then he noticed Marta standing on the curb, watching the blue Prius as it disappeared down the highway. "Weird," she said. "He had the same kind of license plate as you-know-who."

"Seriously?" Nick hadn't noticed.

"Everybody wants to save the poor ol' manatees," Marta remarked.

"I guess," said Nick, pondering the coincidence.

When they reached the store, he realized that he had only fifty-five cents in his

95

pocket, which pretty much blew his cover story about going shopping for his mom.

If Marta figured it out, she never let on. She loaned him a couple of bucks to buy a half-gallon of milk.

Nick walked her back to her block, and then he headed home. Turning the corner of his street, he was surprised to see his mother's car in the driveway. She never got off work early, except for the time that she'd gotten sick after eating a bad burrito in the jail cafeteria.

Opening the front door, Nick called out, "Hey, Mom?"

She wasn't in the living room, or the kitchen. He put the milk in the refrigerator and went down the hall to his parents' bedroom. The door was closed.

"Mom?" He knocked lightly. "Mom, it's me."

"Come on in."

She was sitting on the edge of the bed next to a wad of crumpled tissues. Her eyes were bloodshot, and she was sniffling.

Nick felt his knees turn to rubber. "Oh no!" he said.

"He's not dead, honey. But he's hurt."

"How bad?" Nick rasped.

His mother reached out and pulled him close. "He's on his way home."

"How bad?" Nick asked again, with a tremble.

His mother kissed his forehead and dabbed the tears on his cheeks.

She said, "He's coming home. That's all that matters."

SEVEN

Millicent Winship was seventy-seven years old, ninety-two pounds, ridiculously rich, and as tough as a garfish. Her only daughter, Whitney, had shamed the family by abandoning her husband and son and moving to Paris, where she had opened a cheese shop. Mrs. Winship didn't care much for the fellow Whitney had married, but she felt very bad that he'd been left alone to raise her only grandchild — a burly and rebellious boy named Duane, after his father.

So Mrs. Winship had decided that the least she could do was provide her grandson with the best possible education. Because of his poor grades and occasional behavior problems, the Truman School wasn't exactly eager to have young Duane Jr. as a student. Mrs. Winship solved that problem by sending an extremely large check.

It wasn't often that she got to see Duane Jr. because she divided her time among five different homes in five different states — California, New York, Arizona, South Carolina, and Florida. All of Mrs. Winship's houses were located on championship golf courses; she herself didn't play the game, but she loved watching the players traipse in their colorful outfits down the emerald slopes, pausing every few steps to hack feverishly at a tiny white sphere. Mrs. Winship thought golf was the most amusing spectacle that she'd ever seen, and she would spend hours spying on passing foursomes through the special high-powered binoculars that she kept on the back windowsill at each of her fairway residences.

Mrs. Winship spent only two weeks a year in Naples, but during these visits she always invited Duane Jr. and his father out to dinner. If they failed to respond promptly, Mrs. Winship would command her chauffeur to drive her to the Scrod household so that she could personally raise a ruckus.

Which was her intention on this day as she rapped sharply on the screen door and barked her grandson's name over the notes of a Mozart symphony that was blaring from the stereo speakers inside.

Before long, the music cut off and Duane Scrod Sr. shuffled to the door. He was flustered to see Mrs. Winship and made a halfhearted pass at smoothing the tangle of oily hair under his trucker's cap.

"Afternoon, Millie," he said with false cheeriness. "What brings you here?"

"My grandson. What do you think?" she snapped. "Where is he?"

"Wanna come in?"

"I certainly do not. Why aren't you answering your telephone?" Mrs. Winship demanded. "I left a message about a dinner engagement — that was two nights ago, and I've received no reply."

Duane Scrod Sr. sighed ruefully, and so did the large macaw on his shoulder.

"I see you've still got that stupid bird," Mrs. Winship remarked.

"She's not stupid. She speaks three languages."

"Really? Pick one and have her tell me where D.J. is."

"She doesn't know," Duane Scrod Sr. muttered, "and neither do I."

It was an unsatisfactory answer, as far as Mrs. Winship was concerned.

"We're talking about your one and only child," she said, glaring, "and you don't know where he is?"

Duane Scrod Sr. opened the door and came out on the porch. "He said he was goin' camping somewhere out in the boonies. That was a couple days ago, and I haven't seen him since."

"But what about school?" Mrs. Winship asked.

"He said he needed a break."

"Oh, that's rich."

Duane Scrod Sr. threw up his hands, nearly toppling the macaw from its roost on his shoulder. "What d'you want from me, Millie?" he whined. "The boy has his own agenda. I can't make him do what he doesn't want to do."

"Oh, of course not. You're just his father," Mrs. Winship said sarcastically. "Is he in trouble again? And tell me the truth for once."

Duane Scrod Sr. sat down in a rotting wicker chair and vigorously clawed at an insect bite on one of his bare feet. "A cop was here about an hour ago," he admitted. "Somebody lit a fire out by the Big Cypress, and they think it was Junior."

Millicent Winship closed her eyes and thought: *Not again.*

Duane Sr. said, "They don't have enough to bust him. They're just fishin' is all."

"Is that supposed to make me feel better?"

Duane Sr. reached in a pocket and took out a sunflower seed, which he fed to the macaw. He said, "When D.J. gets home, I'll make sure he calls you. Maybe we can all go to that steak place again, the one up near Bonita Beach."

"Unless he's in jail," Mrs. Winship said, "in which case we can bring him a lovely fruit basket."

"Aw, don't be like that."

"Are you still out of work, Duane?"

"What do you expect? I got no wheels!" Indignantly he pointed at the Tahoe upon which he had painted BOYCOTT SMITH-ERS CHEVY!!!!! "They still won't give me a new transmission," he griped.

"Perhaps it's because you torched their building — you think that might have something to do with it?"

"Beside the point!" Duane Sr. huffed. "I paid my debt to society. I did my time."

Mrs. Winship was more sad than angry. Despite his unattractive personality, Duane Scrod Sr. had always been a hard worker and a good provider, until Whitney had run off to France. Then he'd sort of fallen apart, losing interest in the antique piano shop that he'd owned in Naples. Within a year the place had gone bankrupt, and since then Duane Scrod Sr. hadn't been able to hold a steady job. The low point had come when he'd burned down the Chevrolet dealership.

"Those six months you were locked up," Mrs. Winship said, "I still don't understand why you didn't have Duane Jr. call me. What were you thinking, letting that boy stay out here all alone?"

Duane Scrod Sr. looked up from his bug-chewed foot. "Maybe I was ashamed for you to know what happened," he said in a scratchy voice. "Hey, D.J. took care of himself just fine. He never went hungry, Millie — I had some money put away."

Money that I'd sent you, thought Mrs. Winship, so you wouldn't lose your house to the bank.

"There was plenty for groceries," Duane Scrod Sr. went on. "He did all right, like I've told you a hundred times."

Mrs. Winship shook a finger at him. "Nothing is all right around this place. Not you, not your son — *nothing.* It's time to get a grip on life, Duane. Time to move on."

Duane Scrod Sr. rose with a squeak from the old wicker chair. "Yeah," he said.

"Oui!" chirped the blue-and-gold macaw. *"Ja!"*

Mrs. Winship rolled her eyes. "Would you kindly tell your parrot to shut up?"

"She's not a parrot."

"How did Duane Jr. get out to where he's

103

camping?"

Duane Sr. said, "He drove himself."

"Did he now?"

"He's got his license, Millie. He turned sixteen two months ago."

Mrs. Winship's eyes narrowed. "I'm quite aware of that. I sent a birthday card, remember?"

Duane Sr. looked embarrassed. "I told him to call you and say thanks for the check. I guess he forgot."

"So you bought him a car?"

"Naw. Fixed up a motorcycle that we found in the want ads," Duane Sr. said. "D.J. has a fondness for motorcycles."

"Oh, terrific. Next Christmas I'll get him a helmet," Mrs. Winship said, "and some funeral insurance."

Duane Scrod Sr. frowned. "Now, why do you always have to take that snippy tone?"

"Why? *Pourquoi? Warum?*" cried the macaw.

"Listen to me, Duane," Mrs. Winship said forcefully. "If I don't hear from my grandson soon, life will get extremely unpleasant for you. I'm not paying his tuition so that he can skip class and roast weenies in the woods. That's an insult to me, and I resent being insulted."

Duane Scrod Sr. flinched like a puppy that

104

had just been smacked on the butt with a newspaper. He said, "I'll do my best to find Junior."

"Good idea, because I'm not leaving town until I see him," Mrs. Winship declared. "Now give me a straight answer — do you think he's the one who set fire to the swamp?"

"Truly? I couldn't say."

"Why in the world would he do such a thing?" Mrs. Winship said. "Since you're the only other arsonist I know, I thought you might have some special insight."

Duane Sr.'s eyes flashed in anger. "I never taught that boy to set fires. He knows better."

"Then let's hope the police are wrong." She was halfway down the steps when he called her name.

"Hey, Millie, wait! What do you hear from Whitney?"

The question made Millicent Winship's heart sink.

She looked up at Duane Sr. and quietly said, "She's not coming back from Paris."

"So the cheese business is good?"

"I'm sorry. I really am," said Mrs. Winship. "By the way, your precious bird just pooped all over your shirt."

Duane Scrod Sr. looked down at the mess

105

and nodded bleakly. "What else is new," he said.

On the same Monday morning that Nick had watched Smoke eat Mrs. Starch's pencil, Capt. Gregory Waters was being evacuated from Iraq to an American military installation in Germany. From there he was flown to the Walter Reed Army Medical Center in Washington, D.C., a hospital for soldiers.

Nick and his mother flew up on Thursday morning and waited an hour in the lobby. Finally a doctor came out and introduced himself. They followed him along a maze of drab corridors teeming with nurses and orderlies and patients; Nick had never seen so many young men and women in wheelchairs.

The doctor took Nick and his mother into a private room. Using a cross-section diagram of the human body, he explained that Captain Waters lost his right arm and most of the shoulder when something called a rocket-propelled grenade, or RPG, had struck the Humvee in which he was riding.

"We know," Nick's mother said tightly. "They phoned us from the base in Ramadi. Can we see him now?"

"Did they also tell you that, because of

the severe damage to the shoulder, we might not be able to fit your husband with a working prosthetic?"

"Like a mechanical hook, you mean?"

"It would be difficult," the doctor said, "but we're not giving up hope."

"Can we see him, please?"

The doctor led them up a flight of stairs, then down another long corridor. Every patient they saw was missing an arm or a leg — sometimes both legs. Nick tried not to stare. Before entering his father's hospital room, he paused to brace himself.

Capt. Gregory Waters was propped upright in bed, though his eyes were closed. His chest, wrapped with gauze and heavy tape, moved up and down slightly when he breathed. Nick noticed that his dad's hair had been shaved, and that one side of his face was pink and mottled with welts. A clear tube carried amber fluid into his remaining arm from a plastic bag strung on an aluminum rack beside the bed.

Her eyes welling, Nick's mother stood wordlessly at the foot of the bed. She looked shaky, so Nick put an arm around her waist and walked her to the only chair in the room.

"He's still on lots of pain medication," the doctor said, "so he'll be groggy when he wakes up."

"Could you get my mom a glass of water?" Nick asked.

After the doctor left, another long hour passed before Nick's father awoke. He smiled sleepily when he saw them. Nick's mother hugged him and stroked his face. Nick squeezed his left hand, and his father squeezed back firmly.

Glancing at the bandaged knob where his right arm used to be, he joked, "Now I'll have to sew up the extra sleeve in all my shirts."

Nick's mom said, "Very funny, Greg."

"So I'll have to learn how to throw a curve left-handed. No big deal."

Always a good athlete, Nick's father had been a pitcher in the Baltimore Orioles farm system when he'd first met Nick's mother. According to the newspaper clippings in a family scrapbook, Greg Waters' fastball had once been clocked at 94 mph.

He never made the big leagues, so he'd gone back to college, earned a degree in business administration, and taken a desk job with a sprinkler supply company in Fort Myers. After three years of being bored out of his skull, he returned to baseball as a pitching coach for a minor-league club. He was happy, but the money wasn't great.

That's one reason he'd joined the National Guard — the sign-up bonus had paid for Nick's first year at the Truman School.

For one weekend every month, Greg Waters went to Tampa to train as an army soldier. The country was at peace, and neither he nor his family ever imagined that he'd be sent overseas to face real combat. Everything changed after the invasion of Iraq.

"Did they say when I can go home?" Nick's father asked.

"It all depends. Tomorrow you start rehab," Nick's mother said.

"What fun." Greg Waters blinked heavily. "I'm so damn tired."

Nick's gaze fell upon the rounded white knob of gauze and tape where his father's muscular right arm had once been. The bandages were so shiny that they looked fake, like part of a mummy costume for Halloween.

His mom said, "Greg, you get some rest. We'll come back at dinnertime."

"You're not gonna try to feed me like a baby, are you?"

"No, sir. You're going to feed yourself."

"That's my girl." Nick's father grinned. "Nicky, you holding up okay?"

"I'm good, Dad."

"It's a rough deal, I know, but things could be worse," he said. "I was lucky to get out of that place alive. The guy sitting next to me in that Humvee, he didn't make it."

Nick felt his head start to spin. "Was he your friend?"

"Like a brother."

Nick lowered his eyes. It was almost unbearable to think how close his father had come to dying.

When he looked up again, Capt. Gregory Waters was fast asleep.

After visiting Duane Scrod Sr., who was not especially helpful, Detective Jason Marshall picked up Dr. Dressler at the Truman School, and together they went to the residence of Bunny Starch. The headmaster had requested to come along, which was fine with the detective.

Walking up the creaking steps of the old house, Dr. Dressler exclaimed, "The rat's gone!"

"The *what?*" the detective said.

"She put a stuffed rat on that rocking chair," Dr. Dressler said. "She named it after one of her former students."

Jason Marshall looked doubtful.

"I'm serious," said Dr. Dressler.

The detective knocked on Mrs. Starch's door. Nobody answered. He pressed the doorbell, but it was out of order. They walked around to the other side of the house and rapped on the back door. Still no response.

"Guess I'll come back tomorrow," Jason Marshall said.

Dr. Dressler was disappointed. "Can't you just break in? What if she's ill or she had an accident or . . . something else happened?"

"I can't go inside a house without a search warrant," the detective explained, "and a judge won't give me a warrant unless there's cause to believe a crime's been committed. There's no evidence of that, Dr. Dressler."

Frustrated, the headmaster trailed Jason Marshall back to his unmarked police car.

"That letter I got about a 'family emergency,' I just don't buy it," Dr. Dressler said. "The woman has no family that I can locate anywhere."

The detective leaned against the fender of his car and took out a pack of chewing gum. He offered a piece to Dr. Dressler, who said no thanks.

"Libby's told me all the crazy stories about Mrs. Starch," Jason Marshall said. "Kids love to talk, and normally I wouldn't pay much attention. But now you're telling

111

me she kept a stuffed rat on the porch — this isn't the most normal person in the world, would you agree?"

Dr. Dressler nodded. "She's a bit quirky, for sure."

"Maybe she just freaked out after the fire on the field trip," the detective speculated. "That had to be a scary experience — eventually she finds her way out of the woods and rushes to our house with Libby's asthma inhaler. Then she drives home, looks in the mirror, and says, 'Geez, I could have died out there! I really need some time off.'"

Dr. Dressler was skeptical. "Not Bunny Starch," he said.

"Imagine spending the night all alone in the Big Cypress while it's burning," Jason Marshall said. "I don't care how tough you are, it definitely would shake you up."

"Anything's possible, I suppose."

"Just a theory." The detective took out his cell phone. "What's the number at this house?"

By now the headmaster knew it by heart: "555-2346," he said.

Jason Marshall dialed and waited. Mrs. Starch's phone rang only twice before an answering machine picked up.

"There's a message," the detective whispered to Dr. Dressler.

"What does it say?"

Jason Marshall touched the Redial button and handed the cell phone to Dr. Dressler. The headmaster listened intently to the recorded greeting on the other end:

Hello, people. I'll be away from school indefinitely because of an unexpected family matter. You may leave a message at the tone, though it might be a while before I have time to reply. Please accept my apologies in advance. Now here's the beep!

"Is that her voice?" the detective asked.

"Sure sounds like it," Dr. Dressler said.

"First the letter, now the voice message on her phone. I've got to be honest — there's nothing more the sheriff's office can do. The woman is obviously alive and well," said Jason Marshall.

"Then why no phone calls?"

"Maybe she doesn't feel like answering questions about a 'family emergency' that doesn't really exist. Like I said, she probably just needed a break, so she made up an excuse not to come to school."

"But that's not like her," Dr. Dressler asserted again.

"Some people burn out on their jobs all of a sudden. I've seen it happen before." The detective opened the car door and slid behind the wheel.

"Just a second," said Dr. Dressler. He stepped quickly to Mrs. Starch's mailbox and peeked inside. It was empty.

On the ride back to the Truman campus, the headmaster asked Jason Marshall about the arson investigation. The detective said he'd turned over the information about Duane Scrod Jr. to the fire department.

"So far, they haven't been able to connect him to the crime," Jason Marshall said.

"Did they turn up any clues?"

"Nothing that panned out. Near the scene of the fire they found a ballpoint pen with a name on it — Red Diamond Energy. It's some oil-and-gas company from Tampa that has a small lease out there near the swamp," Jason Marshall said. "Needless to say, young Mr. Scrod is not on their payroll. It's unlikely that the pen was his."

"So what happens to your arson case?"

"Not much, unless we catch a break."

Privately, Dr. Dressler was relieved that Duane Jr. wouldn't be arrested anytime soon, if at all. The ugly publicity would have been damaging to the reputation of the school. Years earlier, a Truman student had

114

been caught driving a stolen sno-cone truck and it had made the TV news all the way over in Miami.

"Do you want me to call you when Duane returns to class?" the headmaster asked Jason Marshall. "Would you still like to speak with him?"

"Might as well — just to let him know he's on our radar."

"Good idea," said Dr. Dressler, although he suspected that Duane Scrod Jr. would not be even slightly intimidated.

EIGHT

The helicopter took off from Naples Airport and headed east. In the front passenger seat was a heavyset man in his mid-thirties named Drake McBride, the president of Red Diamond Energy Corporation. Sitting behind him was his project manager, Jimmy Lee Bayliss. Both men had headsets with microphones attached so that they could hear each other over the din of the engines.

Drake McBride wore a cowboy hat, snake-skin boots, and a pale silk shirt with snap buttons. He was sipping hot coffee from a Styrofoam cup. Jimmy Lee Bayliss was dressed in a tan long-sleeved work shirt and smudged trousers. A map lay open across his lap.

Within minutes the helicopter was circling the Black Vine Swamp. Jimmy Lee Bayliss pointed to a charred, crescent-shaped scar in the scruffy prairie that bordered the ancient cypress strand.

"That's from the fire," he said to his boss. "None of our equipment got damaged, right?"

"Of course not." Jimmy Lee Bayliss thought: *Does he think I'm a moron?*

Drake McBride shielded his eyes from the glare of the sun. "Section 22 is right below us?"

"Yes, sir."

"And Section 21 is over there?"

"That's right," said Jimmy Lee Bayliss.

"Lemme see the danged map."

Drake McBride was not a Texan, although he tried to dress like one and talk like one. It annoyed Jimmy Lee Bayliss, who was from Houston and had spent twenty-six years of his life drilling for oil and natural gas. Drake McBride, on the other hand, was from upstate New York and therefore had no business saying words like "danged."

However, being a fairly intelligent fellow, Jimmy Lee Bayliss knew better than to disrespect the person who signed his paychecks.

"Take us down to two hundred feet," Drake McBride told the pilot.

The helicopter spooked some snowy egrets from the treetops and flushed a deer across the dry prairie.

"Any sign of that danged cat?" Drake

McBride asked Jimmy Lee Bayliss.

"No, sir. The gunshots scared it off for good, I'm sure." Jimmy Lee Bayliss dug into his pants for a roll of Tums. Ever since he'd been assigned to the Big Cypress project, his stomach burned like he'd swallowed a hot coal.

Drake McBride said, "Wouldn't have broke my heart if you'd blasted that hairball to smithereens."

"The law's pretty harsh when it comes to killin' panthers. The feds got no sense of sport, sir."

"Panthers — ha!" Drake McBride snorted. "Out west they're just plain old cougars, and you can shoot 'em down like coyotes."

He pronounced "coyote" with a long "e" on the end, which made Jimmy Lee Bayliss cringe. He wasn't fond of phonies.

"If that cat comes back here and somebody spots it, we got a problem," Drake McBride said. "Last thing we need is nosy game wardens trampin' all over our project site — you follow?"

"The panther's long gone, sir. I fired two rounds over its head with a deer rifle, and you never saw anything run so fast in all your life. Wouldn't surprise me if it's *still* runnin'."

"Hope you're right, friend."

I hope so, too, thought Jimmy Lee Bayliss. Panthers were Florida's most famous endangered species, and public sightings attracted lots of attention. If some overeager wildlife officer decided that Red Diamond's drilling activities were disturbing panther habitat, the whole project could be delayed or even shut down.

The helicopter pilot made one more pass over the scene of the fire. Gazing down at the scorched grass and trees, Drake McBride slurped his coffee and said, "Well, it's the dry season."

Jimmy Lee Bayliss wasn't sure if his boss was trying to be funny.

"Just go on doin' what you've been doin'," Drake McBride told him, "and get us ready to rock-and-roll."

"Yes, sir."

"And don't forget —"

"I know," Jimmy Lee Bayliss said. "Keep a low profile."

"Lower than a rattlesnake's belly," said Drake McBride.

Nick and his mother arrived home from Washington, D.C., on Sunday night. He got up early the next morning to get his arm taped.

When he asked his mother for help, she looked doubtfully at the Ace bandage and said, "What are the other kids going to say?"

"I don't really care," said Nick. "I want to go through the same thing as Dad."

"He won't be home for a while."

"I need to get a head start."

"Nicky, please."

"Just wrap me up, Mom."

As usual, Marta sat next to him on the school bus. She asked what had happened to his right arm, which was bound tightly behind his back, beneath his shirt. The right sleeve of his blue school blazer hung limp.

Nick said, "From now on, I'm doing everything left-handed."

"Writing, too? What about baseball and lacrosse?"

"Everything."

Marta arched an eyebrow. "And there's nothing wrong with your other arm?"

"Nope."

"That's really whacked, Nick. That's, like, making fun of crippled people."

His cheeks flushed. "No, just the opposite," he said sharply. "My dad got hurt real bad by a rocket in Iraq. He lost his right arm all the way past the shoulder."

Marta gasped softly. "God, I am *so* sorry. Is he gonna be all right?"

Nick nodded tightly. "But he'll be a lefty the rest of his life."

"So *that's* why you're switching." Marta smiled and pinched the empty sleeve of his jacket. "Pretty cool."

"Whatever."

"I'm serious," she said. "When's he coming home?"

"Pretty soon, I hope." Nick told her about the trip that he and his mother had made to the Walter Reed military hospital. "That's why I wasn't in school Thursday and Friday."

Marta said, "Nobody told us. I thought you had the flu."

"I wish," he said glumly, and stayed quiet for the rest of the ride to Truman.

His first class of the day was English. The teacher, Mr. Grunwald, was giving a lecture about a famous short story called "The Open Boat," by Stephen Crane. Nick had finished reading it on the flight home from Washington.

When he tried to get his binder out of his book bag, the zipper on the book pocket got stuck. It wouldn't have been a big deal if Nick's right arm hadn't been strapped behind him, but his weaker left hand couldn't loosen the zipper by itself. Every time he jerked on it, the backpack rose off the floor and he lost his leverage.

Mickey Maris, who was behind him, saw what was happening and reached over to help. Nick waved him away. With grim determination he planted both his feet on top of the backpack to hold it in place. Then he yanked with all his might on the zipper hitch, which instantly snapped off in his fingers.

Nick grumbled under his breath. He tugged the book bag onto his lap and, using the tip of a ballpoint pen, separated the teeth of the broken zipper to open the stubborn book pocket. He removed the English binder, slapped it open on his desk, carefully positioned the pen in his left hand, and prepared to take notes.

"This famous tale of a shipwrecked crew," Mr. Grunwald began, "was based on a true episode in the young author's life."

Writing left-handed felt weird, like having a crab claw on the end of his arm. Nick tried hard to guide the pen smoothly. He was trying to spell out the words "based on a true story," but on paper the line came out looking like blue worm tracks — and a dizzy worm at that.

Mickey Maris, who'd been peeking over Nick's shoulder, whispered, "It's okay, dude. You can borrow my notes and scan a copy after school."

Nick firmly shook his head. "Thanks anyway." He wasn't about to give up so easily.

By the end of the period, the letters he was stringing together with such difficulty actually began to resemble those in the English language. The next class was algebra, and its quirky formulas presented a different kind of challenge. Happily, Nick found the numerals and symbols easier to master with an untrained hand than the alphabet.

By the time he got to biology, his left arm throbbed and his fingers were cramping. A substitute teacher stood writing on the board, his back to the students.

"Still no Mrs. Starch?" Nick whispered to Marta.

"She took a leave of absence — you believe that?" Marta said. "Dr. Dressler made an announcement on Friday."

Strange, Nick thought. "Did he say why?"

" 'Family emergency,' whatever *that* means." Marta's cell phone began to vibrate and she turned it off. "He did say that the old witch would be coming back, unfortunately."

Nick wrestled the biology book out of his backpack. "What about Smoke?" he asked.

"Nobody's seen him. He must've quit school, or else Dressler kicked him out," Marta said. "Either way, no great loss."

"Maybe he got busted for setting the fire."

"Libby says no. Her dad's assigned to the case, so she would've heard about it," Marta said. "Hey, how's the arm feel, Lefty?"

"Excellent," Nick lied.

The substitute was spelling out his name in large block letters: DR. WENDELL WAXMO.

Marta inhaled through her teeth. "No way!"

"Not *him*," Nick murmured.

Wendell Waxmo was a legendary wacko. Nick and Marta had never had him as a teacher, but they'd heard all about him. Everybody had.

Because of his peculiar behavior, Wendell Waxmo had been banned long ago from the public school system. However, since private schools such as Truman were usually desperate for substitutes, Wendell Waxmo still got the occasional call.

The students let out a collective giggle when he turned to face them. Wendell Waxmo was wearing a faded black tuxedo with a bright yellow bow tie.

"All right, you little termites, what's so bloody funny?" he asked in a squeaky, brittle voice that was impossible to take seriously. He looked half as tall and twice as wide as Mrs. Starch, and his wispy red hair was arranged in a failed attempt to cover a bald spot the size of a dinner platter.

"Now please rise and sing the Pledge of Allegiance," he said.

The students glanced at each other uncertainly. Nobody stood up. When Graham raised his hand, Wendell Waxmo called on him with an impatient snap of the fingers.

"We only do the Pledge of Allegiance in morning assembly," Graham explained, "and we don't sing it, Mr. Waxmo."

"For me, you do."

So they all got up and sang the Pledge of Allegiance to the tune of "America the Beautiful." It sounded totally ridiculous.

The class sat down, tittering.

Wendell Waxmo announced that he'd be filling in for Mrs. Starch until her return. He also said that he wished to be addressed as *Dr.* Waxmo, as he'd received an advanced degree from Biddleburg State University. Nick had never heard of the school, although Dr. Waxmo described it as "the Harvard of the Dakotas."

Graham again started waving a hand.

"What now?" Wendell Waxmo barked irritably.

"North Dakota or South Dakota?"

"Both. And western Minnesota as well," Wendell Waxmo said. "Now open your textbooks to page 117. Today we're going to conjugate the verb *amar,* which of course means 'to love.' "

Libby Marshall couldn't contain herself. "But this isn't Spanish class. It's biology!" she blurted.

Wendell Waxmo's brow furrowed and he cocked his head. "You think I was born yesterday? You think I just fell off the turnip truck? What's your name, young lady?"

Marta passed a note to Nick: *This is fantastic! He's crazy as a bedbug!* Nick smiled and stuffed the note into his pocket.

Libby Marshall was quaking under Wendell Waxmo's stare.

"I said, what's your name?" he persisted.

Nick raised his left hand and, not waiting to be called on, said, "She's right, Dr. Waxmo. This is a biology class. See, here's our book."

Wendell Waxmo stalked up to Nick, snatched the text, thumbed through it grumpily, and shoved it back at him.

"There's one on Mrs. Starch's desk for you to use," Nick said.

Wendell Waxmo turned to see. "So there is," he muttered, and spun back to face

Nick. "And your name, young man?"

"Nick Waters."

"What's the matter with your right arm, Mr. Waters?"

"Nothing. It's just an experiment," Nick said.

"I broke my right arm once. A dairy cow sat on it," Wendell Waxmo said gravely. "Are you trying to be funny or something?"

"No, sir. It's a serious experiment."

Marta started to raise her hand, but Nick shot her a look. He didn't want everybody in class talking about what had happened to his father.

"Well, you'd better hope that a cloven five-hundred-pound beast never sits on *you,* Mr. Waters, because it's not humorous." Wendell Waxmo strode to the front of the room and hoisted Mrs. Starch's book. "All right, everybody, let's turn to page 117."

The students just sat there. They thought he was joking, but he wasn't.

"What are you people waiting for?" he snapped.

"It's not the Spanish book, Dr. Waxmo," Libby Marshall said in a small but brave voice.

Rachel spoke up. "We're way past page 117."

"Is that right?" Something resembling a

smile crossed Wendell Waxmo's face. "Obviously none of you have ever had the experience of being in my classes. Otherwise you'd know that on Mondays I always teach page 117 — and *only* page 117 — regardless of the subject matter."

Nick had to bite his lip to keep from laughing.

"Earlier this morning, for example, at the Egmont Day School, I substituted in Miss MacKay's advanced world history section," Wendell Waxmo said. "By the time the bell rang, every one of those students had practically memorized page 117 of their history book. And that was a map of the Roman Empire!"

Substitutes were often flaky, but Wendell Waxmo was in a special category. "Every teacher has a system that works best for them," he prattled on. "Mrs. Starch has hers, and I have mine, which is: Pick a page, then focus, focus, focus."

He flipped open the biology text to page 117, skimmed a few paragraphs, looked up brightly, and asked, "So, who can tell me how proteins function in a plasma membrane?"

For once Graham was too flustered to raise his hand. Libby Marshall answered the question in a dull tone: "Proteins release chemicals that allow certain cells to communicate with each other, and they also help move water and sugar through the membrane."

Dr. Wendell Waxmo was overjoyed. "Now *that's* what I'm talking about, folks! This little spitfire is cookin' with gas! I hope everybody's taking notes."

Marta cackled under her breath. "What for? Mrs. Starch tested us on this stuff three weeks ago."

"Don't tell him," whispered Nick.

Whenever Wendell Waxmo spoke, his bony Adam's apple bobbed up and down, causing the yellow bow tie to jiggle.

"Quick now — what's a phospholipid molecule? You there!" He pointed at Graham. "Definition, please."

Graham looked helpless and lost. "I forget," he said.

Wendell Waxmo frowned. "Stand, young man."

Graham rose unsteadily. "Yessir?"

"Lullaby, please."

"But I don't know any lullabies," Graham said, on the verge of blubbering.

Wendell Waxmo sighed. "A day without music is a day without sunshine. Sing after me, please:

Hush, little baby, don't say a word,
Momma's gonna buy you a mynah bird.
And if that mynah bird don't talk,
Momma's gonna buy you a cuckoo
     clock . . ."

Marta leaned close to Nick and said, "That's not how it goes."

"No kidding."

Wendell Waxmo wasn't exactly a born singer. After he finished warbling, the students sat in stunned relief that he mistook for appreciation.

"Your turn, young fellow," he said to Graham.

"No, I can't."

"Pardon me?"

"I just can't," Graham said again.

Wendell Waxmo folded his arms. "I'm in charge of this battleship."

"Yessir."

"And you will do as I say, or face the consequences."

Graham was plainly frightened by the threat, even though substitute teachers had very little authority. "I think I remember what a phospholipid molecule is," he offered gamely.

"Who cares? Now sing," Wendell Waxmo said.

"Hush, little baby," Graham began with a pained grimace, *"don't you cry —"*

Suddenly the door banged open and a boy stepped into the classroom. Nick didn't recognize him at first.

The boy's blazer was pressed and spotless, his khaki trousers were laundered and creased, and his necktie was perfectly knotted. His cheeks looked shiny and scrubbed, his hair was parted and neatly trimmed, and not a speck of grease or grime was visible on his hands.

"And who would *you* be?" Dr. Wendell Waxmo demanded.

"I would be Duane Scrod Jr.," the boy replied.

NINE

Marta jotted another note to Nick: *He's scarier now than he was before.*

Like Marta and the rest of the class, Nick couldn't stop staring at Smoke. The transformation was incredible.

Wendell Waxmo said, "You're tardy, Mr. Scrod."

"Sorry. My bike threw a rod." Smoke set down his backpack and removed a thin plastic binder, which he presented to the substitute.

"Here's my essay," he said. "Five hundred words, just like Mrs. Starch asked for. Actually, it's five hundred and eight."

A ripple of high amusement passed through the room.

Wendell Waxmo opened the binder to the front page, upon which the title of the essay had been centered:

The Curse of the Persistent Pimple

By Duane Scrod Jr.

Wendell Waxmo made the foolish mistake of saying the title aloud, which caused an avalanche of laughter.

"She told me to make it funny," Smoke said defensively. He seemed uncomfortable being so sharply dressed, and the center of attention.

"What kind of nonsense is this?" Wendell Waxmo rolled up the binder and shook it in the air. The tuxedo made him look like an orchestra conductor. "Are you telling me that Mrs. Starch assigned you to write a research paper about pimples? Get serious."

Despite the teacher's hostile attitude, Smoke remained surprisingly calm. "You want me to read it or not?"

"Out loud, you mean?" Wendell Waxmo scowled. "I don't think so, Mr. Scrod. Take your seat."

With a sniff of distaste, Wendell Waxmo deposited the acne essay in his scuffed briefcase.

Smoke sat down and, to the astonishment of his classmates, produced a pen and a notebook. In all the time that Nick had known the kid, he couldn't remember ever seeing him take notes.

"It's not really him," Marta whispered.

"It's gotta be an imposter."

"Or a secret twin brother," Nick said.

Dr. Wendell Waxmo seemed miffed that his limelight had been stolen. He scuttled up to Duane Scrod Jr. and said, "Young man, I intend to find out if you're telling the truth about this preposterous pimple project, or if it's just some prank you thought up to have a few cheap giggles at my expense."

Smoke looked puzzled. "Why would I do a dumbass thing like that?"

"Because kids always try to take advantage of substitute teachers, that's why. To prey on them, as it were. You think we're here just for your sport and entertainment."

Wendell Waxmo inched closer.

"I know your type, son," he said, "but I insist on respect. Why else would I go to all the trouble of dressing up this way?"

Smoke shrugged. "Because you're a total whack job?"

The class exploded, and Wendell Waxmo turned purple. Then he did something that caused the students to swallow their laughter: He jabbed a pale knobby finger at Smoke's nose.

"You," he said, seething, "owe me an apology!"

Nick and the other students fully expected

Smoke to chomp the substitute's offending finger in half, as he'd done to Mrs. Starch's yellow pencil.

But Duane Scrod Jr. shocked them all. He didn't nip, nibble, or even spit on Wendell Waxmo. Instead he clenched his jaws, took a slow, tight breath, and said, "You're right, bro. I'm sorry."

Which prompted Marta to jot another frantic note to Nick: *He's turned into an alien!*

If the truth were known, Dr. Dressler had the names of four other substitutes who were completely sane and normal. He chose Wendell Waxmo instead, knowing full well that the man was more or less out of his mind.

It was Dr. Dressler's belief that once Bunny Starch found out who was teaching her classes, she would immediately terminate her leave of absence and rush back to rescue her students.

In the meantime, the headmaster braced himself for angry phone calls from Truman parents complaining about Wendell Waxmo's distracting wardrobe, bizarre teaching style, and loony impulses to break out in song.

For now, though, Dr. Dressler had a more pressing problem.

"Would you care for some coffee?" he asked Jason Marshall.

The detective said no thanks and took a seat. "Have you spoken to him yet?"

"Not a word. He just showed up for class this morning," Dr. Dressler said, "out of the blue."

"Did you notice anything different about him?"

Dr. Dressler chuckled uneasily. "*Everything* about him is different. He's like a whole new person."

"What do you mean?" the detective asked.

"He looks like a real student is what I mean. He looks like he actually wants to be here."

"But that's a good thing, right?"

"Certainly," Dr. Dressler said, though privately he was both alarmed and suspicious. When the bell rang, he nervously poured himself another cup of coffee.

"You'll see for yourself," he said to Jason Marshall.

Moments later, Duane Scrod Jr. walked into the office. He didn't look like an arsonist; he looked like the future president of the Student Council. He also appeared perfectly fit and healthy, despite having digested Mrs. Starch's pencil.

Dr. Dressler introduced Detective Marshall. "He'd like to ask you a few questions, Duane."

"No problem." Duane Scrod Jr. made himself comfortable on the headmaster's leather sofa.

Jason Marshall took out a legal pad. "I heard about the incident with Mrs. Starch," he began.

Duane Scrod Jr. didn't deny it. "Is it against the law to bite a pencil?"

"Some of the other kids said you also threatened her," the detective said.

"She was making fun of me. I guess I got mad," the boy admitted. "I told her she'd be sorry if she didn't get outta my face. It was wrong, what I said. Definitely."

"So you didn't mean it?"

" 'Course not."

Jason Marshall wrote down Duane Jr.'s answers. Dr. Dressler couldn't get over how *normal* the boy looked; he couldn't imagine what had caused such a dramatic change in grooming and attitude.

"Yet the next day you didn't come to school," the detective said.

"Yeah, I skipped. That was wrong, too," Duane Scrod Jr. said.

"Have you ever been out to the Black Vine Swamp?"

"Sure. Catchin' snakes."

"Did you go there on the day of the class field trip?"

The boy seemed to be expecting the question. "No, I went snook fishin' down at Marco. There was a mullet run and a big tide. You can ask Benjie Osceola — he was on the other end of the bridge."

Duane Scrod Jr.'s story sounded convincing to Dr. Dressler, but the detective wasn't finished.

"Duane, I'm going to ask you something, and you've got to promise not to get upset. It's my job, okay?"

"No sweat."

"Did you sneak out to the Black Vine Swamp and set a fire to scare Mrs. Starch during the field trip?"

The boy was true to his word — he stayed cool. He looked Jason Marshall straight in the eye and said, "I don't do that stuff anymore."

"So the answer is no?"

"Most definitely."

"Did you do *anything* during the last few days that might have frightened Mrs. Starch into believing your threat was real? She hasn't been back to school since the field trip."

Duane Scrod Jr. laughed. "That lady's not scared of anything, especially a kid. I don't want no more trouble from her — that's how come I did that stupid essay she wanted. Sorry, but it *was* stupid."

Dr. Dressler felt obliged to ask, "What kind of essay?"

Duane Jr. rolled his eyes. "She made me write five hundred words about zits."

The headmaster winced.

"Seriously," the boy said.

Dr. Dressler made a mental note to have a diplomatic chat with Mrs. Starch when she returned to school. Disciplining a student was one thing; humiliating him was another.

The detective had heard enough about the pimple paper. "I'm about done here," he said. "Thanks for stopping by, Duane."

The boy rose from the couch.

"Just a second — I have one question," Dr. Dressler said.

Duane Scrod Jr. turned, a trace of impatience in his eyes.

The headmaster said, "I'm just curious, Duane. Did something in particular happen to bring about this major change in you?"

"Whaddya mean?"

Dr. Dressler smiled in a way that he hoped would appear friendly and genuine. "The way you're dressed, the way you're acting — surely you're aware of the difference."

Duane Scrod Jr. looked down at himself and scratched pensively at a radish-colored blemish on his neck. "I went campin' for a few nights. Had tons of time to think about stuff."

"What kind of stuff?" asked Jason Marshall.

"The way I was headed. Mistakes I kept makin', all those wrong turns."

Even the detective seemed touched. "That's just part of growing up," he said.

"Yeah, well, it gets old," the boy remarked, "not carin' about a damn thing in the world. So I decided to try it the other way."

Dr. Dressler nodded sympathetically. "Well, we like the new you, Duane."

"It's a solid move," Jason Marshall agreed.

"I guess," said Duane Scrod Jr., and excused himself.

Dinner was a challenge.

"I should've made fried chicken," Nick's mother said, "something you could pick up with your fingers."

"It's okay. I need to nail this."

Nick was eyeing the pork chop on his plate, trying to figure out how to cut it. He was able to work the knife pretty well with his left hand, but he couldn't keep the meat from sliding around without his other hand there to pin it down with a fork.

"Let me unwrap your right arm," his mom implored, "just for tonight."

"No way. This is how Dad's gotta do it, right?"

Nick's mother said, "I'd cut his food if he were home. You can bet on that."

The disappointing news had come in a phone call that afternoon: Capt. Gregory Waters was fighting an infection in his wounded shoulder. The doctor had told Nick's mother that his dad was responding slowly to the antibiotics.

On a more positive note, the doctor reported that Captain Waters' early rehab sessions were outstanding. Nick was pleased, though not surprised — his father had always kept himself in top physical shape.

"How come they wouldn't let us talk to him?" Nick asked.

"Because he was sleeping. They said he did two hours with his left arm on the weight machine this afternoon."

"That sounds like Captain Studly."

"It does indeed." Nick's mom was watching the pork chop skate back and forth across his plate while he hacked at it with the knife.

"You're gonna starve to death, Nicky. Let

141

me do that," she said.

"No! I'll get the hang of it." In frustration, he put down the knife and reached for a bread roll, which he gobbled in three bites. "It's only my first day left-handed," he mumbled through the crumbs.

"You mean *one*-handed," his mother said. "What'd the other kids have to say?"

"Not much. Marta thought it was cool."

"How was P.E.?"

"Fine," Nick said, which wasn't even remotely true. Lacrosse was extremely difficult to play with your best arm bound behind your back, and Nick had been practically useless to his team.

Later, while he was in the shower, two of the seniors had snatched his Ace bandage from the towel rack and used it to hog-tie an overweight, slow-footed freshman named Pudge Powell IV. Two coaches spent ten minutes unbinding the boy.

So P.E. class basically had been a disaster.

His mother said, "You're going to be hurting tomorrow. You ought to take a hot bath."

Nick didn't argue, though he was embarrassed to admit how sore he was — and it wasn't as if he'd been chopping wood all day. The routine tasks of taking notes, carrying a backpack, opening a few doors, and swinging a lacrosse stick had worn him out.

142

Never again would he take for granted the luxury of having two good arms.

After soaking for half an hour and then rewrapping himself, Nick confronted his homework, which included eighteen algebra problems. At one point his mom came into the room and peeked over his left shoulder.

"I'm impressed. I can actually read your answers," she said. "I've got no idea if they're right or wrong, but I can definitely read 'em."

"Just wait."

"Can I ask you something, Nicky? How long are you going to keep up this lefty routine?"

"Until I get good at it."

"Then what?"

"I don't know, Mom," Nick said shortly. "I haven't thought about it."

In fact, he'd thought about it plenty. The doctors had said that Nick's father would face months of outpatient rehab after returning home. Nick planned to be there with him, practicing all the same left-handed exercises.

After finishing his math homework, Nick read an O. Henry story for English class, which improved his mood. Then he tackled the chore of brushing his teeth, causing only minor bleeding from his gums.

He'd planned to go to bed with his right arm wrapped, but he couldn't get comfortable. His hand kept falling asleep, and Nick became worried that the elastic bandage might cause permanent damage if he dozed off in the wrong position.

With some effort he unstrapped the arm, which felt weak and numb. He made a fist and flexed the muscles several times to get the blood circulating again.

Nick already had the lights off and was listening to his iPod when his mother cracked the door. She said, "Wow. It's only eight-thirty."

"I'm whipped."

She sat down and laid a hand on his forehead, checking to see if he had a temperature. He told her he was fine.

"You bummed about Dad?" she asked.

Nick nodded. "Yeah, it sucks."

"We'll call him tomorrow. I promise."

"The infection must be pretty bad."

Nick's mother told him not to worry. "The doctor said it happens sometimes after a combat amputation."

The last word jolted Nick. The truth was still sinking in: His father was an amputee.

But at least he's alive, Nick said to himself, *and that's what really matters.*

His mother said, "I'll be up watching TV

for a while, in case you can't sleep."

"Thanks, Mom, but I'm ready to crash."

An hour later, Nick was still wide awake. His body was exhausted but his brain was sparking like a high-voltage wire. He couldn't stop thinking about what had happened to his father, imagining the flash from the exploding rocket, the blast of the Humvee bursting into pieces, the flames and the smoke and the screams . . .

Afraid of what he might dream if he shut his eyes, Nick grabbed his cell phone off the nightstand and dialed Marta's number. She answered on the second ring.

"You awake?" he said, keeping his voice low.

"Surfing Facebook. How lame is that?"

"Extremely," Nick said.

"You talk to your dad?"

"Not today. He was rehabbing."

Marta said, "I can't sleep, either. I've been thinkin' about everything that's been happening at school, and here's what I figured out: Mrs. Starch is a witch."

"Not this again."

"No, I mean a *real* witch. Think about it — she and Smoke dropped out of sight at about the same time. Suddenly he's back in school, and it's like he got a complete personality transplant. I bet Mrs. Starch put a spell on him!"

Nick laughed. "This isn't Hogwarts, Marta. It's the Truman School."

"I didn't say she was a wizard. I said she was a witch."

"Whatever —"

"Okay, smartass, let's hear your brilliant theory."

"I don't have one," Nick admitted. "Something weird's going on, that's for sure."

"Thank you," Marta said.

Nick agreed that Mrs. Starch's excuse for taking a leave of absence from school — the so-called family emergency — sounded bogus. The woman hadn't missed a day of teaching since the Stone Age.

Yet even more startling and suspicious had been the appearance in class of the new, improved Duane Scrod Jr. — alert, neatly combed and dressed, academically responsible. A complete stranger, basically.

Nick had the uneasy sense of being in one of those short stories that led you off in one direction, then ended someplace else with a total surprise.

And the weirdness had all started on the day that Smoke ate Mrs. Starch's pencil.

Marta said, "Are you sitting down?"

"I'm *lying* down. In bed."

"Good. Guess what I saw this afternoon

after school? Remember that blue Prius with the 'Save the Manatee' license plate — the one just like Mrs. Starch's car? Well, guess what: it *was* Mrs. Starch's car. Had to be."

"How do you know?" Nick asked skeptically.

"Because I saw it flying out of the parking lot of Ace Hardware going, like, fifty miles an hour. And guess who was chuggin' a Mountain Dew in the passenger seat — Smoke!"

"Get out," Nick said.

"Swear to God. In his Truman blazer!"

"But who was driving?"

"Looked like a guy with a black ski beanie pulled tight over his head — but I bet it was Mrs. Starch. You know, witches can change themselves into anything," Marta said confidently.

"Yeah, well, who changed you into a space case? There's no such thing as witches, so knock it off."

There was silence on the other end of the line. Nick was worried that he'd hurt his friend's feelings.

Marta said, "You don't believe me."

"I just don't believe in all that Harry Potter stuff, okay? But I *do* believe you saw Smoke in the blue car today," Nick said,

147

"and I also believe the car belonged to Mrs. Starch. It's just too freaky to be a co-incidence."

Marta was relieved that Nick didn't think she'd made the whole thing up. "So what do we do now?"

"Now?" said Nick. "Now we've gotta find out who's driving Smoke around town in Mrs. Starch's car, and what they've done with Mrs. Starch."

"Awesome!"

Although Nick stayed awake for a while longer, his imagination was no longer consumed by the Baghdad rocket attack that had maimed his father.

Instead he was thinking about the Black Vine Swamp, and what secrets it might hold.

TEN

Nobody saw the helicopter land, because no bus tours or school classes were visiting the Black Vine Swamp that morning. Drake McBride stepped from the chopper and hurried toward a truck that had the Red Diamond logo painted on its doors. Jimmy Lee Bayliss emerged from the driver's side and greeted his boss with a grim nod.

"What in creation happened out here?" Drake McBride asked.

"Pretty much what I told you on the phone."

"Is that him?" Drake McBride jerked his chin toward a figure huddled inside the truck.

"Yes, sir," said Jimmy Lee Bayliss.

He opened the passenger door and an unhappy-looking young man got out. It was impossible not to notice that he was stark naked under a makeshift robe of clear bubble wrap, the same sort of material used to pack valuables for shipping.

"What the heck?" Drake McBride exclaimed.

"It was all I had in the truck," Jimmy Lee Bayliss said. "That's why I asked you to bring some extra clothes."

Drake McBride shrugged. "Well, I forgot." Addressing the bubble-wrapped man, he said, "What's your name, son?"

"Melton."

"How long you been with us?"

"Three weeks is all," Melton said.

"So you're not on full benefits yet," Drake McBride said. "But don't you worry, we'll make sure all your doctor bills are covered at least sixty percent. Did they hurt you?"

"Not really. But some bull ants chewed up my butt cheeks pretty fierce."

Jimmy Lee Bayliss said, "Go on and tell Mr. McBride what happened. He's a busy man."

Melton didn't seem especially impressed that he was speaking to the president of the company. He looked like he wished he'd never heard of the Red Diamond Energy Corporation.

"I was out here stackin' some pipe," he said, "when they jumped me from behind. Next thing I know, I'm glued to a cypress tree and I can't pull free."

150

"In your birthday suit," Drake McBride said.

"Yeah, they stole my clothes."

"The pipes, too," said Jimmy Lee Bayliss, who'd already eaten an entire roll of Tums since breakfast. He longed to be back in Texas, enjoying the retired life.

On his fingers, Drake McBride began ticking off the crimes committed against poor Melton. "So there's assault, grand theft, indecent whatever — how many of 'em were there, son?"

"I dunno."

"Well, how many'd you *see?*"

"One," Melton said, "but they's had to be more. Ain't no way just one guy could take me."

Jimmy Lee Bayliss didn't say so, but he believed it was entirely possible for one physically fit man to have overpowered the scrawny, chain-smoking Melton.

Drake McBride pulled Jimmy Lee Bayliss aside. "Obviously, we can't tell the police this happened in Section 22, so we're gonna tell 'em it was Section 21, where we're legal. I want you to make sure this young fella gets his story straight."

"Lying to the cops is too risky," Jimmy Lee Bayliss warned his boss, "especially if we rely on Melton. Kid's got the IQ of a baked potato. He's liable to say anything."

Drake McBride let out an aggravated sigh. "We're not s'posed to set foot in Section 22, much less be diggin' a pit and layin' pipe. What other choice do we have, Jimmy, but to lie?"

"That's easy: Don't call the cops." Jimmy Lee Bayliss was trying to conceal his annoyance. From the start he'd been nervous about the scam, even though Drake Mc-Bride had promised that it would make both of them rich beyond their wildest dreams. "Let me handle this," Jimmy Lee Bayliss told his boss.

"But we got, like, bandits on the loose," Drake McBride said. "Outlaws, pirates, whatever."

"You seriously think the cops will come chasing after pipe thieves way out here in the middle of nowhere? They got bigger fish to fry."

"Probably just dope addicts," Drake Mc-Bride muttered. "Meatheads. Where they gonna sell two tons of pipe?"

They walked back to the truck, where Melton was puffing on a dead cigarette butt. "I'm sweatin' to death in this stuff," he complained, and began to strip off the bubble wrap.

"Whoa there!" Drake McBride made a

time-out sign with his hands. "No offense, son, but I'm not in the mood to deal with a buck-nekked man. Keep your plastic jammies on."

Jimmy Lee Bayliss told Melton that he would take him to Wal-Mart on the way into town. "I'll buy you some new clothes, and a hot lunch, too."

"Thanks, man. What about the overtime?"

Jimmy Lee Bayliss looked at Drake McBride, who made a sour face.

"Hey, I spent all night out here," Melton said, "them red ants takin' chunks from my hide. Are you sayin' I wasn't on the company clock?" He held up his arms so that the president of Red Diamond Energy could see the gummy red abrasions left by the hardened glue, which Jimmy Lee Bayliss had pried with a screwdriver from the bark of the tree.

"I think you'll live," Drake McBride remarked.

Jimmy Lee Bayliss said, "Tell us about the man who attacked you."

Melton admitted that he hadn't gotten a clear look at the guy. "He had a ski cap pulled down to his eyes, so I couldn't really see his face all that great."

"Was he young or old?"

"I couldn't say," Melton replied. "But he

was real strong — and real crazy."

Drake McBride frowned. "Dope fiend. What'd I tell ya?"

"No, man, he wasn't high or nuthin'. Just whacked-out mean," Melton said. "When he pasted me to that damn tree, he said I was bear bait. That's what he called me. Real nice, huh?"

Jimmy Lee Bayliss asked, "Did he have a weapon?"

"I dunno. Probably."

Meaning the answer was no, thought Jimmy Lee Bayliss. Melton was too embarrassed to admit that he'd been captured by — and lost a load of expensive pipes to — an unarmed intruder.

"Listen to me, son," Drake McBride said. "We're not gonna call the cops, okay? Red Diamond will deal with this situation, I promise. We'll catch this creep and make sure he doesn't do it to anybody else."

Melton said, "Sooner the better."

"Meantime, you gotta promise to zip your lip, okay? You can't tell anybody what happened out here," Drake McBride said, "not even your wife and kids."

"All I got is a girlfriend."

"Not her, either," Jimmy Lee Bayliss interjected firmly. "Don't mention this to a living soul. Understand?"

"Gotcha." Melton was idly popping the bubbles in his see-through plastic coat. "Hey, when we go by the Wal-Mart, can you buy me some cigarettes? That wacko got my last pack when he swiped my pants."

"Sure," Jimmy Lee Bayliss said.

"One more thing — I ain't never been up in a helicopter before. . . ."

Drake McBride's expression turned stony. "Sorry, pardner."

"Just a quick spin? Aw, come on."

"You can't get on a chopper if you're not wearin' clothes. Strict FAA rules."

"What? You're kiddin' me," Melton said.

"Yeah, tough break."

Then the president of Red Diamond Energy Corporation turned on one boot heel and signaled for his pilot to fire up the engines.

Duane Scrod Sr. was attacking a twenty-ounce sirloin steak, cooked rare. Duane Scrod Jr. contemplated a large, steaming plate of linguini. Millicent Winship picked at a fresh shrimp cocktail; at her age, she had no patience for chitchat.

"D.J., how are your grades at Truman this term?" she asked her grandson.

"Not so great," he said, "but I aim to do better."

"Do you have any homework tonight?"

"No school tomorrow — it's a teacher work day."

"Sounds like a good opportunity to catch up with some of your studies," Mrs. Winship said.

"Yes, ma'am. I brought my books home."

"I must say, you look very serious and handsome."

Embarrassed, Duane Jr. shoveled pasta into his blushing cheeks.

Mrs. Winship turned to Duane Sr. "It's quite a difference. I'm impressed."

"Don't look at me, Millie. It was all D.J.," he said, slurping a cup of coffee. "He came back from that camping trip and, I swear, it's like there's a stranger in the house. Picks up his dirty clothes, brushes his teeth twice a day, stays up late doin' his homework. It's like he turned into a grown-up overnight."

"Maybe you should take a lesson." Mrs. Winship wore a frosty smile.

"Aw, lay off," the boy's father said.

They were sitting at an outside table overlooking a marina that was filled with yachts and sailboats. The restaurant was called the Silver Dolphin and the food was excellent, though expensive. Mrs. Winship was paying the tab, as usual, and happy to do it. She couldn't get over the promising

156

change in her grandson.

Duane Sr. was another matter. He showed absolutely no interest in improving himself, or his life. Earlier, Mrs. Winship had caught him stashing packets of oyster crackers in his pockets to take home to his obnoxious pet bird.

She said, "Tell me, D.J., can you see yourself in college someday?"

"Yes, ma'am. It's possible," Duane Jr. replied.

"I'm so pleased to hear that. Have you given any thought to what subject you might like to study," Mrs. Winship said, "on the path to a career?"

Chewing loudly, Duane Sr. interjected, "It's too early for all that. Cut the boy some slack, Millie. . . ."

"Environmental science," said Duane Scrod Jr.

"Really?" His grandmother beamed and looked cuttingly at Duane Sr., whose jaw hung open.

"I really like the outdoors. It's quiet and pretty," Duane Jr. said. "Plus I'm into animals and fishin' and stuff."

"Ever since you were little, you were an explorer. And fearless, too," Mrs. Winship said fondly.

Duane Sr. began jabbing at his molars

with a toothpick, trying to liberate a string of meat. "I'm sorry, but I just don't see Junior as a 'scientist.' Heck, he's flunkin' biology for the second or third time."

"Second," Duane Jr. said crossly.

Mrs. Winship glowered at Duane Scrod Sr. "You listen to me, and listen well. This boy can be whatever he chooses to be, once he finds the right role model."

"Ouch," Duane Sr. said, responding not to the insult but rather to a small hole that he'd punctured in his gums.

Duane Jr. put down his fork. "If they wipe out the Everglades and all, people like me won't have anywhere to go except for big cities. And I hate big cities."

Mrs. Winship thoughtfully appraised her grandson. "Tell me about your camping trip," she said.

He cleared his throat. "Caught some bass. Saw an otter with two pups, and about a jillion gators, as usual." He started eating again.

"Were you there all alone?"

"Pretty much." Duane Jr. didn't look up from his plate.

"Your dad told me about the fire. The headmaster called me as well."

"What fire?"

"Out at the swamp," Duane Sr. cut in.

"Now don't act like you never heard about it."

The boy spun some linguini onto his fork. "Oh, yeah. *That* fire."

Mrs. Winship dabbed her mouth with her napkin, which she then refolded neatly on her lap. "D.J., I'm seventy-seven years old," she said, "which doesn't make me a dinosaur, but I'm not so young anymore, either. Time isn't something I can afford to waste, do you understand?"

"Yes, ma'am."

"So just tell me if you set that fire. Yes or no?"

"No, ma'am."

"Yet the police think you did it. Why is that?"

Again Duane Sr. spoke up. "They can't prove a flippin' thing. Otherwise the boy'd be locked up in juvie hall right now."

Mrs. Winship shot Duane Sr. a peeved look. Gently she asked her grandson, "Did you have a chance to give your story to the authorities?"

"Yes, ma'am. I straight-up told 'em I didn't do it," Duane Jr. said.

"Those days are over, right?"

"Yes, ma'am. No more fires."

"It's not something that a future environmental scientist should do, burning a

159

swamp."

"No, ma'am."

His grandmother said, "There was a field trip from Truman out there that morning. Somebody could've been hurt badly, D.J., or even killed."

Duane Jr. looked her straight in the eye. "It wasn't me, Gram. I swear."

"All right. I believe you."

"Thank goodness that's settled," said Duane Sr., scanning the restaurant impatiently. "Where did our waiter disappear to? I can't wait to have a peek at that dessert tray."

It was only her love for Duane Jr. that prevented Mrs. Winship from smacking his father on the top of his hopelessly thick head.

To the boy she said, "Your mother told me she wrote you."

He seemed surprised. "I didn't get a letter."

"Nothing?"

"Nope."

"Me neither," Duane Sr. piped.

Mrs. Winship was ashamed to think that her daughter could be so selfish and neglectful. "I'm sorry, D.J. I'll speak with her."

"It's not your fault, Gram."

"How about some dessert?"

"No thanks."

"Well, *I* saved plenty of room," Duane Sr. announced heartily, patting his stomach.

Millicent Winship eyed him as if he were a cockroach on a wedding cake. "We've all had enough," she said sharply, and called for the check.

Before Marta's mother dropped them off at the mall, she asked, "What's the name of the movie?"

Marta faked a cough and turned to Nick, who got the hint.

"It's *Spider-Man VII,*" he said to Mrs. Gonzalez. *"Revenge of the Web Slinger."* He had no idea if there was such a film — he'd lost count of all the Spider-Man sequels.

"PG?"

"Yeah, Mom, it's PG," Marta said.

"I'll see you back here at ten-thirty sharp. Don't be late."

"Bye, Mom," Marta said impatiently.

"Have you got enough money?"

"Goodbye, Mom!"

Lying about the movie made Nick and Marta feel sneaky and low, but there had seemed to be no other choice — their parents never would have allowed them to spy on Mrs. Starch's house, especially after dark.

161

"According to MapQuest, it's only 2.4 miles," Nick said, studying the map that he'd printed out. He'd gotten Mrs. Starch's address from Libby, who'd found a faculty directory in her father's den after the detective had visited Dr. Dressler's office.

Marta said, "I can't believe I forgot a flashlight."

Nick had brought one in a pocket of his jacket. "Let's go," he said, and they headed off across the vast parking lot, toward the road.

Before long, the bright lights of the mall were behind them. Sticking closely to the MapQuest directions, they walked five blocks to Mockingbird Court, then seven more blocks to Grackle Drive. When they reached Mrs. Starch's street, Nick said, "We go west here until the road ends."

Marta laughed. "No way! The old buzzard actually lives on Buzzard Boulevard — how perfect is that?"

"Number 777," Nick said. "The very last house."

"Naturally."

The streetlights ended when the pavement ran out. As Nick and Marta continued down the dirt road, the night deepened. Nick took out his flashlight.

"Doesn't anybody besides her live out

here?" Marta said nervously.

They walked past a couple of houses that were under construction, and another that was roofless and abandoned, probably a hurricane casualty. The woods hummed with crickets and cicadas, and rustled with other, heavier sounds that might have been rabbits or raccoons. Whenever Nick heard something, he aimed the light into the woods to see what it was, but the critters always stopped moving, remaining invisible among the pines and the scrub.

Nick assured Marta there was nothing to be afraid of, but he was jumpy, too. Usually he loved hiking through the outdoors, but it was a totally different experience in the black of night.

"Do me a favor," Marta said. "Take off the Ace bandage."

"Why?"

"Because you're gonna need both arms to carry me back to the mall after I pass out."

"You are *not* going to pass out."

"No, I'll probably just drop dead from fright," Marta said, "when a rabid bear comes chasing after us."

"Or a panther," Nick joked, trying to lighten the mood.

"Shut up."

Every now and then they would glance

163

back, watching for oncoming headlights, but Buzzard Boulevard was as quiet as a graveyard. Nick wondered if he'd be able to run as fast as normal with one arm bound clumsily behind him.

"How much farther?" Marta asked.

Nick didn't know. The distance seemed longer than it had appeared on the map. He picked up the pace, the white beam of the flashlight bobbing ahead of them. A layer of clouds hung overhead, blocking out the stars and the moon.

When a small animal scampered across the road ahead of them, Marta let out a yip and grabbed Nick. "This was a really terrible idea. Let's go back," she said.

"Shhhh. We're here."

His flashlight illuminated a plain metal mailbox with three 7's on the side but no name.

"Where's the house?" Marta asked.

"This way." Nick led her along an overgrown trail no wider than a car. He nearly stepped on a coachwhip snake that, fortunately, slithered into the shadows before Marta noticed it. At the end of the trail, he dropped to a crouch. Marta knelt behind him.

Mrs. Starch's house stood alone in the middle of a clearing. Nick counted three

164

stories, although the old wooden structure appeared smaller than that, hunched and frail. A bare bulb flickered from the ceiling of the porch, but no lights shone in the windows. In the yard there was no sign of the teacher's blue Prius.

"Nobody home," Marta said, clicking her teeth nervously.

"We'll see."

"Where are you going?"

"To spy," Nick said. "That was the plan, right?"

Marta stayed close. They darted around the house to the back porch, which was unlit. After creeping up the steps, they searched fruitlessly for a window in which to peek. All the shades were drawn.

"Oh well. We tried," Marta said, turning to leave.

"Get back here."

"Come on, Nick. I'm totally creeped."

"Something's not right."

"Thank you! Now can we please go?"

"What I mean is, look at this place. She hasn't been here for a while." Nick shined the flashlight back and forth. "Check out all the spiders."

Marta cringed, but she got the point. Mrs. Starch was a notorious neat freak, yet her porch looked untouched by a broom or

165

mop. Shimmering spiderwebs hung like tapestries in the corners of the ceiling, while the floor was littered with pine needles and moth casings and lizard poop.

Nick said, "She hasn't been home since the field trip. I'll bet you twenty bucks."

"Then who's picking up her mail? And driving her car?" Marta said.

"Exactly. That's the mystery."

"Smoke knows everything."

"He's next on our list. Meantime . . ."

Marta ducked and covered her head. "A bat just buzzed me, I swear to God!"

"Don't be such a wuss." Nick jiggled the knob on the back door, which was locked.

"We should go. It's a long walk back," Marta said, apprehensively eyeing the sky.

Nick scanned the porch until he spotted a large clay pot that contained a wilted palm. "Give me a hand," he said, pocketing the flashlight. "We're going to lift that thing."

"Okay, now you're officially insane."

"Hurry up. On the count of three . . ."

The pot budged only a few inches, but that was enough. Nick pointed to a dusty circle on the wood planks, and there lay a key. He smiled.

"Way to go, Sherlock," Marta said.

The key fit easily into the door, and the lock turned with a crisp click.

"You coming?" Nick asked. "Or would you rather stay out here with the bats and black widows?"

ELEVEN

Nick wasn't sure if sneaking into Mrs. Starch's house was the bravest thing he'd ever done, or the dumbest.

But he felt certain that the world's meanest biology teacher wasn't really absent from school because of a family crisis. Something else had happened, something serious, and Duane Scrod Jr. had to be involved.

"What if she's croaked?" Marta whispered as she closed the door behind them. "What if we find the body?"

The same awful thought had occurred to Nick, although he didn't say it aloud.

"Then the cops'll think we did it! We'll spend the rest of our lives in prison!" Marta said.

"Keep it down, okay?"

"This is the darkest place I've ever been. Give me your hand."

"I've only got one," Nick reminded her, "so you carry the flashlight."

It had been a long while since he'd held hands with a girl — fifth grade, Jessie Kronenberg. The following summer her family had moved to Atlanta, and Nick hadn't heard from her since.

"Where do you think the old witch keeps all her snakes?" Marta asked, squeezing his fingers.

"That's just another lame rumor."

"Maybe it's a true rumor. Maybe she whacked her husband, too. They say he disappeared, like, twenty years ago."

Nick and Marta hadn't moved three steps since coming through the door.

"I'm totally sketched out," she said.

"I know — you're crushing my knuckles."

Nick pulled free of her grasp and took back the flashlight. The moment he turned it on, he saw that at least one of the many crazy stories about Mrs. Starch was true. The house was filled with stuffed animals — and not the soft, huggable type that are found in toy stores.

Marta said, "We . . . are . . . outta here."

"Hold on."

"It's, like, a zoo for the dead!"

Nick, too, had never imagined such a scene — a herd of taxidermied creatures displayed in wild disorder, from wall to wall and from the floor to the rafters. There were birds, mammals, reptiles, and amphibians of many sizes, suspended in poses of coiling, leaping, lurking, snarling, soaring, and pouncing. The animals stared with blank glass eyes through Nick and Marta, into infinity.

"I told you she was a psycho," Marta whispered.

Nick played the beam of the flashlight across the lifeless menagerie. Every mount was identified by a handwritten tag.

"I think I know what she's done here," he said.

"Besides losing her marbles?"

Nick approached a tawny spotted cat the size of a golden retriever. Beside it was a small mottled bird, perched sprightly on a stick of driftwood. Mounted overhead on the wall was a homely brown fish with armored ridges. Nick checked the tags on each of them.

"They're all endangered species," he told Marta. "That's a panther cub, that's a Cape Sable seaside sparrow, and that ugly thing up on the wall is a shortnose sturgeon. I know they're endangered because Mrs. Starch has a list in her class syllabus."

"You actually *read* her syllabus? Are you, what, king of the geeks?"

"She said it would be on the final."

170

"Whatever, Nick. We gotta get back to the mall before —"

"Look here." He fixed the light on a short-eared brown bunny. "A Lower Keys marsh rabbit. And there," he said, pointing to a stubby-legged lump the size of a hockey puck, "is a baby leatherback turtle. And this little guy is a —"

"Rat," Marta interrupted irritably. "A nasty, smelly rat."

"Wrong." Nick pronounced the name slowly from the name tag. "It's a Choc-taw-hatch-ee beach mouse."

"That was my next guess," she said dryly.

"Hey, here's one with a collar." Nick grinned as he read it aloud: " 'Chelsea Evered.' Must be somebody special."

Marta looked around uneasily. "This place is too freaky."

Nick approached a weather-beaten old steamer trunk. The lid was so bulky and warped that he was unable to raise it one-handed.

"Help me out," he said to Marta.

"No way! What if that's where she stuffed Mr. Starch's body?"

"Quit whining."

Together they prized open the antique chest, which, to Marta's relief, was empty.

She crinkled her nose. "Smells like my

grandpa's attic."

A car door slammed outside. Nick instantly clicked off the flashlight.

"Get down!" he said, tugging Marta to the floor.

The glow from the car's headlights lit the edges of the window shades. Nick and Marta heard someone clomping up the steps, making no effort to be stealthy. The next noise was the rattle of the doorknob.

"We're *so* busted," Marta groaned.

Nick motioned toward the open trunk. "After you."

"Nope. Not happening."

"Get in!"

They clambered inside and pulled the top shut. The only sound was the thump of footsteps on the pine floor, and the footsteps were not dainty. It could have been Mrs. Starch, who wasn't a dainty woman, or it could have been Smoke.

Or possibly some other sizeable person.

"I can't breathe," Marta said wretchedly.

"Yes, you can."

"Turn on the flashlight, Nick, or I'm gonna scream."

"Don't tell me you're claustrophobic."

"Big-time."

Nick said, "Oh, that's great." He, too, had a fear of confined spaces. The flashlight wouldn't come on until he jiggled the batteries.

"Is that better?" he asked.

Marta was as pale as wax and drenched with sweat. She looked terrible.

The steamer trunk was barely wide enough for the two of them to wedge side by side, sitting with their knees against their chins. For Nick, the cramped fit was as painful as it was unnerving. His taped-up arm was pinned at an unnatural angle against his shoulder blade — he felt like a hawk with a broken wing.

Still, he was more concerned about Marta. "It's all my fault. I'm really sorry," he whispered.

She shut her eyes and took a deep, labored breath. "You'll *really* be sorry if I hurl all over both of us."

The person who'd entered the house was moving around, opening cabinets and cupboards. Gradually the sounds of the footsteps came closer, making the planks shudder beneath the trunk.

Nick wished he'd listened to Marta when she had told him to remove the Ace bandage — it would have been helpful to have two good hands available, if needed. He was furious at himself for taking such a foolish risk by entering Mrs. Starch's house. The last thing his mom needed right now was a phone call from the police or, worse, the hospital. And how would she break the bad news to his father?

As the footfalls got heavier, Marta's eyes popped open. "Can he see that light inside this thing?"

"I doubt it," Nick said. The sides of the old chest appeared solid and seamless.

"Better turn it off, just in case."

"You won't spaz out?"

"Nope."

Nick killed the flashlight. He could sense Marta trembling at his side. In the smothering blackness, he reached out and found one of her hands. She squeezed back fiercely. By now they could hear the cadence of human breathing outside the steamer trunk — whoever was in the house, man or woman, was standing only a few feet away.

Time seemed to stop dead. Nick felt trapped in his own skin, helpless and on the brink of panic. Taking care of Marta was the only thing that kept him steady; she was in worse shape than he was.

His escape strategy was simple because he was short on options. If they were discovered inside the trunk, Nick planned to spring straight upward, shrieking like a lunatic jack-in-the-box. The idea was to scare the pee out of the person in the room, in the hope that he (or she) would either run away or have a stroke, at which point Nick and Marta could bolt safely out the back door.

Nick figured that the shock tactic had a fifty-fifty chance of working on Mrs. Starch, who wouldn't be expecting nocturnal intruders. He wasn't so sure about Smoke; it was hard to picture the kid being afraid of anything, except possibly a SWAT team.

Marta's hand went limp and clammy. Nick gave it a little pinch, but she didn't respond. In the pitch-darkness of the steamer chest, he groped frantically for her face to make sure she was still breathing.

"Watch it!" she burst out. "Your stupid thumb went up my nose."

"Not so loud."

But it was too late. There was a heavy thud, and the trunk moved.

"Come out of there!" a male voice commanded.

Nick and Marta were too frightened to respond. They felt another hard jolt — the guy was kicking the sides of the wooden chest.

So much for the element of surprise, Nick thought. Marta poked him sharply, as if to say: *Do something!*

Nick shifted his weight to his heels and prepared to launch himself against the balky lid. At that moment the trunk went over backwards and the top flew open, spilling him and Marta in a tangled, terrified heap.

Standing over them was the man who had overturned the chest.

"Get up," he snapped.

Nick rose first and helped Marta to her feet. He noticed that they'd landed on the mount of an endangered wood stork, snapping its long spindly legs so that it was now the same height as a duck.

The stranger carried a flashlight of his own, which he aimed harshly in their eyes. "This must be your first burglary," he said, "because you stink at it."

"We didn't come to steal anything. That's the truth," Nick blurted.

He couldn't see the face behind the flashlight, but the voice didn't sound like Duane Scrod Jr.'s.

"Let's go for a ride," the man said.

"No, wait!" cried Marta. "We're looking for our teacher, that's all."

"Move it."

They exited through the back door, the stranger prodding them from behind. Outside, there was enough starlight to see that

176

the man was shirtless and wore scuffed trousers and muddy hiking boots. A black ski cap covered his hair, forehead, and ears. He stood about the same height as Smoke, although he was leaner and more muscle-bound.

Nick didn't even consider trying to get away, because Marta was still so wobbly that she couldn't possibly have outrun the stranger.

Mrs. Starch's blue Prius was parked next to the house.

"Hop in the backseat," the man told them.

Marta froze on the spot. "No way."

"Just let us go," Nick pleaded. "We won't tell the police."

The man chuckled dryly. "I'm the one who oughta be calling the cops. Now you two can either get in the car or be *thrown* in the car, it's your choice."

Reluctantly, Nick and Marta got in. The stranger whipped the Prius around and drove down the trail to Buzzard Boulevard. He didn't bother switching on the head-lights.

"What'd you do with Mrs. Starch?" Nick heard himself ask.

The man eyed him in the rearview mirror. "The question is, what'm I gonna do with *you?*"

Marta reached over and slugged Nick's leg.

"My name's Twilly," the man said, a sure sign — or so Marta believed — that he intended to murder them and dump their bodies in a drainage canal. Otherwise why would he so casually identify himself and risk being turned in to the authorities?

"I'm Nick Waters," said Nick. "My friend's name is Marta."

"What happened to your arm, son?"

Nick was pretty sure that the man named Twilly wouldn't believe the truth — that Nick was training to be a lefty — and, in any case, Nick didn't feel like getting into a detailed discussion of his father's war injury.

"Lacrosse," he said. "I sprained it at lacrosse practice."

"Mmmm," said the man.

Marta interjected, "Seriously. I was there when it happened."

"Whatever you say."

"Where are you taking us?" Nick asked.

"Depends."

"My mom's meeting us back at the mall," Marta said. "If we're not there, she'll go nuts. I swear to God, she'll call the White House!"

The stranger named Twilly said, "I wish I'd had a mom like that."

Nick decided that because he was the one who'd gotten them into this awful mess, it was his duty to get them out. And since he couldn't very well overpower the guy and hijack the car, the next best option was to talk some sense into him.

"Mister, you don't want to go to jail for kidnapping."

"No, and I don't intend to," the man said evenly.

"Honest, if you'd just let us go, we won't nark you out —"

"So, Mrs. Starch is your teacher?"

Marta spoke up. "We're in her biology class."

"And you adore her so much that you busted into her home just to make sure she's all right? That's your story?" The man named Twilly was smiling behind the wheel.

"Not exactly," Nick said. "We didn't break in. There was a key on the porch."

"Ah."

"What were *you* doing there?" Nick asked, not expecting to receive a straight answer.

"Looking for some powdered cocoa," the man replied, flicking on the headlights, "and a book. Ever heard of a writer named Edward Abbey?"

Nick and Marta admitted they hadn't.

"No surprise," the stranger said. "I'm sure they don't teach his stuff in that uptight private school of yours. Ed was sort of a bomb thrower, only the bombs were ideals and principles. He liked the earth more than he liked most humans."

A Hannah Montana ring tone went off, and Marta sheepishly smothered her cell phone. "That's gotta be my mom. She's supposed to pick us up outside the movie theater."

"Answer it," the stranger said. "Tell her you'll be right on time — and if you say anything else, I'm turning this car around and we're going to Miami. Or maybe Key Largo."

Marta did as she was told.

After hanging up, she said, "Ten-thirty sharp. She'll freak if we're not there."

"Understood," said the man named Twilly.

Nick was relieved to see that the car was heading in the direction of the mall, which raised the welcome possibility that they weren't actually being kidnapped.

"How do you know Mrs. Starch?" he asked the stranger.

"None of your business, Nick Waters." The man tugged the ski cap even tighter on his head.

"We're worried about her, that's all.

Nobody's seen her in, like, a week," Marta said.

"Yeah? Then take out your cute little pink phone again, princess, and dial this number: 555-2346."

Marta switched on the cell phone's speaker so that both she and Nick could hear the recording:

Hello, people. I'll be away from school indefinitely because of an unexpected family matter. You may leave a message at the tone, though it might be a while before I have time to reply. Please accept my apologies in advance. Now here's the beep!

"That's her," Nick said.

"Definitely," Marta agreed.

"Did she sound the least bit dead to you?" the man named Twilly asked. "Gravely ill? Mortally wounded?"

"Not really."

"Then quit worrying," he snapped, "and quit nosing around places you don't belong."

He pulled over a block from the mall, in front of a seedy pawnshop. He stepped out of the Prius and ordered Nick and Marta to do the same. Standing in the glow of a gaudy neon sign, the man looked to be in his late thirties, with an athletic build that reminded Nick of his father.

The stranger said, "It would be best if I never set eyes on you two again."

"Oh, don't worry," Marta assured him.

Nick was staring at Twilly's belt, which was made of tanned cowhide and stitched with a row of small sleeves designed to hold bullets. It looked very much like the one worn by the mysterious figure in Nick's video from the field trip to the Black Vine Swamp.

The man tapped the face of his wristwatch. "You've got six minutes and thirty seconds before your momma shows up. Get a move on."

"Thank you," Marta said with a grateful sigh. "Thank you, thank you."

"For what?"

"For not killing us and tossing our bodies into a ditch."

"You're welcome," said the man named Twilly. "I'll tell Aunt Bunny you asked about her."

Nick rocked back on his heels. "Mrs. Starch is your aunt?"

With a thumb, the stranger popped two shiny bullets out of his ammo belt. He began tossing them from hand to hand, like jellybeans. "I hate repeating myself," he said. Nick and Marta started running. They didn't stop until they reached the mall.

TWELVE

Drake McBride had stumbled into the oil business after failing at many other jobs and ruining many other companies. He enjoyed spending money much more than he enjoyed working for it, and this was the secret to his lack of success. It also helped to be lazy, easily distracted, and not very good at math.

Every time Drake McBride got himself into trouble, his wealthy father would simply buy a new company for him to noodle with. But now, after several wasted years and millions of wasted dollars, Drake McBride's father finally had lost patience with the free-spending poser who happened to be his youngest son. The Red Diamond Energy Corporation was to be Drake's last chance.

"If you screw up this one," his father had warned, "you won't get another nickel from me."

"Have you checked out the price of gas,

Dad?" Drake McBride had chortled with confidence. "Only an idiot could lose money in the oil business."

"You said the same damn thing when you were selling real estate," his father had reminded him coldly, "or *trying* to sell real estate."

"It's not my fault the market went sour —"

"Get real, boy. You couldn't sell an igloo to an Eskimo," his dad had said. "Red Diamond is my last act of charity. If you come crawling back here with another lame sob story, you might as well change your name to Drake Chowderhead and sign up for bartender school, because I'm done with you. Now go find some oil. Hurry up!"

Because the competition in Texas was fierce (and also because he owned a waterfront condo on Tampa Bay), Drake McBride chose Florida as headquarters for the new Red Diamond Energy Corporation. His first move was hiring Jimmy Lee Bayliss, recently retired from ExxonMobil, to teach him about oil exploration and run the day-to-day operation so that Drake McBride could concentrate on waterskiing and fishing.

It was Jimmy Lee Bayliss who'd explained to Drake McBride that Florida's richest petroleum deposits lay miles offshore and were controlled by giant companies who'd been battling for years to get drilling permits. The drilling was opposed by most Floridians, who didn't want to risk having their beaches choked with black tar in the event of an accidental oil spill.

"Aw, forget about what's under the ocean," Drake McBride said, and handed a newspaper clipping to Jimmy Lee Bayliss. "Here's where the fast money is, my friend."

Jimmy Lee Bayliss frowned at the headline. "The Everglades?"

"Keep readin', pardner."

According to the article, the U.S. government had announced a plan to buy up the drilling rights for oil and natural gas beneath the vast Big Cypress Preserve to protect the vanishing wetlands from future damage.

"All we've got to do is find some oil, any oil," Drake McBride said excitedly, "and Uncle Sam will pay us a fortune *not* to pump it. Isn't that the wildest danged thing you ever heard of?"

"Sure is," said Jimmy Lee Bayliss, who was immediately leery of the scheme.

"Tell me this isn't a great country!" Drake McBride exclaimed.

"But we don't own any drilling leases in the Everglades."

"Your job is to get me one," Drake Mc-

Bride said, poking Jimmy Lee Bayliss in the chest, "and make it a winner."

The task turned out to be frustrating and complicated. All but a few of the oil leases were held by huge corporations or rich old geezers who practically laughed at Jimmy Lee Bayliss's offers. Eventually he was able to obtain a single 640-acre parcel from a troubled soul named Vincent Trapwick Jr., who was facing trial for embezzlement and was frantically selling everything he owned to pay his lawyers.

The Trapwick parcel, known as Section 21, was located east of Naples at a promising location near the Black Vine Swamp. Yet after months of ground testing and half a dozen boreholes, Jimmy Lee Bayliss had reached the grim conclusion that Section 21 held barely enough oil to fill a goldfish bowl.

The news set badly with Drake McBride, who kicked at his desk so viciously that he tore the python skin on one of his cowboy boots.

"Too bad we don't have Section 22," Jimmy Lee Bayliss remarked.

"What?" Drake McBride perked up. "Is there serious oil in Section 22?"

"That's what the geologists think, but it doesn't matter. The state owns the land,"

Jimmy Lee Bayliss said, "and they ain't sellin'. It's part of some wildlife preserve."

"But there's oil, they said. How deep?"

"Eleven, twelve thousand feet is their guess. But as I told you, the state's got the property —"

Drake McBride snapped his manicured fingers. "I got an idea. We sink a pirate well on Section 22, totally secret, then run the pipe underground to our rig on Section 21."

Jimmy Lee Bayliss's gut started to churn. "Sir, it's not worth the risk. The geologists say there's no more than nine hundred barrels a day. And it's poor quality, sir, gooey and full of sulfur —"

"I don't care what it looks like, or how bad it stinks," said Drake McBride, "as long as it's oil. All I need — or, I should say, all *we* need — is genuine Florida crude to drip on some sucker's desk at the Department of the Interior, who will then give us such a gi-mongous wad of money for our drilling rights that even my old man will be impressed. You with me?"

"Do I have a choice?"

"Not if you care to remain employed," said Drake McBride.

And that's how the Section 22 scam had been born.

Now Jimmy Lee Bayliss squinted through

the open hatch of the helicopter, his line of vision following a row of small pink flags that marked the path under which the illegal pipeline would travel from Section 22 to Section 21. The small drill rig would be concealed in a tall stand of bald cypress and would be practically invisible, even from the air.

Because Section 22 was so wild and remote, Drake McBride didn't worry about getting busted for hijacking the state of Florida's oil. Jimmy Lee Bayliss, however, was highly concerned. If just one wayward hiker made a wrong turn in the Black Vine Swamp, the Red Diamond drilling scheme might unravel — and Jimmy Lee Bayliss could wind up sharing a ten-by-ten jail cell with Drake McBride. The thought made Jimmy Lee Bayliss's stomach pitch, and had pushed him to take extreme measures.

He wasn't a crook by nature, but the lure of making millions of dollars by *not* pumping oil had been too juicy for even him to resist. Still, ever since agreeing to Drake McBride's sleazy scheme, Jimmy Lee Bayliss hadn't had a good night's sleep. The disturbing incident involving Melton had only worsened his jitters. Gluing a man naked to a tree didn't seem like something an ordinary thief would do.

189

So Jimmy Lee Bayliss had decided to make daily patrols by helicopter over the wetlands, scouting for signs of intruders. So far, he'd turned up nothing.

"You 'bout ready to head back?" the pilot asked.

"Sure. Drop me off at my truck," said Jimmy Lee Bayliss.

As the chopper gently touched down on the dirt road, Jimmy Lee Bayliss was surprised to see a cherry-red SUV parked next to his pickup. The SUV had a set of emergency lights mounted on the cab and the initials "CCFD" painted on the sides.

It took a few moments for Jimmy Lee Bayliss to realize that the letters stood for "Collier County Fire Department." He chewed up four more Tums tablets before climbing out of the chopper.

The fire investigator's name was Torkelsen. He had thinning blond hair and a handshake that could crush walnuts. He wanted to chat about the fire in Section 22.

"We work in Section 21," Jimmy Lee Bayliss said quickly.

"Yes, I know. We were wondering if you or your men saw anything suspicious in the area that day."

"Like what?"

"Like any person or persons who weren't

190

supposed to be there." Torkelsen spoke in a mild, official tone that made Jimmy Lee Bayliss uncomfortable.

"My crew was on another site when the wildfire broke out," he said. "I was with them."

"It wasn't a wildfire, Mr. Bayliss. It was arson."

"What?" Jimmy Lee Bayliss tried to hide his shock so that the fire investigator wouldn't know that he was in danger of soiling his pants. "Arson? That's crazy!" he said with a weak laugh. "What's the point of torching a swamp?"

Torkelsen shrugged. "People do crazy things sometimes. Do you recognize this?"

He held up a plastic ballpoint pen stamped with the name of Red Diamond Energy. For a moment, Jimmy Lee Bayliss thought he might puke his breakfast muffins all over the fire investigator's shoes.

"Yeah, that's mine," he croaked. "It must've fell from my pocket while I was shootin' pictures from the helicopter."

Which was a lie, of course. Torkelsen seemed to buy it.

"No big deal. We're just trying to run down every lead," the investigator said. "We found the pen about a hundred and fifty yards from where the fire flashed up."

"Well, you can keep it. I got a whole box of 'em." Jimmy Lee Bayliss was trying to sound casual and unworried.

Torkelsen dropped the Red Diamond pen into a large manila envelope and took out a small photograph. "Could you take a look at this, too?" he asked.

It was a police mug shot of a pimply teen-aged kid whom Jimmy Lee Bayliss didn't recognize. In the picture, the kid looked surly and uncooperative, a pose that reminded Jimmy Lee Bayliss of his own boys when they were that age.

"This is the guy who started the fire?" he asked Torkelsen.

"He's a person of interest."

"Is that the same thing as a 'suspect'?"

"Between you and me? Yes, he's a suspect," Torkelsen said. "His name is Duane Scrod Jr., a local punk who likes to play with matches. He's been arrested before. The sheriff's office gave us a tip that he might have been in this area on the day of the arson."

By now Jimmy Lee Bayliss had steadied himself. As he examined the photograph of Duane Scrod Jr., an idea took root in his mind.

"He got into a hassle with one of his teachers," the fire investigator went on.

"The next day there was a school field trip to the swamp, but our boy Duane didn't show up for the bus. We're trying to find out if he snuck out here and set the fire."

"As payback, you mean," Jimmy Lee Bayliss said.

"That's the theory," said Torkelsen. "Apparently this kid is somebody you definitely don't want to piss off."

Jimmy Lee Bayliss beheld the photo of the student as if it were a gift from the heavens: a real arsonist was exactly what he needed now.

Never had Jimmy Lee Bayliss expected anyone to figure out that the blaze at the Black Vine Swamp was intentional, because he'd worked so hard to make it look like a wildfire.

The purpose was to scare off the kids on that field trip before one of them blundered into Section 22 and spotted Red Diamond's mud pit and drilling equipment. The students were never in serious danger, in Jimmy Lee Bayliss's view. It was a controlled burn, with a dirt berm and a watery slough providing a barrier between the flames and the hikers.

A whiff or two of smoke had done the trick; the teachers had lined up the kids and filed out of the swamp in less than ten minutes. Jimmy Lee Bayliss had watched through his binoculars, a red bandanna covering his mouth and nose.

Afterward he'd stayed until the fire burned itself out, and then he cleared the scene of all evidence — or so he'd believed. He was furious at himself for having dropped that stupid ballpoint pen while setting the fire. How could he have been so careless? Drake McBride would blow a gasket if he found out.

"You're sure it was arson?" Jimmy Lee Bayliss asked Torkelsen.

"We found a suspicious line of flash marks in the underbrush," the investigator said.

Jimmy Lee Bayliss was glad that he'd taken the trouble to throw his butane torch into a canal along Route 29 on the way home that night. As a result, the only direct evidence linking him to the arson was now rusting in thirty feet of muddy, alligator-infested water.

The best news of all, however, was that the fire department had zeroed in on a suspect other than Jimmy Lee Bayliss. This Scrod boy was obviously a bad egg — maybe he was the one who'd attacked poor Melton, thought Jimmy Lee Bayliss. Getting a goon like that off the streets would be a public service.

"Well, what do you think?" Torkelsen nodded toward the photograph in the oilman's hand, which was now barely shaking at all. "Ever seen that young man hanging around out here?"

"I believe I have," Jimmy Lee Bayliss said, furrowing his brow in fake concentration. "Matter of fact, I'm sure of it."

THIRTEEN

Nick spent most of the teacher work day exercising his free arm, washing his mother's car, and helping her scrub the oven. Luckily, she didn't ask how he and Marta liked the movie that they never went to see. Later Nick rode his bike to the public library and checked out a book by Edward Abbey, the writer mentioned by the stranger who'd caught Nick and Marta inside Mrs. Starch's house.

The afternoon was sunny but cool, so Nick practiced pitching left-handed into a net until dark. His arm felt like cement by the time he went to bed. He was so exhausted that he fell asleep after reading only a few pages of the book, which was called *The Monkey Wrench Gang*.

He woke up early the next morning and called the army hospital in Washington, D.C. He was eager to know if the infection in his dad's injured shoulder had gotten better. A nurse who answered the phone in the hospital room told Nick that Capt. Gregory Waters was gone, but said she wasn't allowed to give out any other information.

Nick immediately tried to reach his mom at work, with no luck. Deep in worry, he sat by himself on the bus to Truman, barely mumbling hello to Marta and his other friends.

All morning Nick remained so preoccupied that he was unable to focus on his schoolwork, including the topic of "punctuated equilibrium." That was the featured term on page 329 of Nick's biology book, and on Thursdays Dr. Wendell Waxmo always taught page 329, and *only* page 329.

Punctuated equilibriums had something to do with how animal species change over time, but even Libby Marshall was having difficulty explaining it. Wendell Waxmo scanned the room for a fresh target and called not once but three times on Nick, who was in a fog.

"All right, Mr. Waters, stand up," Wendell Waxmo barked finally, "and sing along with me."

Jarred into alertness, Nick was too mortified to move.

"Even with one arm tied behind your back, I'll bet you can carry a swell tune," said Wendell Waxmo.

"No, I can't. Honest."

" 'Bridge over Troubled Water'?"

"I don't know all the words to that one. Sorry," Nick said. The whole class was watching him except for Smoke, whose nose was buried in his textbook.

" 'White Christmas'?" the crazy substitute said. "For heaven's sake, every human over the age of three knows 'White Christmas' by heart."

"Please don't make me sing. Not today."

Nick had the strange sensation of physically shrinking at his desk, growing smaller with each agonizing moment. He thought: *If only I could make myself disappear . . .*

"Well?" said Wendell Waxmo.

"I just can't do it."

"And why not, Mr. Waters?"

"Because . . . I just . . . I . . ."

"Because why?"

"Because he's not in the mood!" It was Marta, shooting to her feet. The other students sat stunned and gaping.

Even Wendell Waxmo was briefly flustered. He fiddled with his bow tie — today's color selection was lime green — before collecting his wits and boring in on Marta.

"Miss Gonzalez, it's nice to have you participating, finally, in a class discussion.

Would you mind telling us how you happen to know that Mr. Waters isn't in the mood for singing?"

Marta glanced sideways at Nick, who nodded for her to sit down. He appreciated what she was trying to do — spare him from an incredibly awkward moment — but he didn't want her to get in trouble.

"I'm waiting, Miss Gonzalez." Wendell Waxmo brushed at the lapels of his tattered old tuxedo. "Kindly tell us why your friend doesn't feel like belting out a song."

"Because his father got blown up in Iraq," Marta said quietly, "and nearly died. So leave him alone, okay? Just leave him alone."

Wendell Waxmo looked as if a bowling ball had been dropped on his toes. His mouth froze in the shape of an "O," and the sound that emerged was a long faint hiss, like a tire going flat.

Nick didn't know what to do. Most of the kids were looking at him with expressions of sympathy and sorrow; even Smoke had closed his book and was studying Nick from across the room.

Marta sat down, her eyes glistening with tears. She scribbled a note and thrust it at Nick: *I want Mrs. Starch to come back!*

Gradually the color returned to Wendell Waxmo's face, and he cleared his throat much too loudly and moistly. Once again he'd been upstaged in his own class, only this time the circumstances didn't allow for a witty retort.

"Mr. Waters, our sincere prayers are with your father, and your family. War is a tragic event," the substitute said, "but life does go on. So, people, please return your attention to page 329 and the theory of punctuated equilibrium."

Nick raised his left hand.

"Yes, Mr. Waters?"

"My dad's going to be okay," Nick declared in a strong voice. "The doctors say he'll be fine."

Wendell Waxmo hoped the boy's upbeat attitude would energize the rest of the class. "What good news!" he said. "I think that calls for a round of applause!"

The students stared at the man as if his pants had fallen down. Wendell Waxmo looked at the clock on the wall: nine long minutes until the bell.

"One piece of unfinished business," he said briskly. From his battered briefcase he removed the essay written by Duane Scrod Jr., upon which the brutal grade of D+ had been scrawled supersized with a bright red marker. It was painfully visible to all members of the class, even those in the back row.

Wendell Waxmo waved the paper in Smoke's face and said, "Pimples indeed, Mr. Scrod." The essay was covered with crimson slashes, circles, and scribbles.

"It wasn't even my idea," the boy said. "Mrs. Starch is the one who made me write it."

"Well, she's not here, is she?"

"But how'd I mess up so bad?"

"In a word: scholarship, or lack thereof. I'm going to leave this disaster in Mrs. Starch's desk so she can see for herself." Wendell Waxmo returned to the front of the class and placed the pimple paper in Mrs. Starch's top drawer.

The other students remained silent, but the mood was definitely hostile. Nick saw Marta trying to write another note, the veins in her neck pulsing with anger. Finally she crumpled it and mouthed the words "I hate him!"

Nick, too, felt bad for Smoke, who seemed floored by the D+ grade. Crazy Dr. Waxmo should have waited until after the bell to return the essay instead of embarrassing the kid in front of everybody.

Smoke raised his hand.

Wendell Waxmo called on Graham, who wasn't expecting it. "Mr. Carson, tell the class how punctuated equilibrium relates to the concept of speciation."

Graham stood up and confidently gave a totally wrong answer, as usual.

Smoke raised his hand higher. Wendell Waxmo looked the other way and called on Mickey Maris.

Nick couldn't stand it. He cleared his throat and spoke up. "Duane has a question, Dr. Waxmo."

"What?" The substitute wheeled around and speared Nick with a glare. "Are you interrupting me, Mr. Waters?"

Nick gestured toward Smoke. "Duane's had his hand up."

"I'm not blind, am I?"

"No, sir."

"Whatever Duane wants to ask can wait, I'm sure."

Nick said, "That's not right."

"Yeah, answer his question," said Marta.

Wendell Waxmo's ears turned pink and his bald spot began to tingle and his tuxedo shirt began to itch. What had gotten into these kids? It was unbelievable!

He banged a pudgy fist on the desk and said, "Quiet, you little termites —"

At that moment there was a firm rap on the door, and Dr. Dressler entered the room. He pointed at Nick and said, "Mr. Waters, I need to see you in my office.

Right away."

Twilly Spree had been born in Key West thirty-four years before the Red Diamond Energy Corporation came probing around the Big Cypress. Twilly's father was a gung-ho real estate salesman; his mother grew bonsai trees and wrote a dreadful romance novel that she published under the pseudonym Rosalee DuPont.

When Twilly was eighteen, his grandfather had died suddenly, leaving the young man a generous inheritance of $5 million. Twilly had invested wisely and was now wealthy enough to buy his own private jet, if he wanted one.

He didn't. He seldom left the state of Florida, a place that he loved, a place that was breaking his heart because it was disappearing before his very eyes.

Twilly Spree had good intentions but a rotten temper, which occasionally got him into hot water. He didn't like high-rise buildings and freeways and ugly housing subdivisions named after nonexistent otters or eagles. He didn't like concrete and asphalt, period, and he especially didn't like the people who were burying the wilderness under concrete and asphalt.

And although he gave away thousands of

dollars to conservation groups, Twilly Spree sometimes got personally involved in the causes in which he believed — too personally involved. One time Twilly witnessed a driver tossing hamburger wrappers from a car, and he followed the man a hundred and three miles down the turnpike, all the way to Fort Lauderdale. That night, the litterbug was flabbergasted to find four tons of raw garbage on top of his red BMW convertible. Twilly, watching from the top of a pine tree, wasn't the least bit ashamed of himself.

While he could easily afford to book penthouse suites at the finest hotels, Twilly preferred a pup tent under the stars. For a month or so, he'd been camping east of Naples, in a marvelous cypress strand known as the Black Vine Swamp.

On the day of the fire, Twilly had been deep inside the tree line, observing a group of school students on a nature hike. An unexpected turn of events had prevented him from chasing down the arsonist at the time, though Twilly was confident he would eventually catch the culprit.

The helicopter now circling above the swamp didn't concern Twilly, because his campsite was so well concealed that it could not be seen from the air. He was aware that the chopper was leased to the Red Diamond

Energy Corporation, and that Red Diamond was preparing to drill for oil in the wetlands. Twilly did not approve.

As a first warning, Twilly had captured one of Red Diamond's workers, stripped off the man's clothes, and then glued him to a tree trunk. The fellow had not been harmed, but he'd been made to feel extremely unwelcome. The iron pipes that he had been unloading were already on a freighter bound for Haiti, where they would bring much-needed water to the vegetable fields of poor farmers. Twilly had the funds and the connections to make such miracles happen.

After the glue incident and the pipe disappearance, Twilly had expected Red Diamond to beef up security. Therefore the appearance of the helicopter was no surprise. As soon as the aircraft flew away, Twilly slipped out of the trees and made his way across a grass prairie until he reached the precise longitude and latitude of a way point that was logged on his handheld GPS. There he sat down cross-legged and amused himself by watching a line of bull ants carry off a dead cricket.

Within minutes a different helicopter flew in from the south and stopped to hover directly above Twilly, the backwash from the rotors disrupting the ant parade and making the soft grass dance and flutter crazily.

It was a helicopter paid for by Twilly himself. He waved to the pilot, who opened the door and pushed out a bundle that landed with a damp thud ten yards from where Twilly waited.

With a pocket knife, he sliced open the thick outer binding and pried off the slatted lid to make sure that the important contents of the package weren't damaged. Inside, he counted two dozen small plastic bottles, each filled with a whitish liquid. The bottles had been packed on a bed of dry ice, to keep them cold.

Twilly Spree smiled and thought: *Hope springs eternal.*

He flashed an "okay" sign to the pilot and the helicopter buzzed off, leaving the prairie silent in the slanted morning light.

Nick didn't want to hear bad news about his father from Dr. Dressler, who was practically a stranger, but why else would the headmaster have pulled him out of class?

Dr. Dressler didn't say a word as they walked to the administration building. Nick felt like turning around and running away as fast as he could. If his whole life was about to fall apart, he wanted to be at home when it happened. He wondered if his mom had already been notified. If so, where was she? And who was there to comfort her?

"Have a chair, please," the headmaster said when they got to his office.

Nick needed to sit down. The room seemed to be spinning, and Dr. Dressler sounded as if he were speaking into a bucket.

"Can I call my mother?" Nick asked.

"Why?"

"Oh. So she already knows."

Dr. Dressler looked puzzled. "Knows what?"

Nick had never fainted, but he was pretty sure that he was going to keel over any second. With his free hand, he clutched the arm of the chair to keep himself upright. He squeezed his eyes shut, hoping that the room would stop moving.

Is my dad dead? He couldn't make himself ask the question. He was too afraid.

"Are you all right?" the headmaster asked.

"No, sir, not really."

"Is your arm bothering you?"

Nick said, "There's nothing wrong with my arm. I strapped it up this way because I'm training to be left-handed."

"That's an interesting project." Dr.

207

Dressler was trying to sound supportive, which didn't make Nick feel any better.

"Still, you look pale," the headmaster said. "Let me call the nurse —"

"Please don't. I'll be okay." When Nick opened his eyes, he saw that Dr. Dressler was holding an envelope.

"This came to the school, Nick, addressed to you."

"From who?"

"Read it closely. Then I have some questions," Dr. Dressler said.

When Nick took the envelope, he saw that somebody already had opened it. That's not cool, he thought angrily. What if the letter was personal?

Sensing that Nick was miffed, the headmaster said, "It's just a precaution. We have to make sure that undesirable persons aren't trying to contact our students on campus."

"So you read my letter?"

"We're just being careful, Nick. As you can see, there's no return address."

That was the first thing Nick had noticed, too, and with huge relief. He was sure that the Army National Guard wouldn't send a death notice in an unmarked envelope, especially a lavender-colored envelope. He unfolded the letter:

Dear Mr. Waters,

I've learned that you and Miss Gonzalez have taken a strong interest in my health and well-being. Let me assure you that I am just fine, and I intend to return to my teaching duties at the Truman School as soon as possible.

You and Miss Gonzalez are the only students to express any concern for me, and I'm grateful for that. However, I must firmly ask you not to probe any further into my personal affairs or to visit my home without a proper invitation.

Instead, both of you should focus on your academic studies (which, as I recall, could stand some improvement).

Sincerely,
Mrs. Starch

The message had been typed on stationery bearing Mrs. Starch's name. If it was fake, Nick thought, the imposter had done an excellent job of imitating Mrs. Starch's stern tone. In any case, Nick was overjoyed that the letter had nothing to do with his father's medical condition.

The headmaster wasted no time getting to his questions. "Did you and Marta really go to Mrs. Starch's house?"

209

Nick nodded. "Nobody's seen her since the field trip. It just seems so weird."

"She had a family emergency," Dr. Dressler said, "and she informed the school that she'd need some time off. There's nothing weird about that."

Dr. Dressler didn't sound very sure to Nick. In fact, he sounded like he was trying to persuade *himself* that Mrs. Starch's sudden disappearance was normal.

"How did you and Marta even get to her place? It's way out near the mall," the headmaster said.

"We walked from the movie theater."

"And what did you find when you got there?"

Nick considered his response carefully. He and Marta had promised each other not to tell anyone about the man who called himself Twilly and said that Mrs. Starch was his aunt.

"Well, she wasn't home," Nick said. "It looked like she hadn't been there for a while."

Dr. Dressler folded his hands in a mechanical way. It seemed to Nick that he wanted to appear unruffled.

"Did you see anything unusual?" the headmaster asked.

Nick immediately thought about the

creepy gallery of stuffed animals inside Mrs. Starch's house. "It was dark," he said, dodging Dr. Dressler's question without having to invent a lie.

"But clearly she knew that you and Marta had been there, or else she wouldn't have written the letter."

It had to be Twilly who'd told Mrs. Starch about encountering the two students. However, Nick saw no reason to inform Dr. Dressler that he and Marta had been captured by an odd stranger wearing a ski cap and an ammo belt full of live bullets.

"Maybe she peeked out and spotted us from an upstairs window," Nick said. "Just because she didn't answer the door doesn't mean she wasn't home."

"Yes, that's true," said the headmaster.

"Have you talked to her since she's been gone?"

Dr. Dressler stiffened behind his desk. "As I mentioned before, she's been in communication with the school."

"But have you actually *talked* to her? Has anyone?"

"I'm certain that she'll call," Dr. Dressler said curtly, "as soon as her family situation is taken care of."

The phone rang, and the headmaster picked it up. After listening for a moment,

211

he excused himself from the office. Several minutes passed, and Nick grew restless.

He noticed a thick file marked "B. Starch" on a corner of Dr. Dressler's desk. Nick flipped open the file and hurriedly started skimming the pages. Normally he wasn't a snoop, but he was still highly annoyed about his letter being opened without his permission. He figured that Dr. Dressler owed him one.

Nick was searching for a particular piece of information, but the paperwork in Mrs. Starch's file was mostly dull and routine. He found what he was looking for just as he heard the muffled voice of the headmaster, speaking to someone outside the door. Nick shut the file folder barely half a second before Dr. Dressler walked in.

"I only have one more question, Nick."

"Yes, sir."

"Can you absolutely guarantee that you and Marta will follow Mrs. Starch's wishes? Please give her the privacy she needs at this time. It's only fair."

"We were worried about her, that's all. We didn't mean to cause any hassle."

Dr. Dressler seemed to be struggling with the notion that any of Bunny Starch's students cared that much about her.

"Look, I know she's not the most popular

teacher at Truman," said Nick. "In fact, just the opposite. But after what happened on the field trip . . ."

The headmaster nodded. "Yes, it was very courageous of her to go back for Libby's medicine while that fire was burning. And don't worry, Nick, the school will honor her appropriately when she returns."

Dr. Dressler escorted him out of the office, apparently believing that Nick had promised not to concern himself further with the whereabouts of Mrs. Starch. In fact, Nick had made no such pledge.

"Did you talk to any of her family?" he asked the headmaster.

"No, I didn't."

"I heard she had a nephew," Nick remarked in an innocent tone.

"Not that I'm aware of," Dr. Dressler said. His curious expression confirmed what Nick had seen in Mrs. Starch's employment file. She had no sisters or brothers, which meant it was biologically impossible for her to have a nephew named Twilly — or Joe or Fred or Engelbert, for that matter.

In fact, Mrs. Starch's file didn't list any living relatives, which made her excuse of a "family emergency" seem highly suspicious.

Nick was eager to show Mrs. Starch's note to Marta, but he didn't make it back to biology class. As he hurried out of the administration building, he heard a car horn honking, and then somebody shouted his name. It was his mother, waving from the parking lot. Nick couldn't see whether she was crying or not. He swallowed hard, and ran to meet her.

FOURTEEN

It had been on a creek deep in the Everglades where Nick had learned that his
father would be leaving for the Mideast.
They were in a small flat-bottomed boat being poled along the shallows by a guide who
was hunting for redfish and snook. The fishing trip had been an early Christmas present
to both of them from his mother.

Nick sat on a cooler in the center of the
boat, watching his dad cast a fly rod with an
easy, flawless rhythm that was almost hypno-
tizing. Fifty feet of line would snap straight
behind him and float in midair, then loop
tightly and shoot forward, dropping the fly
as softly as a snowflake. It was a marvelous
sight to see.

"My Guard unit's been called up," Nick's
father said, his eyes fixed on the water.

"To fight, you mean?"

"I guess we'll find out when we get there."

"How long will you be gone?" Nick tried

215

to keep the emotion out of his voice.

"A year is what we heard, but hopefully not that long."

On the very next cast, Nick's dad hooked a good snook that jumped twice and then streaked into the mangroves, cutting the leader. The guide cursed loudly, yet Nick's father seemed as pleased as if he'd landed the fish.

"Your turn, Nicky," he said, reeling up his line.

"No, Dad. Keep casting."

"Come on, I had my chance."

"Catch the next one," Nick said.

The truth was, he didn't feel like fishing. He was satisfied to sit back and watch his father work the fly rod, whipping airy ribbons in the sky. Nick wanted a memory to keep fresh, something that would stay with him while Capt. Gregory Waters was away in combat.

"You tell Mom yet?" Nick asked.

"Last night."

"Is she all right?"

"She had a feeling it was coming. She watches the news."

"Aren't you scared?"

"A little," his father said. "But mostly I'm bummed because I'm going to miss your soccer season. Maybe lacrosse, too. But they let us do e-mail over there."

"Cool. I'll send you the scores."

"Nicky, I guess there's no need to give you the big speech."

"About taking care of her?"

"Right."

"Don't worry," Nick said.

"I won't."

Nick's father tossed another long cast. Instantly there was a flash on the surface and the line came taut. Five minutes later, the guide slipped his net under a hefty snook that was dark and coppery from the swamp water. Nick's dad lifted the sleek fish by its lower jaw and held it up while Nick snapped a picture.

His father was beaming. "What do you think — ten pounds?"

"More," said Nick. "At least twelve."

Late that night, after his parents were in bed, Nick had gone on the Internet and Googled "Iraq" in order to learn what the war was all about. Seven months later, he still wasn't sure.

Nobody could find the terrible weapons supposedly stashed by the Iraqi government, while many of the terrorists who were attacking American troops had turned out to be Iraqi citizens. It was hard for Nick to understand why good soldiers like his dad were being blown up by some of the same people they were trying to help.

Nick was a mild and levelheaded person who seldom lost his temper, but lately there were times when he'd get mad about what had happened. Running toward his mother in the school parking lot and fearing the worst possible news, Nick felt the anger boil up again. Maybe it was selfish, but he didn't want to lose his father to a war that nobody seemed able to explain.

Nick ran up to his mom and pulled her close. He blinked away hot tears and almost choked when he tried to speak.

"It's okay, Nicky," she said, sounding amazingly strong and calm.

"I called the hospital and they said Dad was gone."

"Yes, I know."

"But I thought he was getting better! What happened?" Nick cried.

"You should ask him yourself."

His mother spun Nick around to face the car. Capt. Gregory Waters sat in the front passenger seat, grinning and giving a thumbs-up sign with his left hand.

Every evening Dr. Wendell Waxmo set out a dozen bowls of food for stray cats, a gesture that annoyed his human neighbors but was greatly appreciated by the wild raccoons, squirrels, and opossums that would amble out of the woods to gorge themselves on stale Meow Mix.

Wendell Waxmo lived in a small apartment five blocks from the Naples beach, a lovely place that he never visited because his sinuses got inflamed by salt water and his skin was ultra-sensitive to ultraviolet rays. Wendell Waxmo was strictly an indoor person. Yet, for a teacher (even a substitute), he spent little time reading books or polishing his skills in science, math, and English.

Instead Wendell Waxmo preferred to drown his brain in bland television, especially the shopping networks and infomercials. He purchased every goofy, worthless gimmick that he saw advertised on cable — cheese curlers, mayonnaise whippers, personalized oven mitts, ear-hair trimmers, electronic sock deodorizers, reusable dental floss, and even a flashlight that stayed on for three straight years, night and day.

Wendell Waxmo got so caught up channel-surfing in search of clever new items that he'd tune out everything else in his peculiar little world, from the tuba ring tone of his cell phone to the yowls of the cats being roughed up by hungry raccoons behind the apartment building.

As it happened, Wendell Waxmo was once again glued to the phone, excitedly ordering a solar-powered raisin peeler for $49.92 (to be paid in twelve monthly installments of $4.16, not including handling and shipping), when he glanced up and saw a stranger standing in his living room.

"That's quite a tuxedo," the man remarked.

Gripping the phone fiercely, as if the intruder planned to snatch it away and order the raisin peeler for himself, Wendell Waxmo stammered, "I'll b-b-be with you in a m-m-minute."

The man sat down and waited. Wendell Waxmo gathered his wits, completed his transaction, and put down the phone. He decided that the stranger didn't look like a chain-saw killer.

"How'd you get inside my apartment?" he asked.

"The door was unlocked. You should be more careful." The man wore a dark ski cap, khaki clothes, and what appeared to be a Western-style ammunition belt.

"If you're going to rob me, take whatever you want," Wendell Waxmo said with a sweep of an arm. "Just don't hurt me."

The intruder smiled wryly as he scanned Wendell Waxmo's vast assortment of useless gadgets and gizmos, which cluttered the shelves and the tables and the floor.

"As much as I'd love to own a three-speed sonic artichoke juicer," the man said, "I think I'll pass."

"Then what are you doing here?"

"A small favor for the youth of America."

Wendell Waxmo nervously loosened his bow tie. "What does *that* mean?"

"It means you're about to retire from the teaching profession."

"What?"

"Your services are no longer needed at the Truman School. Today was your last day."

Wendell Waxmo's piggy eyes narrowed. "Who are you, anyway?"

The stranger said, "Bunny Starch takes her responsibilities very seriously, and she expects her substitutes to do the same. She's been receiving some very disturbing reports from her classroom, Wendell."

"I've no idea what you're talking about."

"Teaching the same page over and over on the same day every week. Asking students to get up and sing, for no good reason." The man shrugged and rose. "By the way, what kind of nitwit *sings* the Pledge of Allegiance?"

"Is that it?" Wendell Waxmo asked resentfully. For one foolish moment he considered

221

trying to defend his teaching methods.

"I get results!" he declared.

"No, you get laughed at," the stranger said. "Some kid grinds out a five-hundred-word essay, a kid who's never written anything before in his life, and you tear him down in front of the whole class. Not cool."

"You mean the pimple paper?"

"Another kid, his old man gets torn up in Iraq and you want him to do 'White Christmas'?" The intruder shook his head in disgust. "The only thing worse than a whack job, Wendell, is a clueless whack job. I recommend you find another line of work."

Wendell Waxmo huffed. "From what I've heard, Mrs. Starch can be just as tough on her students."

"Oh, I don't doubt that," the man said, heading for the door, "but at least they learn the whole book."

"You can't fire me! Only the headmaster can do that."

The man stopped, walked back to Wendell Waxmo, seized him by the shoulders, hoisted him out of the chair, and said to his face: "I'm much, much crazier than you are. Do *not* give me a reason to return here."

Finally Wendell Waxmo was frightened, a

sane and normal reaction. The intruder's arms were rock-hard, and his eyes were cold and weary. He acted like a man with absolutely no fear and no doubts.

"I'll call in sick tomorrow," Wendell Waxmo peeped.

"Permanently."

"Right. I'll think of something awful and contagious."

"Good idea." The stranger in the ski cap lowered Wendell Waxmo back into a sitting position.

"I don't suppose you want to hear me sing," the substitute said. "It might change your mind."

"Highly unlikely."

"Then just tell me this — are you a spy for Bunny Starch?"

"Good night, Wendell." The intruder stalked out the back door and down the steps, scattering the whiny throng of stray cats.

When Duane Scrod Jr. got home from school, his father handed him a short grocery list that included milk, cereal, and five pounds of sunflower seeds — too much to haul back on a motorcycle. Duane Jr. took one of the pickup trucks and headed for the store, the wheels spraying gravel.

Jimmy Lee Bayliss, who was waiting down the street, recognized the boy from the photograph shown to him by Torkelsen, the fire investigator. As soon as the pickup was out of sight, Jimmy Lee Bayliss pulled up to the house and parked next to a Tahoe that bore angry graffiti: BOYCOTT SMITHERS CHEVY!!!!!

Ironically, Jimmy Lee Bayliss himself was driving a Chevrolet, a four-door sedan that he'd rented because he didn't want to be seen in the company truck. On this mission, it was crucial that Jimmy Lee Bayliss's connection to the Red Diamond Energy Corporation remain secret. He planned to talk his way into the Scrod house and secretly swipe something — anything — that belonged to the boy.

The windows were dark yet wide open. A symphony was playing loudly, which Jimmy Lee Bayliss found strange. From the rough, unfinished look of the place, he would have expected to hear the blues or country music, his own favorite.

A man who could only have been Duane Scrod Jr.'s father answered the door. He was barefoot and had three days' growth of beard. He wore smudged reading glasses, a dirty red cap, a camouflage hunting shirt, and no pants — only leopard-print boxer shorts.

"Are you here about the taxes?" the man asked.

That sounded to Jimmy Lee Bayliss like an excellent cover story, much better than his original idea of posing as a septic-tank inspector.

"That's right," Jimmy Lee Bayliss said to Duane Scrod Sr. "I'm from the tax collector's office."

"Well, I've been expectin' you," said Duane Scrod Sr., who whipped out a pair of rusty needle-nose pliers and, quick as a viper, clamped the lips of his startled visitor.

Jimmy Lee Bayliss would have let loose the loudest scream of his life, if only he could have opened his mouth. But all he could do was moan and remain motionless, because even the slightest movement worsened the pain from the pinching pliers.

"Oh, Nadine?" Duane Scrod Sr. called out.

A tremendous flapping noise erupted, and a very large, gaily plumed bird came to rest with a squawk on Duane Scrod Sr.'s shoulder. Jimmy Lee Bayliss, whose eyes were watering because his lips hurt so much, studied the bird anxiously.

"Hello," it said. *Bonjour! Hallo!*

"Hhhnnngggg," replied Jimmy Lee Bayliss.

Using the pliers to tow his prisoner, Duane Scrod Sr. walked to the living room and turned off the stereo. "Man's home is his castle," he grumbled. "Says so, right in the Good Book."

Jimmy Lee Bayliss was in no position to argue. Frantically, he tried to think of a means to escape.

"What if I yanked off your lips and fed 'em to Nadine? Would that make you think twice about invadin' a person's privacy?" asked Duane Scrod Sr.

"Nnnnuuuuggh!" Jimmy Lee Bayliss pleaded.

"She's a blue-and-gold macaw. Speaks three languages. One time she got so hungry, she ate a beer can," Duane Scrod Sr. recalled proudly. "We're talkin' top-grade aluminum — gobbled it down like an oatmeal cookie."

Jimmy Lee Bayliss understood how Duane Scrod Sr.'s son could have become a troubled youth. He felt a pang of sympathy for the boy, whom he intended to frame for arson.

"Whaddya say, Nadine baby? Wanna snack?" Duane Scrod Sr. teased the macaw, who was eyeing the prisoner with great interest. Jimmy Lee Bayliss carefully reached into his pocket and pulled out a small wad of cash, which he held out to his captor.

Duane Scrod Sr. counted the money and said, "Nineteen dollars? You think you can buy your freedom for nineteen lousy bucks?"

He began feeding the dollar bills, one at a time, to his bird. "I told you people about a thousand times, I'll be happy to start payin' my taxes again, soon as somebody puts a new transmission in my Tahoe."

"Aaaccchhhhh," warbled Jimmy Lee Bayliss, who'd heard enough. He kicked hard at one of Duane Scrod Sr.'s bare kneecaps and made solid contact. The man hollered and let go of the needle-nose pliers, which hung momentarily from Jimmy Lee Bayliss's face before dropping to the floor.

As Duane Scrod Sr. hopped in circles, swearing and clutching his bruised knee, the macaw squawked furiously and took flight. Jimmy Lee Bayliss ran for the screen door, but he was too slow — the bird caught him from behind and locked its jagged beak on his scalp, trying to shuck him like a coconut.

Jimmy Lee Bayliss fell to his knees and flailed at the vicious devil bird, which refused to let go. Dragging himself across

227

the moldy shag carpet, Jimmy Lee Bayliss came upon a heavy nylon satchel with arm straps. He picked it up and began beating himself about the head, a painful but effective strategy. Several of the blows struck Nadine, scattering blue and gold feathers. The bird cursed in German, released Jimmy Lee Bayliss, and flew back toward Duane Scrod Sr., who by now was searching madly for his pliers.

Dizzy from clobbering himself, Jimmy Lee Bayliss lurched down the front steps and dove into his rental car. He was halfway to the interstate before he came to his senses and noticed that he still had the bulky backpack with which he'd fought off the killer macaw. It was right there on the front seat next to him: a camo-patterned book bag.

A kid's book bag.

Jimmy Lee Bayliss thought: *This is too good to be true.*

From the parking lot, Nick's mother phoned Dr. Dressler, who gave permission for Nick to leave school early. On the drive home, Nick peppered his father with questions until his mom told him to slow down and catch his breath.

"So the infection must be gone, right?"

Nick asked.

"It's getting better," Capt. Gregory Waters said. "There's a V.A. outpatient clinic in Fort Myers where I can get my checkups."

Nick noticed that the welts and burn marks on his dad's face were healing, and that his hair was slowly starting to grow back.

"How's the rehab?"

"Good, Nicky. I hear we're going to be partners." Nick's father pointed at Nick's wrapped right arm. "What kind of exercises are you doing with your other one?"

"Mostly trying to write and do math," Nick said. "It's harder than I thought."

His mother interjected: "You should see him on the computer, Greg. He can type almost as fast with one hand as he could with two. And last night he was throwing the baseball!"

Nick's father lit up. "Pitching lefty? That's fantastic."

A bit embarrassed, Nick said, "I look kind of spazzy on my windup."

"You do *not* look 'spazzy,' " said his mom emphatically. "You're doing great."

"I can't wait to see," his father said.

"No way, Dad, I'm not ready."

"Come on, I could use the inspiration."

"Maybe later," Nick said.

229

When they arrived at the house, Nick and his mother helped Greg Waters walk to the bedroom, where he quickly lay down and zonked out. He slept all afternoon and woke up hungry.

Over his wife's objection, he declared that dinner would be a left-handed speed-eating contest, with five dollars to the winner. He and Nick made a total mess, mangling their salads and stabbing at their ravioli and green beans. By the end of the meal, they were laughing so hard that they couldn't swallow their food. Nick's mother declared the race to be a tie, and for dessert she served chocolate milkshakes so that both Nick and his dad could rest their arms.

Afterward they went out to the backyard. His father sat down in a patio chair and said, "Let's see what you've got."

Nick picked up the ball and approached the homemade pitcher's mound. The framed net stood about forty feet away, and Nick eyed it apprehensively. He and his father had been playing catch since Nick was three years old, and he'd never felt any pressure — until now.

This wasn't about baseball, it was about hope. Nick wanted to show his dad that you could do practically anything with one arm that you could do with two.

"Relax. Take it smooth," his father advised.

"Don't laugh if I screw up."

"In Double-A I played with a guy who was ambidextrous — he could throw out a base runner with either arm. He played right field left-handed and left field right-handed."

"Are you serious?" Nick said.

"Incredible athlete. Unfortunately, he couldn't hit a curveball to save his life," Greg Waters said. "Now he's selling washing machines in Pensacola."

Turning the baseball in his free hand, Nick lined up his first two fingers with the stitches. Having his other arm bound to his back made him feel out of balance, almost tippy.

"Nice and easy," his dad said.

Nick uncoiled and heaved the ball as hard as he could. It bounced six feet in front of the net and rolled into the mesh.

Blushing, he kicked at the ground. "God, I throw like a girl!"

His father chuckled. "Don't let your mom hear you say that — she was the strikeout ace on her college softball team. Now do it again, only slow your motion."

Nick retrieved the baseball and tried throwing with an easier rhythm. This time

231

his pitch caught the lower half of the net.

"That's better. Take a longer step toward your target," Greg Waters suggested.

By the tenth throw, Nick was consistently hitting the strike zone. The pitches weren't very fast, but at least they were straight.

His father said, "Nicky, that's pretty darn good. I mean it."

"Thanks, Dad."

"Can I give it a shot?"

"Sure."

But as soon as Greg Waters stood up, he began to sway. Nick rushed over and steadied him.

"Let's wait till tomorrow, Dad. You've had a long day."

"I'm all right. Let me have the ball."

"You sure?" Nick glanced back toward the house and saw his mother watching anxiously from the kitchen window.

"Ball, please." Greg Waters held out his left hand.

Nick gave him the baseball, and he headed for the mound. His uncertain gait and heavily bandaged shoulder made him appear bulky, almost bearlike.

"Remember — nice and easy," Nick called out.

"You bet."

His father stared down an imaginary bat-ter, nodded at an imaginary catcher, and then rocked back into a jerky version of his normal windup motion. The pitch flew wildly past the net, through the hedge and over the fence. They heard a distinct *gong* as the baseball bounced off their neighbor's barbecue grill.

"Oh, crap," Greg Waters muttered.

Nick didn't want him to be discouraged. "You've still got plenty of heat, Dad."

"Could you go get it? I want to try one more time."

"Not tonight. You need to rest."

"Nicky, go find the ball," his dad said sharply.

It was floating in the neighbor's pool. Nick hurriedly fished it out and scrambled back over the fence. He was glad to see that his mother had come out of the house; he hoped that she would talk his dad into taking a rest.

"There's someone at the front door to see you," she said to Nick.

"Who is it?"

Greg Waters reached for the baseball, but Nick's mother grabbed it first. "You're benched for the night, big fella," she told him.

"Who's at the door, Mom?" Nick asked again.

"Some boy with a motorcycle," she said. "He says he's in your biology class."

FIFTEEN

Duane Scrod Jr. stood motionless in the driveway, his back to the house. He appeared to be watching the sun go down.

"Hi, Smoke. What's up?" said Nick.

When the kid turned around, Nick saw that he was still wearing his Truman School blazer and necktie.

"Hey, Waters." Smoke looked uneasy about being there, almost shy. "Listen, dude, I need to borrow your biology book. I'll give it back tomorrow."

"No problem," Nick said. "I missed the last part of class today. Did Wacko Waxmo give us homework?"

"Don't worry about him. He's no longer a factor."

"What do you mean?"

"He's history, man." Smoke made a slashing motion across his throat. "Gone. Done. Over."

That didn't sound good. Nick experienced

235

a moment of dread. "What happened? Did he die or something?"

Smoke chuckled. "Relax, man. Waxmo ain't dead — nobody laid a finger on him. But after what he did to you today, why do you care?"

Nick was mildly embarrassed to hear the kid mention the scene in class when the lunatic substitute had ordered Nick to sing a Christmas song and Marta had piped up in his defense. Nick half expected Smoke to make fun of him for letting a girl fight his battles.

He said, "It was no big deal. I don't want anything bad happening to the guy."

"That's real sweet. Can I have the book now? I'm late somewhere."

"Sure," Nick said, and he went into the house.

His mother intercepted him before he got to his room. "Who's that boy?" she asked. "Why don't you invite him in?"

"It's Duane Scrod Jr."

"The pencil-eater? But he looks so neat and normal."

"Neat, maybe. Definitely not normal," said Nick.

The biology book was at the bottom of his cluttered backpack. He hurried back outside and handed it to Smoke, who was waiting on the motorcycle. He'd put on leather riding gloves and also a helmet with a black plastic face shield. Nick could no longer see his expression.

"Smoke, can I ask you something — how come you need to borrow the book?"

" 'Cause I lost my backpack."

"What I meant is, why do you need the book if we don't have any homework?"

Smoke didn't answer right away. He tucked the book under one arm and kick-started his motorcycle. " 'Cause I gotta study," he said.

Nick could barely hear him. "What?"

"I GOTTA REVIEW FOR THE EXAM!" he shouted through his face mask.

What exam? Nick wondered, and he motioned for the kid to wait. Nick wanted to ask him about the fire in the Black Vine Swamp, and if he was the person that Marta had seen riding shotgun in Mrs. Starch's blue Prius, and also if he was acquainted with the man called Twilly who claimed to be Mrs. Starch's nephew. . . .

But most of all, Nick wanted to find out if Duane Scrod Jr. knew where Mrs. Starch was.

"Can you shut off the bike for a minute?" he yelled.

The kid revved the engine louder.

"Please? It's important!"

"How's your dad?" Smoke shouted, catching Nick off guard.

"He's doing good. He came home today," Nick hollered back. "Hey, I really need to talk to you —"

Smoke gave a slight wave and roared down the street.

Nick's mother opened the door. "What did he want?" she asked.

"To borrow a book," Nick said. "And I have no idea why he picked me to ask."

"Maybe he doesn't have any other friends."

"But he's hardly said five words to me since elementary school. I wouldn't exactly call him a friend."

"Well, maybe he thinks you are," Nick's mom said. "Now go help your father. He's determined to have a shower, and I don't want him falling down and breaking his butt, along with everything else."

"Who's gonna watch him while I'm at school and you're at work?"

"He says he's going to take care of himself, Nicky."

"But what about rehab?"

"Guess what he asked me to buy for him."

"Baseballs?" Nick said.

"Yep." His mother made a pitching motion. "Four dozen baseballs is what he wants. I guess he's going to throw at that darn net all day long. Can you believe it? He just got out of the hospital!"

"I believe it," said Nick. He couldn't have been any happier.

When Dr. Dressler arrived at the Truman School early the next day, he found a note stuck to his office door asking him to call Wendell Waxmo as soon as possible.

Dr. Dressler had no desire to speak to Wendell Waxmo first thing in the morning. In truth, he preferred not to speak to Wendell Waxmo at all. The man was a total flake, a menace in the classroom.

Not a day went by that Dr. Dressler didn't receive irate phone calls from parents complaining about Wendell Waxmo's nutty antics and demanding that he be fired or hauled off to a psychiatric institution. Dr. Dressler always assured them that he would look into the matter promptly and take appropriate action.

He was only stalling, of course, hoping that word of the daily chaos would reach Bunny Starch and that she'd come charging back to Truman to rescue her pupils from the clutches of the world's worst substitute.

Yet so far, nearing the end of Wendell Waxmo's first week, Mrs. Starch remained silent and out of sight. Dr. Dressler didn't know how much longer he could fend off the angry mothers and fathers before they took their complaints to the board of trustees. The headmaster had even called Mrs. Starch's answering machine and left a message, pretending to complain about Wendell Waxmo's bad behavior and inquiring (in a gentle but urgent tone) when Mrs. Starch might return to school.

Yet again there was no response.

And now Wendell Waxmo himself had called, requesting to speak with Dr. Dressler. As the headmaster reluctantly dialed Wendell Waxmo's phone number, he anticipated being trapped in a conversation that made no sense whatsoever, just like the substitute's teaching practices.

So he was surprised when Wendell Waxmo straightforwardly stated: "I won't be coming back to Truman. I'm afraid you'll have to find another teacher to handle Mrs. Starch's classes."

"You haven't left me much time — the first bell is only an hour away."

"It can't be helped, Dr. Dressler. I'm afraid I'm quite ill."

"I'm sorry to hear that. Is it serious?"

"*Very* serious. It's the Burmese jungle rot."

240

"Excuse me?"

"Burmese jungle rot!" snapped Wendell Waxmo. "Surely you've heard of the disease."

"Of course," the headmaster lied. Not that it mattered, but Wendell Waxmo didn't sound sick at all.

"It's a terrible condition, Dr. Dressler. Makes your skin turn green and fall off."

"Really?"

"And the doctors believe I caught it at your school! From unsanitary conditions in the cafeteria!"

Dr. Dressler seriously doubted that. On his desktop computer he had called up Yahoo and typed in the term "jungle rot."

Wendell Waxmo said, "I'm in pretty bad shape here. Pretty bad shape."

"But it's a foot fungus," the headmaster remarked after reading the definition. "You can treat it with topical antibiotics, according to these medical Web sites I'm looking at."

"No, no, no — that's *regular* jungle rot. Burmese jungle rot is a hundred times worse. There's no known cure!"

"Hmmmm," said Dr. Dressler. "How in the world would you catch something like that in our cafeteria?"

"From the salad bar, no doubt."

241

"Did you put your feet in our salad bar, Wendell?"

"The point is, I'm an extremely sick person."

No kidding, thought Dr. Dressler. Sick in the head.

"Sadly, I won't be returning to teach at Truman — ever," Wendell Waxmo continued. "Kindly remove my name from your list of available substitutes."

No great loss, mused Dr. Dressler, but now how do I lure Bunny Starch back to school?

"I've got a long, painful struggle ahead," Wendell Waxmo said dramatically.

"We'll all be praying for your jungle rot to go away."

"I appreciate that, Dr. Dressler."

"But don't even *think* about suing us."

"Good heavens, no!"

"Because things would get ugly, Wendell. No offense, but you haven't made many friends here at Truman."

"Well, I march to the tune of my own tuba," Wendell Waxmo said.

"That's one way of putting it, I suppose." The headmaster didn't know the true reason Wendell Waxmo was leaving, nor did he intend to waste his time trying to find out.

Nothing the man said or did seemed very logical.

"Oh, I almost forgot," Wendell Waxmo said. "Please inform my replacement that the students are on page 263."

"In which class?" Dr. Dressler asked.

"In all the classes," Wendell Waxmo replied matter-of-factly. "Today's Friday, and on Fridays we always study page 263. No exceptions."

The headmaster rolled his eyes but restrained himself from saying something cruel into the phone. "Every Friday, the same page?"

"Of course. Focus, focus, focus!"

"Goodbye, Wendell. Get well soon."

"Thank you, Dr. Dressler."

Jimmy Lee Bayliss hadn't said a word to his boss about the arson investigation, but Drake McBride found out anyway. Apparently the helicopter pilot was a blabbermouth.

"When did you plan on telling me — or did you?" Drake McBride asked tartly.

"I didn't think it was necessary, sir. I got everything under control," Jimmy Lee Bayliss said.

They were sitting in Drake McBride's office, which had a grand view of Tampa Bay.

In the distance, sailboats tacked back and forth across the choppy water.

"But you told me you cleared the scene. You told me they'd never suspect we did it," Drake McBride said.

"There's nuthin' to worry about. Honest."

"Don't worry?" Drake McBride raised his palms skyward. "Arson is a big-time felony, pardner. They put people in prison for it!"

Jimmy Lee Bayliss said, "I made friends with the fire investigator, and we've got no problems. They're after some local kid, a known pyro."

Drake McBride rose from his desk and poured himself a cup of black coffee. He didn't offer any to Jimmy Lee Bayliss, which was just as well because Jimmy Lee Bayliss's stomach was a wreck and his lips were still sore from the encounter with Duane Scrod Sr.

"I don't understand what's the big deal," Drake McBride fumed. "It's not like an orphanage got torched — just some worthless damn swamp. This time next year, you won't be able to tell it ever got burnt."

"Lightning strikes all the time in those woods," Jimmy Lee Bayliss remarked.

"*Exactamente!* Now, are you tellin' me these arson guys rush out and investigate every single wildfire? No way." Drake Mc-

244

Bride was indignant. "Now all of a sudden it's *CSI: Everglades.* Talk about a waste of taxpayer dollars!"

Jimmy Lee Bayliss knew exactly why the authorities had taken an interest in the fire at the Black Vine Swamp. "It's only because there were kids out there," he said.

"Yeah, well, none of the little buggers got hurt, did they? Nobody even got their eyebrows toasted." Drake McBride stood at the picture window and stared pensively out at the bay. "Bottom line: We had to do somethin' to keep 'em away from Section 22. And it worked, did it not?"

"Yes, sir. No harm done."

"And by the way — is that a stupid place for a field trip, or what? Way out in the middle of nowhere? If that was my class, I'd take 'em all to SeaWorld to watch those killer whales do ballerina dances, or whatever."

Jimmy Lee Bayliss said, "Or Weeki Wachee. They got all these girls dressed up like mermaids, ridin' water skis."

"Now you're talkin'!" Drake McBride finally smiled, though he became serious again when he returned to his desk. "Jimmy Lee, please tell me they've got no evidence that can tie Red Diamond to the arson. Please tell me I don't need to start lookin' for a lawyer and a bail bondsman."

"They haven't got diddly, sir." Jimmy Lee Bayliss failed to inform his boss that he'd dropped a company pen at the crime scene.

Drake McBride sat forward and peered at him curiously. "What the heck happened to your face? Somebody punch you out?"

Jimmy Lee Bayliss chose not to admit that a lunatic with a rabid parrot had tried to remove his lips with a pair of pliers.

"I cut myself shavin'," he said.

"Shaving with what — a weed whacker?"

"No big deal," mumbled Jimmy Lee Bayliss, covering his mouth.

Drake McBride fixed him with a steely look that he practiced often in the mirror. "Look here, pardner — you say the situation is under control. Does that mean I can take the afternoon off and go run King Thunderbolt?"

"Absolutely."

In his quest to look like a Texan, Drake McBride had bought a horse named Dumpling, renamed it King Thunderbolt, and was now taking riding lessons. Jimmy Lee Bayliss fully expected the animal to throw Drake McBride out of the saddle and stomp on him once it figured out what a phony he was.

"The arson investigator and I had a real

good talk," Jimmy Lee Bayliss said, trying to put his boss at ease.

Drake McBride leaned back and propped his shiny snakeskin boots on the desk. "That kid you mentioned, he sounds like a prime suspect."

"Definitely," Jimmy Lee Bayliss said. "A bad actor."

"They should take a real hard look at him."

"Oh, they are."

"Any assistance that Red Diamond Energy can offer —"

"They got our full cooperation," Jimmy Lee Bayliss said.

Drake McBride winked. "Give 'em whatever they need, okay?"

"I'm all over it."

"One more thing, pardner."

"Sure." Jimmy Lee Bayliss hated it when Drake McBride called him "pardner." The guy watched too many old Westerns on cable TV.

"If somethin' else bad happens," Drake McBride said, "I don't want to hear about it from my helicopter pilot. Understand? I want to hear about it from *you*."

"Yes, sir. Speakin' of the chopper, I need a lift out to the drilling site."

"Sure thing — after you drop me off at

the . . . whatchacallit. You know, the horse place?"

"You mean the stable," said Jimmy Lee Bayliss.

"Right." Drake McBride adjusted the tilt of his cowboy hat. "The stable," he said.

SIXTEEN

On the bus ride to school, Nick told Marta about Smoke's surprise visit.

She said, "You mean that maniac knows where you live? That's not cool."

"He just wanted to borrow my biology book."

"I'm so sure," Marta said.

"To study for an exam, is what he said."

"What exam? There's no exam . . . is there?"

"Not that I know of. It was weird," Nick said. "Then he took off before I could ask about Mrs. Starch."

Marta frowned. "Don't go there, Nick. Just let it drop."

After their encounter with the man called Twilly, Marta had lost some of her enthusiasm for solving the mystery of Mrs. Starch's disappearance.

Nick said, "I checked out a book by that writer Twilly talked about, Edward Abbey.

It's called *The Monkey Wrench Gang,* and the hero is this wild dude named Hayduke who wants to blow up a dam."

"What for?" Marta asked.

"Because it's plugging up this huge wild river. So he and these other guys launch, like, an underground war."

"All guys, huh?"

"No, there's a lady in the gang, too."

"Stick with comics, Nick."

"Seriously, it's a good story. And funny."

"But what's it got to do with Mrs. Starch?"

Nick shook his head. "Who knows. Maybe nothing."

"Look, I really don't care where she is, or what she's doing," Marta said. "I just want her to come back to Truman so we don't have to deal with Waxmo anymore. A witch that knows how to teach is better than a fruitcake from Mars."

"Smoke said Dr. Waxmo's gone."

"No way!" Marta exclaimed jubilantly.

"Whatever happened, Smoke acted like he had something to do with it," Nick said. "Sort of sketched me out."

Marta clapped her hands. "I can't believe we're really rid of Wacko Waxmo. It's too good to be true."

"We'll find out soon."

Sure enough, a different substitute was

sitting at Mrs. Starch's desk when Marta and Nick walked into third-period biology. They exchanged glances and took their seats. Graham was already waving his hand at the teacher, whose name was Mrs. Robertson. Most of the kids knew her, because she substituted regularly at the school.

"Dr. Waxmo has called in sick," she began. "Some sort of nasty flu bug, according to Dr. Dressler. So it looks like I'll be teaching this class until Mrs. Starch returns."

When the students broke out in grateful applause, Mrs. Robertson tried not to smile. Wendell Waxmo's unstable personality was legend among other substitutes.

When the celebrating was over, she said, "All right, let's get down to business. You have a question, Graham?"

The boy lowered his hand and said, "I'm ready with page 263."

"Oh?"

"I memorized the whole thing, like Dr. Waxmo told us to. Gametes and chromosomes!"

"That's good," Mrs. Robertson said patiently, "but I use a different teaching method than Dr. Waxmo's. I find it's more helpful to study chapter by chapter, instead of choosing random pages."

Graham looked crestfallen as Mrs. Robertson instructed the students to open their textbooks to Chapter 10. It was then Nick noticed that Smoke was absent, which meant that Nick's biology book was absent, too. He would have to share with somebody else.

Marta passed him a note: *Where's your new friend?*

Nick shrugged. Maybe the new, improved Duane Scrod Jr. was back to his old ways.

Torkelsen parked his SUV on the dirt road and approached the helicopter where the oilman was waiting.

"Hop in," he said to the fire investigator.

Torkelsen strapped himself in one of the back seats. "When did you find it?" he asked.

"About an hour ago. I called you right away," Jimmy Lee Bayliss said.

The chopper ride took only about three minutes. Torkelsen looked out the window while Jimmy Lee Bayliss chewed up a handful of Tums and hoped that the fire investigator wouldn't ask about the tool marks on his lips. The helicopter touched down in a dry clearing and the two men stepped out, Jimmy Lee Bayliss leading the way.

"Watch out for rattlers," he warned.

"You bet," the fire investigator said.

They made their way to a hammock of cabbage palms. The camo-print book bag lay on the ground, partially concealed by dead fronds. Jimmy Lee Bayliss thought he'd done a very convincing job of planting the evidence.

Torkelsen picked up the bag and examined it.

"We were doin' a fly-by when I saw some wild hogs runnin' through these trees," Jimmy Lee Bayliss said, "so I had the pilot set her down and I took off with my rifle. Didn't catch those darn pigs, but I came across this thing and figgered you'd be interested."

The fire investigator unzipped the pockets of the satchel and carefully sorted through the contents.

"What the heck's in there?" asked Jimmy Lee Bayliss, as if he didn't know. He'd been careful to remove any assignment papers that were dated after the arson; otherwise Torkelsen would have figured out that the book bag couldn't have been left at the scene on the day of the crime.

"Schoolbooks, pencils, a calculator," Torkelsen said. "And this —"

From one of the compartments he pulled out a small butane torch.

Jimmy Lee Bayliss whistled. "You hit the

jackpot!"

Torkelsen used a digital camera to take pictures, placing the book bag and the torch on a mat of palm fronds.

"This isn't far from where the fire was started, right?" Jimmy Lee Bayliss said, again as if he didn't know. "The kid must've stashed his stuff here before he took off."

"Sure looks that way."

Torkelsen jotted down the brand and model number of the butane torch, which Jimmy Lee Bayliss had purchased at his favorite hardware store on the way home from the Scrod household. Jimmy Lee Bayliss had tested the device by using it to burn up the sales receipt so that it could never be traced to him.

The fire investigator repacked the book bag, slung it over one shoulder, and followed Jimmy Lee Bayliss back to the helicopter. The pilot lifted off and made an extra-wide turn to avoid flying over the area of Section 22 where Red Diamond Energy was erecting its illegal oil-drilling platform. Even though the site was well concealed among the woods, Jimmy Lee Bayliss wasn't taking any chances, especially with a sharp-eyed passenger such as Torkelsen.

When the chopper landed on the dirt road, Jimmy Lee Bayliss got out and walked with the fire investigator to his SUV.

"Is there a name tag on that backpack?" Jimmy Lee Bayliss asked innocently.

"Yep," said Torkelsen. "It's that same kid I told you about — Duane Scrod Jr."

"Then you've got your arsonist!"

Torkelsen placed the incriminating bag in the back of the SUV. "This is a big help, Mr. Bayliss. Thanks a million."

"Call me anytime." Jimmy Lee Bayliss silently congratulated himself as he returned to the chopper, though he wouldn't have had such a merry spring in his step if he'd known that he was being spied upon at that very moment.

Perched halfway up a cypress and shielded by branches, Twilly Spree sucked on a slice of store-bought grapefruit and waited for the Red Diamond helicopter to fly away. Then he climbed down and waded slowly out of the strand.

The spiders and mosquitoes didn't concern him, nor did the poisonous snakes and the snapping turtles. Twilly was utterly at ease in the Black Vine Swamp, as he was in almost any wilderness. He felt much safer hiking among a few hungry gators and bears than driving down Interstate 75 at rush hour.

As he did every morning before the oil company workers arrived, Twilly went searching for signs of a particular panther. He would have been elated to see one measly paw print, but he found nothing. Twilly hadn't laid eyes on the animal since the day he'd heard two rifle shots in the area. He never came across its body or any spots of blood, so he'd concluded that it had safely gotten away.

On the day of the fire, Twilly had heard a panther scream — there was no mistaking the hair-raising wail — and he chose to believe that it was the one that he'd been seeking. The sooner the feline returned to its territory, the better. This was truly a matter of life and death, although not Twilly's own.

On the trail leading back to camp, he encountered the kid.

"You're supposed to be in school," Twilly said.

"I dreamed I saw the cat."

"Where?"

"On the boardwalk," said Duane Scrod Jr. "I had to check it out, in case it was, like, an Indian dream. But it wasn't."

"Too bad." Twilly himself rarely dreamed, but he knew Seminoles and Miccosukees who had visions that sometimes came true.

Facing the sun, Duane Scrod Jr. squinted out across the swamp. "So you didn't find anything? No tracks?"

Twilly shook his head. "A bobcat and some deer, that's all. You saw that chopper, right?"

"Don't worry," Duane Scrod Jr. said. "They didn't see me. I hid the bike real good, too."

"You need to get your butt to school. The alternative isn't pretty."

"Yeah, I know."

"Did your book bag ever turn up?"

"Nope. I swear I took it home," the kid said, "but I can't find it anywhere. Weird."

"You ask your old man?"

Duane Scrod Jr. snorted. "He's locked inside his music room with that crazy bird. Says he chased off a government tax man and next they're gonna send the FBI. There's no use talkin' to him when he gets like this."

The boy clearly had a rocky situation at home — his mother had run off to Europe and his father didn't always have both oars in the water. Twilly Spree felt bad for him, although not bad enough to risk blowing the mission.

"Hey, I saw the bottles got here," Duane Scrod Jr. said.

"Yep. Everybody's okay, for now."

"That was a cool thing you did."

"Go to school," Twilly told him. "Don't make me say it again."

"Right. Later, dude."

Watching the boy walk away, Twilly wished that he were better qualified to give out advice and wisdom. However, he'd spent most of his own life following his gut impulse instead of his brain, so he was hardly the proper model of a sensible grown-up.

He headed back toward camp, moving quietly by habit through the marshes and prairies and tree islands. On a soggy stretch he came upon something dark in the middle of the trail, something that hadn't been there earlier in the morning.

Twilly dropped to the ground and put his face closer in order to be sure. Eagerly he studied the fresh find. He poked it with a twig. He turned it with a leaf. He even sniffed it.

There was no doubt: panther poop!

Dr. Dressler's day turned sour when his lunch was interrupted by the arrival of George and Gilda Carson. They had come to make their weekly plea to have their "brilliant" son Graham moved up one or two grade levels at Truman.

Based on Graham's most recent report card, which Dr. Dressler held in his hand, Graham was exactly where he should have been.

"He has a C-plus average," Dr. Dressler reminded the Carsons. "There's nothing wrong with that, but it tells me that your son has all the challenges he can handle right now."

"What do you mean by that?" huffed Gilda Carson.

"Yes, what are you driving at?" George Carson chimed in.

Part of Dr. Dressler's job was putting up with the unreasonable demands of parents, but sometimes it wasn't easy to be polite.

"We don't normally advance a student unless he or she has straight A's," he explained, "and only then if they pass a series of tests showing that they're ready to skip ahead of all the other students their age."

Gilda Carson said, "We told you to give Graham those tests."

"And I did." Dr. Dressler handed her a copy of the not-so-brilliant results, which she showed to her husband.

"So he had one bad day. Big deal," said George Carson. "Let him take the tests again."

Dr. Dressler glanced wearily at the brass clock on his desk. He said, "Graham is a fine young man. He pays attention in class. He asks lots and *lots* of questions. He tries hard, but —"

"But what?" sneered Graham's mother.

"But he's a C-plus student."

"Which is the fault of his teachers, Dr. Dressler. Clearly Graham is underachieving," George Carson said, waving the test paper, "and that shouldn't happen at a place like Truman. We pay an arm and a leg for tuition here. . . ."

Dr. Dressler tuned out the arm-and-a-leg speech, which he'd heard dozens of times from parents who'd decided to blame the school because their children were falling short of their expectations. More often than not, the students improved with a little extra help and went on to graduate with solid marks.

However, the Carsons were in no mood for a pep talk, and Dr. Dressler was in no mood for the Carsons. He was on the verge of saying something very frank to them when his assistant cracked open the door.

"Sorry to interrupt, Dr. Dressler, but Detective Marshall is here to see you."

"Certainly. Right away." The headmaster was relieved to be rid of the Carsons (who departed, grousing), but he was worried about this new visit from the sheriff's detective. It probably wasn't a social call.

Once Jason Marshall entered the office, he got directly to the point. "I'm here to arrest Duane Scrod Jr.," he said.

"For the fire in the swamp?"

The detective nodded soberly.

Dr. Dressler's spirits sank as he envisioned the awful headline: TRUMAN STUDENT BUSTED FOR ARSON.

Because he was still a minor, Duane Scrod Jr. could not be openly named by the authorities, although it hardly mattered. The news that anyone enrolled at Truman was being charged with such a serious crime would bring horrible publicity, and Dr. Dressler anticipated a strong reaction from the school's board of trustees, not to mention some of the wealthy donors.

"The fire department called about an hour ago," Jason Marshall said. "It sounds like they've got all the evidence they need."

Dr. Dressler didn't bother asking for details. Given the boy's history of setting fires, the headmaster had no doubt that Duane Scrod Jr. was guilty. Obviously there was a good reason why the other students called him Smoke.

"It's only twenty minutes until school's

261

dismissed," Dr. Dressler said. "Can't we wait?"

The detective said, "No, let's get it over with."

Dr. Dressler checked the schedule and saw that Duane Scrod Jr. was in Mr. Riccio's English seminar.

"It's probably better if you stay here," the headmaster told Jason Marshall, who agreed.

The classroom was on the other side of the campus, and Dr. Dressler hurried to get there. Duane Scrod Jr. showed little emotion when the headmaster tapped on the door and summoned him outside.

Halfway to the administration building, the boy finally asked why he'd been called out of class.

"We've got a problem, Duane," said Dr. Dressler.

"Whaddya mean?"

"A man from the sheriff's department wants to speak with you."

"Again? How come?"

"Is your father home? Because you'll probably want to give him a call later."

"When hell freezes over," the boy said.

The Truman School had a strict rule against cussing, but Dr. Dressler let it slide. Duane Scrod Jr. was a large person, and the headmaster didn't want to rile him. He knew that the detective was far more experienced at handling such situations.

Jason Marshall, it turned out, was waiting with a set of handcuffs.

"No way," muttered Duane Scrod Jr. when he realized what was happening.

"I'm sorry, son," the detective said. "Turn around, please."

The boy didn't move. He sighed heavily and rolled his eyes toward the ceiling. "This is so wrong," he said.

Dr. Dressler was now extremely nervous. Nobody had ever been arrested in his office before. "Duane, please do what Detective Marshall says."

Slowly, very slowly, the boy turned around.

Thank goodness, thought the headmaster.

Then, just as Jason Marshall stepped forward to snap on the handcuffs, Duane Scrod Jr. bolted out the door.

"Hey!" shouted the detective, charging after him. "Stop!"

Dr. Dressler stood there alone, dumbfounded and flustered. He felt like he was in an episode of *Cops.*

The headmaster looked out the window in time to see Duane Scrod Jr. sprinting toward the athletic field. For such a stocky kid he was very quick, and he steadily widened the gap between himself and the detective. Dr. Dressler wondered why nobody had ever talked Duane Scrod Jr. into playing for the Truman football team, which was in dire need of a fullback.

A lacrosse squad was practicing at the west end of the field, and Duane Scrod Jr. made a beeline for one of the players. Even from a distance, Dr. Dressler easily identified the student as Nick Waters because of the bulky sling contraption that he wore on his right shoulder.

The headmaster watched in puzzlement as Duane Scrod Jr. pulled Nick aside and spoke to him briefly. Then the boy again dashed away, jumping a chain-link fence and vanishing into a deep stand of pine trees. Detective Jason Marshall ran far behind, waving and hollering.

Dr. Dressler didn't think that Duane Scrod Jr. had any friends at the Truman School, so he wondered why the kid had singled out Nick Waters to speak to — and what message could have been so important as to prompt him to interrupt his escape.

Had Dr. Dressler been able to hear every word that Duane Scrod Jr. said on the practice field, he might have reserved his opinion about the arson in the Black

264

Vine Swamp.

The first thing that the boy called Smoke told Nick Waters was: "Your biology book's in my locker. The combination is 5-3-5."

And the second thing he said was: "I didn't do that fire, man. I'm innocent."

SEVENTEEN

When Nick got home from school, he saw his father in the backyard throwing baseballs left-handed into the pitching net. Nick dropped his blazer on a chair, yanked off his necktie, and ran outside.

"How's your . . . you know . . ." He pointed at his dad's bandaged shoulder.

"My stump, you mean." His father smiled ruefully. "Actually, it's more like a stump of a stump."

Nick thought: *At least he hasn't lost his sense of humor.*

His dad said, "The infection's almost gone, but I'd be lying if I said I felt like a million bucks."

"Then you should take it easy."

"No, sir." Capt. Gregory Waters grabbed another ball from a bucket by his feet. "Take off your sling, Nicky, and we'll play some catch."

Nick knew it was useless to argue. "Throw

it here," he said.

"Unstrap your right arm and go get your glove."

"Come on, Dad, just throw it."

"Suit yourself." His dad wound up and pitched. The ball made a smack when it landed in Nick's bare hand — and it stung.

"Whoa!" Nick whistled and shook his fingers. "That's pretty good."

"I'm gettin' there," his father said.

Nick tossed back the ball, which went straight enough, though not terribly hard. He still felt awkward throwing with the wrong arm.

"Dad, how long have you been out here practicing?"

"Four hours and change."

"Geez, you're not tired?"

Greg Waters laughed. "Are you kidding? I'm whipped," he said, "but it's the best way to build up my strength and get some muscle memory."

His next pitch was low and off the mark. Nick scooped it off the grass, took a big step, and hurled it back — five feet over his father's head.

Greg Waters chuckled and said, "Even when I had *two* arms I couldn't jump that high."

Nick retrieved the baseball from a bed of

geraniums and jogged back to the other end of the yard.

"Who's your favorite lefty of all time?" he asked his dad on the next throw.

"Steve Carlton of the Phillies, way before your time. But you should've seen his fastball."

"Better than Johan Santana's?"

"Ask me again when Johan is in the Hall of Fame." He zipped another one back at Nick, who didn't mind the sting. It was exciting to see his dad throwing so hard and so accurately from what was once his weak side.

"So, Nicky, what's the hot news at Truman?"

Nick had planned to tell his parents about Smoke at dinner. They would have heard about it eventually anyway.

"Libby's dad came to arrest a kid at school, only the kid ran off into the woods and got away," Nick said.

Greg Waters stopped in the middle of his pitching motion. He lowered his arm but hung on to the ball.

"What was he being arrested for?"

"That fire in the swamp that I told you about, the day we went on the field trip," Nick said. "But here's the thing, Dad — I don't think he did it."

"How do you know?"

The back door opened and Nick's mom came outside wearing a first-baseman's mitt as big as a ham. She pounded a fist into the pocket and called out to Nick's dad: "Come on, soldier boy, let's see what you've got!"

Greg Waters grinned and hurled the ball, which she snagged easily and threw underhanded — but with plenty of juice — to Nick. His mother hadn't played softball since college, but she still had an excellent arm.

"How long have you been home?" Nick asked her.

"About thirty seconds. I saw you two rookies out here in the yard and figured you needed some backup or else you were gonna break out some windows on Mrs. Storter's house."

"Not me!" Nick's father said, pretending to be insulted. "Nicky's the wild one."

For half an hour they played three-way catch in a breezy, pleasant silence, just as they used to do before Greg Waters had been sent to Iraq. To Nick it seemed unreal that not even two weeks had passed since his dad had been seriously wounded — yet he was already back home, slinging the baseball! It was like a miracle, Nick thought.

Then again, his father was no ordinary patient.

Greg Waters said, "Nick, tell your mom what happened at school today."

"Oh, I already know about it. Gilda Carson text-messaged every parent in the phone book," said Nick's mother. "That boy who ran from the police is the same one who stopped over last night to borrow Nick's biology book."

"Really? Nicky didn't mention that." Greg Waters looked concerned, but he kept on throwing.

"His name is Duane Scrod Jr.," Nick's mother said. "His dad did a stretch in jail for arson, so I guess the apple doesn't fall far from the tree —"

"Mom, he didn't do it," Nick cut in firmly.

"What makes you so sure?"

"He told me so," Nick said. "While he was running away from Detective Marshall, he stopped me at lacrosse practice and said he was innocent. Why would he bother to do that if it wasn't true?"

Nick's mother tossed him the baseball. "People do lie, Nicky, especially when they're in trouble."

"But I believe him! You guys didn't see the look in his eyes, but I did." Nick heaved the ball to his dad, who bobbled it and then dropped it on the grass. Obviously he was distracted by what he was hearing.

Nick's mom said, "Tell your father what the other kids call Duane Jr."

"Aw, it's just a nickname," Nick protested.

"Let's hear it," said his dad.

"Smoke," Nick said quietly, knowing it would be harder than ever to convince his parents that Duane Scrod Jr. was innocent.

"Smoke?" Greg Waters picked up the baseball and turned it over and over in his hand. "Let me guess why they call him Smoke."

"Because that's what he likes to be called. Nobody knows why," Nick said. Then he added: "Okay, the police said he set two fires a long time ago — but that doesn't automatically mean he did this one."

Nick assumed that his mother had already learned about Smoke's previous arsons from Mrs. Carson, who'd probably gotten the information from Graham.

"Nicky, this doesn't sound good," his father said.

"But what happened in the past shouldn't matter — if he didn't start *this* fire, he shouldn't be arrested for it," Nick said. "That's not right, Dad."

Nick's mother walked over and put an arm around him, her softball mitt resting

271

behind his back on the lump that was his wrapped-up right arm. She said, "According to Mrs. Carson, they've got real strong evidence that Duane Jr. did it."

"Like what?"

"She didn't say in the message. But she made it sound solid."

Nick pulled away and sat down in a patio chair. "Well, I don't believe that. Anyway, you're supposed to be innocent till proven guilty, right?"

If Smoke was lying to me on the lacrosse field, Nick thought, then that kid is the world's greatest actor.

"Did the police catch him?" he asked.

"Not yet," his mom said. "I'd better go start dinner. We can talk about this later."

Capt. Gregory Waters sat down, flexing the fingers in his left hand. He looked sore and exhausted. "Maybe tomorrow I'll try the fly rod," he said.

Nick found himself staring at the empty right sleeve of his father's shirt — getting used to the sight of him without one arm would take time. His dad even joked about how "lopsided" he appeared in the mirror.

"Can I ask you something about the war?" Nick said.

"Sure."

"That man who died when the rocket hit

272

your Humvee — you said he was like a brother to you."

"It's true. He was," Nick's father said.

"How long did you know him before then?"

Greg Waters thought for a moment. "Two weeks. Maybe three."

"That's not a very long time," Nick said.

"Well, sometimes you make a connection right away."

"And not just because you're, like, in battle together?"

"No, the same thing would happen when I played ball in the minors," said Nick's dad. "You'd start talking to a new player the first day of spring training, and right away you knew he was okay. And then some other guy would walk up, and in two seconds you could tell he was a complete ass."

"I know what you mean," Nick said. "It's like a weird radar."

"Yeah, sort of."

Nick stood up. "I need to make a phone call before dinner."

His father said, "This boy that the police are hunting for — is he a friend of yours?"

"That's a good question," said Nick. "I think maybe he is."

After setting the table for his mom, Nick went to his bedroom, shut the door, and called Libby Marshall on her cell. She was out walking her dog, Sam.

"No, they didn't catch him yet," she said, anticipating Nick's question. "But they will. And my dad is *so* not amused — he pulled a hamstring while he was chasing him!"

Nick had to be careful what he said to Libby. It was natural for her to believe that Smoke was guilty, because that's what her father surely told her.

Libby said, "He's still on probation for torching that billboard on the interstate, so they can lock him up until his next trial, my dad says. Six months, maybe longer."

No wonder he ran away, Nick thought. "Are they still out there looking for him?"

"Nah. He's not, like, a serial killer or something," Libby said. "They'll bust him as soon as he goes home. Dad says that's where they usually find juvenile fugitives."

"But what if he doesn't show up?"

"Right, Nick. Where else is he gonna go?"

Nick thought: *I wish I knew.*

"Why are they so sure he did it?" Nick was hoping that Libby's father had mentioned something about the mysterious new evidence.

And luckily, he had.

"Somebody found Smoke's book bag near the place where the fire was started," Libby said. "Guess what was in it — a portable torch, just like the arsonist used! He's toast, Nick. Case closed."

"His book bag from school? The camo one?"

"Hang on a second," Libby said. "Sam, no! Bad dog! BAD DOG!"

While she hollered at her pet, Nick held the phone away from his ear. It didn't make sense that Smoke's backpack had suddenly turned up at the Black Vine Swamp.

When Libby came back on the line, she was out of breath. "Sorry, Nick, I gotta go. Sam's cornered a humongous ol' tomcat and it's about to scratch his nose off. . . . No! Bad boy! I said NO!!!"

Nick hung up and immediately called Marta.

"What are you doing first thing tomorrow?" he asked.

"Sleeping," she replied. "It's Saturday, remember?"

"We're going on a bike ride."

"I don't think so, Nick."

"Be ready at eight."

"Get serious," said Marta. "I plan to be snoring like a polar bear at eight o'clock in the morning."

"No, this is important. I'll explain everything when I see you."

275

"Don't you dare take me back to Mrs. Starch's house! I don't want to end up with glass eyeballs and a tag around my neck, like all those other dead animals."

Nick said, "Don't worry. That's not where we're going."

The next morning, as Duane Scrod Sr. crept into the kitchen to get some sunflower seeds for Nadine, he heard a knock at the front door and then a voice calling, "Duane? Are you there?"

It sounded too young to be an FBI man, but Duane Scrod Sr. wasn't taking any chances. He scrambled back to the music room and barricaded himself inside. His macaw, who was famished, peevishly latched on to one of his earlobes, yet Duane Scrod Sr. gritted his teeth and remained silent in spite of the pain.

He didn't want to go back to jail, although he realized that the odds were stacked against him. Attacking that tax man wasn't the brightest move he'd ever made, and he figured it was only a matter of time before his house was surrounded by heavily armed agents of the U.S. government.

Earlier in the day, Duane Scrod Sr. had hidden from another stranger, a man who had knocked repeatedly and identified himself as a sheriff's deputy searching for Junior. Duane Sr. had snatched Nadine from her cage and run to cower under a quilt in the music room.

"Duane, open up! It's me — Nick Waters," the new visitor shouted.

Then a girl's voice said, "I told you so. He's not even here."

It occurred to Duane Scrod Sr. that the persons on the porch might actually be looking for his son, but he quickly dismissed the idea. Except for one or two Miccosukee Indians, Junior didn't have any friends his own age.

No, thought Duane Scrod Sr., this must be a trap. The FBI could be extremely sneaky.

As soon as the voices outside stopped, Nadine let go of Duane Scrod Sr.'s ear. After a few minutes he cautiously approached the small spinet piano that was blocking the music room door and prepared to push it aside.

"Ich habe Hunger!" Nadine complained. *"J'ai faim!"*

"Hush up, bird," Duane Scrod Sr. whispered, "or I'll sell you to Colonel Sanders."

A female voice from behind piped, "Don't do that."

Duane Scrod Sr. wheeled around and

cowered beside the piano. Framed in the open window were two faces — a boy and a girl, watching him.

"What do you want?" he demanded. "Did the guv'ment send you, too?"

The boy said, "We go to school with Duane. We need to find him."

"Yeah, well, get in line."

"He's in our biology class," the girl added.

Nadine screeched and flapped around the room two or three times before alighting on a dusty chandelier.

"Go away!" Duane Scrod Sr. barked at the kids. He still wasn't convinced that they weren't FBI agents in disguise.

The boy said, "Duane's running from the police. They're going to arrest him for arson, but we don't think he did it."

"No, Nick," the girl interrupted, "*you* don't think he did it."

"Whatever. We've got to talk to him."

Duane Scrod Sr. said, "Even if I knew where he was — which I don't — I wouldn't tell ya. So kindly take a hike. And I mean *now*."

But the two kids didn't move.

What's wrong with this world? thought Duane Scrod Sr. When did the grown-ups stop being in charge?

"That's a nice piano," the girl remarked.

"I've been taking lessons since I was four."

"How thrilling for you," Duane Scrod Sr. grumbled. "Now get lost."

He was astounded to see both kids calmly climb through his window to enter the room. The girl said, "You know what I played at our fall recital? Rachmaninoff's Prelude number 4 in D."

"You're kidding," Duane Scrod Sr. said. Rachmaninoff was one of his all-time favorites. He slid the spinet away from the door and the girl sat down on the piano bench and played the whole piece from memory.

"That's downright lovely," Duane Scrod Sr. admitted.

She said, "My name's Marta. And this is Nick."

"I'm Duane's dad. But I still can't tell ya where he's at, 'cause I don't have a clue. Besides, you might be undercover FBI."

The girl said, "That's the dumbest thing I ever heard. I didn't even make the J.V. cheerleader squad."

Duane Scrod Sr. reddened.

The boy named Nick said, "Didn't you hear what happened at school yesterday?"

"Nope. Junior never came home is all I know."

"That's because he's a fugitive from

justice," the girl named Marta said dramatically.

"Oh, that's great," Duane Scrod Sr. muttered.

The boy described what had occurred when the sheriff's detective went to the Truman School to arrest Duane Scrod Jr. for the arson at the Black Vine Swamp.

"But D.J. said they didn't have any evidence!" his father objected. "He promised me!"

"They didn't have a thing until yesterday," said the boy named Nick. "Then they found his book bag at the scene of the fire."

Now Duane Scrod Sr. was really puzzled. "D.J. had a book bag?"

The girl sighed impatiently. "For school, Mr. Scrod."

"It was camo-colored," the kid named Nick went on, "like a hunter's backpack."

"Okay. Yeah." Now Duane Scrod Sr. remembered the bag.

"When's the last time you saw it?" the boy asked.

"Day before yesterday."

The two kids whispered to each other; then the girl turned to Duane Scrod Sr. and asked, "Are you a hundred percent sure?"

"You bet I am. It was when the guv'ment tax man was here, violatin' my personal privacy. He grabbed Junior's bag off the floor and tried to murder my dear sweet Nadine with it — ain't that right, darlin'?"

"Oui," replied the macaw, rocking the chandelier.

"So where's the backpack now?" the girl asked.

"Beats me. Maybe the tax guy ran off with it." Duane Scrod Sr. wondered how long he could put off calling Millicent Winship to tell her that her grandson was in trouble with the law again.

The boy named Nick said: "I don't think Duane is guilty."

Duane Scrod Sr. coughed. "I'd dearly like to believe that's true, but D.J.'s got what they call a 'history' with fires."

"Well, this time he didn't do it," declared the boy. "That's what he told me, and I believe him."

"And what do you 'spect *me* to do? Go march at the courthouse?" Duane Scrod Sr. shrugged. "Junior won't come out of the woods till he's good and ready, and they'll never find him out there. Not in a trillion years."

"When you hear from him —"

"Who says I will?"

"But if you do," the girl named Marta said, "tell him to quit running and turn

281

himself in. That's the only way he'll clear his name."

Duane Scrod Sr. cackled bitterly. "This ain't the movies, you know. Life doesn't shake down so simple."

The boy went out the window first. The girl followed, pausing briefly on the sill. She said, "That's a sweet little piano. Do you play?"

Smoke's father shook his head. "Not in years."

"Well, you should take it up again."

"Yeah? What for?"

"Because you'll feel better," the girl said, and dropped out of sight.

On the ride home, Nick was so agitated that he had trouble keeping his bike on the sidewalk.

"Don't you see? It's a total setup!" he exclaimed to Marta. "Smoke couldn't possibly have ditched his book bag in the swamp on the day of the fire, because his father saw the same bag in the house two days ago. You know what? *I* remember seeing it under Smoke's desk in biology class the first day Waxmo was there!"

Marta said, "Easy, dude. You're gonna hyperventilate."

"I'm serious: somebody stole his backpack, stashed a torch inside, and left it at the scene of the arson. Smoke's been framed!"

"But why? That's crazy."

Nick had to agree — some vital pieces of the puzzle were missing. Although Duane Scrod Jr. kept to himself at Truman, he didn't seem to have made any enemies. Nick couldn't think of a single person who'd want to see the kid wrongfully locked up in jail.

"Don't forget," Marta said, "the guy's dad is a major screwball, too. I mean, come on: Why would a tax collector steal a kid's book bag?"

"What if he wasn't really a tax collector?" Nick said. "What if he went to Smoke's house just to take something that he could plant at the Black Vine Swamp, something incriminating?"

Marta gave a skeptical grunt. "Now, don't get mad," she said, "but here's another what-if."

"Okay."

"What if Smoke had two book bags, Nick? One for his school stuff and one for his pyro gear."

Nick was growing frustrated with Marta — why couldn't she see what was happening? "But he came over Thursday night to

283

borrow my biology book, remember? He said he'd lost his backpack. I told you about it the next day."

"He also said he needed to study for a nonexistent exam," Marta pointed out. "The whole story was pretty sketchy. You said so yourself."

Nick braked his bike under the shade of a tree and tried to gather his thoughts. Nothing about the fire in the Black Vine Swamp made much sense, from the disappearance of Mrs. Starch to the appearance of Duane Scrod Jr.'s backpack.

Marta stopped her bicycle beside Nick's. "What if Smoke heard his book bag had been found where the fire was set, and what if he was trying to make an alibi for himself by coming over and telling you that he'd, quote, 'lost' it. Then he gets his dad to lie and say the bag was in the house two days ago but some stranger conveniently ripped it off."

Nick said, "I like my theory better."

"If he's not guilty, why did he run from Libby's dad?"

"Because he was scared of getting arrested. He freaked out, that's all."

Marta said, "Everybody says they're innocent, no matter what. Don't you watch Court TV?"

To himself Nick admitted that it was possible that she was right, and that Smoke was playing him for a sucker. But Nick's father always said to go with your gut, and Nick's gut said the kid was telling the truth.

"Marta, I still say he didn't do it."

"Fine. Then tell me one good reason why anyone in town would want to frame him. Name one person, okay? . . . Nick?"

He wasn't listening. He had gotten off his bicycle and started jogging across the street. "Come on," he called back to her.

"Are you cracking up, or what?" she shouted.

"Hurry!" Nick motioned excitedly toward a strip mall. Marta hastily locked both bikes to the tree and ran after him.

Mrs. Starch's Prius with the "Save the Manatee" license plate was parked outside a pizza joint called Little Napoli. The car was empty and unlocked.

Nick checked around to make sure nobody was watching. Then he dove into the backseat, leaving the door open for Marta.

"What exactly are you doing?" she demanded, anxiously looking over her shoulder.

"Waiting for that Twilly guy, or whoever's driving this thing. Get in."

"But he said he never wanted to lay eyes

285

on us again! Or did you forget?"

Nick hadn't forgotten. He said, "This is the only way we'll get some answers. I don't know about you, but I'm tired of being confused."

Marta grimaced and clutched the sides of her head. "Are you completely, totally, hopelessly nuts? I'd rather be confused than, like, dead. The dude had *bullets* in his belt, Nick. Real live bullets, which means he probably has a real live gun to put 'em in."

"I'm not moving," Nick said flatly. "Either go on home or get in the car with me. But you'd better make up your mind fast, because here he comes."

Marta got in the car.

EIGHTEEN

The man named Twilly showed no reaction when he saw Nick and Marta in the backseat of the Prius. He sat down behind the wheel, placed two pizza boxes on the seat beside him, and started the car.

"Can you take us to Mrs. Starch?" Nick said.

Twilly didn't respond. In the rearview mirror they could see that he was counting to himself.

"What are you doing?" Marta asked him.

"You've got until the count of twenty to clear out of this car."

Nick said, "We're not moving till we get some answers."

"And if you try to throw us out," Marta added, "I'll scream until somebody calls the cops."

Twilly sighed and said, "Such drama." He turned in his seat and started backing the Prius out of the parking space.

Marta pointed at him. "What is *that?*"

"Vulture beaks. A friend gave them to me," Twilly said, "for good luck."

Sun-bleached and crusty, the two beaks were tied to a frayed leather lanyard that dangled against his bare chest. Marta made a face at Nick and mouthed the word "Yuk."

Twilly eased the car into traffic. Trying to mask his nervousness with conversation, Nick said, "I'm reading one of Edward Abbey's books. It's sick."

In the mirror Twilly eyed him. "I assume that means you like it."

"Yeah, he's funny. Was there a real Monkey Wrench Gang?"

"God, I wish." Twilly laughed to himself and pulled his ski cap down to his brow. "How about you?" he said to Marta. "What do you read?"

She said, "All the Harry Potters — three times. Seriously, did those gross things come from vultures?"

"Yep."

"So your friend —"

"No, he didn't shoot 'em," Twilly said. "They were roadkills."

Marta nodded, fascinated. "Aren't the beaks, like, magic or something?"

"That I wouldn't know."

As they passed the ramp to the interstate

highway, heading farther and farther away from town, Nick wondered if he'd made a big mistake. They knew practically nothing about this man; he could be driving to Belle Glade to dump them in Lake Okeechobee.

Nick said, "Mrs. Starch isn't really your aunt, is she?"

"Of course not," Twilly replied.

"So is she, like, your prisoner?" Marta asked bluntly. "We know you were out at the swamp during the school field trip because you're on a video that Nick took — wearing the same ammo belt that you've got on now. Are you the one who set the fire?"

Nick sunk down in his seat. Once Marta got comfortable, she was capable of saying anything. To Nick it seemed like a bad time to accuse Twilly of being a kidnapper and arsonist.

Yet he didn't get mad. "So many pesky little questions," he said with a note of amusement. "First of all, I'm not holding dear Aunt Bunny prisoner. Anybody who tried to do that would live to regret it, I'm sure. And you're right: I was in the Black Vine Swamp that day. But I didn't light that fire. Somebody else did."

"It wasn't Smoke, was it?" Nick heard himself say.

289

"Smoke?"

"His real name is Duane Scrod Jr.," Nick said. "Marta saw him riding in this car the other day — with you."

Twilly said, "I've been known to pick up hitchhikers."

Nick went on: "Duane's in Mrs. Starch's biology class with us. Yesterday a detective came to arrest him for the arson, but he got away."

Marta was impatient. "He told Nick he's innocent, but the fire department found his book bag at the scene."

In the mirror Twilly's expression had grown serious. "The fire department didn't find it. A civilian found it and called the arson squad."

"What's the difference?" Marta said.

"Huge difference, princess."

"How do you know all this?" Nick asked excitedly. "Have you seen Smoke?"

Twilly said, "That's enough chitchat." He handed one of the pizza boxes to Marta.

"One more question, please," Nick implored, "and then we'll shut up. Won't we, Marta?"

She gave Nick a sarcastically polite smile before attacking the pizza. Twilly drummed his hands on the steering wheel.

"Who really started that fire?" Nick asked.

"If I knew that, I'd . . ."

"You'd what?"

"Nothing," Twilly said, and turned up the radio very loud.

By the time Jimmy Lee Bayliss arrived at the emergency room, Drake McBride was no longer bellowing at the nurses. This was because they'd given him an injection of special medicine to make him settle down and behave. They told Jimmy Lee Bayliss that Drake McBride probably had a concussion from landing on his head, and possibly some broken ribs.

"King Thunderbolt threw me off," Drake McBride complained woozily. "Then he did a danged tap dance on my chest!"

Jimmy Lee Bayliss sat down and said, "You're gonna be fine."

"They won't even let me see a doctor!"

"You've gotta wait, same as everyone else."

"But why? I'm not *like* everyone else," Drake McBride whined. "I tried to give 'em some cash to let me go first, but they got all snotty and mad. . . ."

Jimmy Lee Bayliss was glad he'd missed that scene. "You can't bribe a nurse. Hospitals don't work that way."

"It wasn't a bribe. It was a tip." Drake McBride paused to vomit in a plastic bedpan. Looking up, he said, "Do me a favor, pardner. Go out to the barn and shoot that no-good nag for me, would you? Before he cripples somebody, namely yours truly."

"Yes, sir," said Jimmy Lee Bayliss, who had no intention of harming Drake Mc-Bride's horse.

As on most Saturdays, the hospital emergency room bustled. Among those in the waiting area with Drake McBride were a middle-aged woman who'd crashed her moped into a mailbox, an older gentleman who'd been beaned by his doubles partner during a tennis match, and a surly young burglar (handcuffed to his chair) who'd been bitten by a police dog in a very sensitive area of his body.

"That shot made me dizzy," said Drake McBride. "And my head's still killin' me."

Even though his boss was groggy and in pain, Jimmy Lee Bayliss decided to go ahead and tell him. "Sir, I've got good news and bad news," he said.

Drake McBride groaned. "Lemme explain somethin': If you've got bad news, then there ain't no possible good news. The bad always cancels out the good."

Jimmy Lee Bayliss lowered his voice. "They're gonna charge that pyro kid with doing the fire in Section 22," he said to

292

Drake McBride. "That means we're in the clear."

"Okay, what else? Don't hold back just 'cause I'm sittin' here with, like, nine fractured ribs and a major brain injury."

Jimmy Lee Bayliss told him first about Melton. "That bozo got ambushed again. This time they spray-painted him blaze orange from head to toe and tied him to the hood of his truck."

"Buck nekked, same as before?" Drake McBride asked weakly.

"Yes, sir."

"Was it a Red Diamond company truck?"

"Lucky it was me who found him and not some outsider," Jimmy Lee Bayliss said. "Otherwise it could've made the newspapers or even Fox TV — a naked orange guy in the middle of a swamp."

Drake McBride nodded somberly. "Yeah, that's a winner. Thanks for ruinin' my day, which was already ruined pretty bad by that stupid horse."

Jimmy Lee Bayliss wasn't finished. "Whoever did it, they took the front axle off the pickup."

"The company pickup."

"Yes, sir."

"I need to lie down." Drake McBride slid off the chair and sprawled on the floor. The other patients, sitting with their relatives, ignored him.

"There's more," Jimmy Lee Bayliss said. "A game warden called me this morning at the car wash. That's where I took Melton to scrub off his paint job."

Drake McBride groaned. "State or federal game warden?"

"The feds. A wildlife agent, he called himself."

"Oh, don't tell me."

"Yeah, he got a report of a wild panther near our lease. He wants to come out and check around as soon as possible."

Drake McBride raised up. "So what's the problem? You told me the cat was gone. You said the gunshots did the trick."

Jimmy Lee Bayliss knew that his boss didn't have the quickest mind, but being dumped on his head had made Drake McBride unusually slow.

The wildlife officer wouldn't need to find a live panther on the property in order to cause major problems for Red Diamond Energy. If he saw even a partial paw print or the tiniest, moldiest lump of scat, the government might step in to supervise the oil-drilling operation, perhaps even halt it.

"The Endangered Species Act is a tough one," Jimmy Lee Bayliss reminded Drake

McBride, who cursed under his breath and collapsed once more on the dingy floor.

"And what if Officer Game Warden goes wanderin' off into Section 22," said Drake McBride, "and discovers our little private project there? I imagine we'd have some ex-plainin' to do, since that land belongs to the great state of Florida and not us."

"I'll think of something," Jimmy Lee Bayliss said. "It'll be at least ten days before we can sink the transfer pipe, so we'll be okay as long as we keep the guy focused on Section 21."

"And in the meantime, tell me your secret plan for cleanin' up any old doo-doo that rotten cat left behind."

Jimmy Lee Bayliss had no strategy for locating and removing panther poop. He said, "There's six hundred and forty acres. About all we can do is pray for a good hard rain."

"During a drought? That's very funny." Drake McBride covered his face with his hands and rocked sideways on the floor. "I might just die here," he said miserably.

Jimmy Lee Bayliss wasn't feeling especially happy and carefree himself. Only two weeks earlier he'd been looking at real estate brochures from Costa Rica, daydreaming about how he'd spend the millions of dollars he was going to make from the Red Diamond oil scam. Now he was worrying about staying out of prison.

"We should give Melton a nice raise," he suggested. "He's really ticked off about what happened, and we sure don't want him blabbing all over town."

"The orange paint come off?" Drake McBride asked.

"Most of it. Certain places were hard to get to."

"You gotta find out who keeps doin' this stuff and put a stop to it. Whatever's necessary."

Jimmy Lee Bayliss said, "I aim to, don't worry."

A stern, broad-shouldered nurse walked up and told Jimmy Lee Bayliss to move his boss back onto the chair. "He's next up to see the doctor," she said, "after the lady with the wasp sting and the man with the barbecue burn."

"Glory be," murmured Drake McBride, and struggled to his knees.

Twilly Spree wasn't an outgoing person, and while he generally preferred the company of animals to that of human beings, he tried to be cautious in all relationships. Once he had become too fond of a dopey dog that he'd kidnapped from a knuckle-head who had needed to be taught a hard lesson — several lessons, in fact. When the time came to say goodbye to the dog, Twilly had found himself so sad and empty that it was alarming. Such sentimental feelings, he believed, could only distract him from his missions.

The two kids in the backseat of the car weren't too obnoxious and probably meant well, yet Twilly remained guardedly quiet during the drive to the Black Vine Swamp. His thoughts were on the boy who called himself Smoke, now a fugitive and in need of help.

It was disturbing that Duane Scrod Jr. was being framed, and Twilly suspected that the Red Diamond Energy Corporation was behind the plot. Someone working at the company's drilling site had summoned the arson investigator, a brief meeting that Twilly had observed the previous day from his distant roost in a cypress tree. At the time, he hadn't known about the stolen book bag, but he put the whole story to-gether after speaking with young Duane on the run, and later with a talkative secretary at the sheriff's office.

Twilly reasoned that Red Diamond's only motive for pinning a bogus felony rap on an innocent kid was to hide its own involvement in the arson. Twilly didn't know why Red Diamond would ignite a brush fire to scare away school kids on a field trip, but he was working on theories.

Because it was a new company, little information about Red Diamond was available on the Internet. However, private investigators hired by Twilly had dug up the name of the president and chief operating officer — Drake W. McBride — which was a beginning.

Meanwhile, Twilly continued his sneak forays to the Section 21 lease, where the same poor dunce had twice confronted him, and both times had been dealt with somewhat firmly.

Twilly Spree felt a tap on his shoulder. From the backseat, the boy named Nick Waters asked, "Could you please turn down the radio?"

"Nope," said Twilly.

"Then at least change the station," said the girl named Marta.

"Negative." Twilly's driving music was classic rock, nothing else.

Nick, hovering at his shoulder, asked: "Do you work for Mrs. Starch?"

"I told you, no more questions. Eat some pizza."

Marta said, "He doesn't like mushrooms or olives."

"Too bad." Twilly opened the windows to blow out the cheesy pizza smell. "For your information, I don't work for anybody," he said. "I'm what's known as 'unemployable.' "

"Are you, like, homeless?" asked Marta.

"Just the opposite. I can live anywhere." Twilly was half tempted to pull over on a remote stretch of road and abandon the two kids, but he thought they might be helpful later. At the very least, it would be good for Duane Jr. to know that somebody else cared about him.

Twilly turned off Route 29 onto a dusty farm road. A few minutes later, the Prius was inching down a bumpy, overgrown passage that had once been a railroad spur for a logging operation. The path ended at a broken gate that bore a rusty "No Trespassing" sign. Twilly parked beneath a giant strangler fig, shut off the radio, and instructed his passengers to be still. He listened for the high-pitched whine of the oil company's helicopter, but the sky was quiet.

Quickly he got out and began concealing the car with tree branches and palm fronds that he'd cut and stacked for that purpose.

One-armed Nick Waters pitched in to help, but the girl named Marta apprehensively stood apart, brandishing her cell phone for Twilly to see.

"Libby Marshall is number two on my speed dial and her dad's a sheriff's detective, so don't get any crazy ideas," she warned.

Twilly smiled. "I'll try to control myself. You ready to hike?"

"Definitely," the boy said.

"How far?" asked the girl.

Twenty minutes later, knee-deep in swamp water, she asked again in a much louder voice.

Twilly raised a finger to his lips and continued wading. He led them along a boggy trail through a treeless marsh until they entered dry pine flatlands. There he saw recent signs of white-tailed deer, bobcats, and raccoons, although he didn't stop to point out the various tracks and scat. Twilly had no time to play nature guide; he was in a hurry.

Balancing the pizza boxes on his free hand, the boy named Nick came up beside Twilly. In a hushed voice he said, "Are there panthers out here?"

"Didn't you hear one scream while you were on the field trip?"

"No, that was you," Nick said. "Wasn't it?"

Twilly winked and shook his head.

"No way!" The boy looked thrilled.

A few paces behind, the girl named Marta was griping. "Why can't we use the boardwalk like normal people? My brand-new Converses are totally trashed!"

A red-shouldered hawk clutching a mouse in its talons passed overhead. Once more Twilly paused to listen — the only sound from above was a woodpecker making holes in a dead tree.

When Marta caught up, she said, "This is ridiculous. Where's Mrs. Starch?"

Twilly inserted two fingers in his mouth and whistled. There was no response, which was the agreed-upon signal for him to proceed.

Suddenly Marta blurted, "Nick, what if he's not really taking us to Mrs. Starch? What if he's gonna chop us to pieces and feed us to the alligators?"

"Human flesh is tough. Gators prefer fish," Twilly noted, and resumed walking.

Nick remained at his side. "She's just scared is all," he whispered.

Twilly understood. He was the first to admit that he wasn't a reliable-looking person.

"Soon everything will become clear," he said. "More or less."

"I trust you."

"Well, Nick Waters, I wouldn't go *that* far."

"My father always says to stick with my gut instincts."

"He got hurt pretty bad in Iraq, right?"

Nick looked taken aback. "How'd you know that?"

"Duane mentioned it," Twilly said. "You didn't mess up your arm playing lacrosse, like you told me, did you?"

"No, that was a lie."

"I figured. I never saw a back-assward sling like this before." Twilly flicked the odd hump in the boy's shirt behind his right shoulder.

He said, "There's nothing wrong with my arm. I'm teaching myself to be a lefty."

"Like your old man's gotta do."

Nick nodded and grew quiet.

"Good for you," Twilly said.

He tried to recall if he'd ever cared about his own father as deeply as Nick Waters cared about his. The emotions were complicated, as were his childhood memories.

From behind them, the girl called out, "I hope you're both happy. I got blisters on my blisters!"

They were now close enough that Twilly

Spree could smell the woody haze from last night's campfire.

"When's the last time you saw a wild panther?" he asked Nick.

"Never."

"Then this is your lucky day."

NINETEEN

The secret camp was in shadows, beneath a tangled canopy of trees. There were two pup tents and a fire pit. Pegged to the ground was a faded green tarp, covering a chest-high stack of supplies.

A flap opened on one of the tents, and a gangly figure crawled out. It was Mrs. Starch. She rose slowly, brushing herself off, her eyes blazing at the sight of Nick and Marta.

"What's the meaning of this?" she demanded.

"They carjacked me," Twilly said. "Sort of."

Mrs. Starch scowled. "Oh, please."

Despite the chilly reception, Nick was relieved to see his biology teacher unharmed and still as ornery as ever. Except for the straw hat, she had on the same clothes from the field trip: baggy long-sleeved shirt, canvas pants, and wading boots. Still, Mrs.

Starch looked different — older, and more tired. Her heavy makeup had worn off, and a stripe of coffee-brown roots bisected her mass of tinted blond hair, which was tied in a ragged ponytail. There was no sign of her huge dragonfly sunglasses.

"It's your turn to entertain them. I'm heading out on poop patrol," Twilly told her, and sauntered back into the woods. Nick assumed he was taking a bathroom break.

Mrs. Starch began pacing, as she did in class. It had the same nerve-wracking effect on Marta as always; she turned greenish and queasy. Nick set the pizza boxes on a tree stump.

"What do you have to say for yourselves?" Mrs. Starch said.

Marta was in no condition to speak, and Nick had not yet composed a presentation. The best he could muster was: "We were worried."

"Worried, or just plain nosy?" Mrs. Starch shot back. "It's rude enough that you broke into my home. Now this?"

Nick thought he heard a faint, muffled cry, but he couldn't tell where it came from. Still clutching her phone, Marta sat down on a log near the fire pit and took deep breaths to ward off the nausea.

The wind picked up from the north, putting a cool bite in the air. Mrs. Starch's footsteps crunched on crisp twigs and leaves as she stalked back and forth in front of them. She seemed not quite as tall as Nick remembered.

"You have no right to be here. No right," she said.

Marta raised a limp hand. "It was all Nick's idea."

"Undoubtedly," said Mrs. Starch.

"We just want to know what's going on," Nick heard himself say.

"Get more specific."

"Okay, the fire. Tell us about the fire."

"Ah," said Mrs. Starch.

"And Smoke — I mean Duane Jr."

The teacher stopped pacing and planted her knuckles on her hips. "Anything else?"

"Yes," Nick said. He had so many questions.

Marta peeped: "Your house — all those stuffed animals . . ."

Mrs. Starch wagged a bony forefinger in protest. "Now, that's personal. Way too personal."

Again Nick heard an odd cry — like a bird trapped in a pillowcase. "What *is* that?" he asked Mrs. Starch.

She glanced worriedly behind her. In the

dappled shade, the anvil-shaped scar on her chin was so dark that it looked almost purple.

"I didn't hear anything," Marta said.

Mrs. Starch bent down until she was nose to nose with Nick, and up close her nose wasn't especially attractive. It was smudged with mud and freckled with what appeared to be tiny insect bites.

"I'm going to show you something extraordinary," she said, "but if either of you tells a living soul, if you blab a single word about this, then I swear I'll . . . I'll . . ."

"Flunk us?" said Nick.

"Kill us?" asked Marta.

"Worse!" exclaimed Mrs. Starch. "I'll lose all respect for you. All respect."

Nick blinked. It was news to him that Mrs. Starch had *any* respect whatsoever for them, and judging by Marta's baffled reaction, it was news to her as well.

"Nobody else besides you two must know," the teacher said forcefully. "Not your mummy or daddy, not your gabby little pals on Facebook, not your third cousin in Goose Falls, Arkansas, *nobody.* Is that clear?"

"As a bell," Marta murmured.

Mrs. Starch grabbed Nick's left shoulder. "This is life-or-death," she whispered. "Can

307

you understand that?"

"We won't tell anyone," said Nick.

"Life-or-death," Mrs. Starch repeated. Then she dropped to all fours and scurried into her tent.

As expected, the local newspapers and TV stations identified Duane Scrod Jr. as "an unnamed juvenile" with previous arrests for arson. But even if the authorities had released the boy's full name, the impact on Dr. Dressler's steady, well-organized existence would have been no more shattering.

TRUMAN STUDENT, SOUGHT FOR ARSON, FLEES COPS

That was just one of the unpleasant headlines that prompted the school's board of trustees to call an emergency meeting on a Saturday. The board members were highly distressed and asked many tough questions of Dr. Dressler, who answered as best he could.

Some of the remarks were quite unfair, in the headmaster's opinion, yet he didn't waste energy trying to defend himself. The mood in the room was too tense, which he could understand. It was disgraceful enough that a Truman student had been charged with a serious crime, but the sensational media accounts of Duane Scrod Jr.'s escape and mad dash across campus — leaving the sheriff's detective panting in defeat — had pitched the board of trustees into a fever.

Although technically it wasn't his job to arrest and handcuff arsonists, Dr. Dressler expected to be punished, possibly even fired, for allowing the detective to confront the boy while classes were in session.

In the end, the board voted to reprimand the headmaster and ordered him to expel Duane Scrod Jr. from school, effective immediately. When Dr. Dressler pointed out that Duane Jr.'s grandmother donated large sums of money to Truman every year, the board members quickly huddled for another vote. This time they decided that the boy should be "suspended temporarily" until his criminal case went to court, at which point his status at the Truman School would be reviewed.

Dr. Dressler faced two undesirable chores. One was to notify Millicent Winship, Duane Jr.'s wealthy grandmother, and the other was to notify Duane Scrod Sr., his kooky father. The headmaster had flipped a coin, and now he was driving to the Scrod residence.

Turning down the road, he noticed a sheriff's deputy sitting in a squad car parked on one corner. At the other end he could see a black sedan with tinted windows — probably another officer in an unmarked car. They were waiting to grab Duane Scrod Jr. if he tried to sneak home, although Dr. Dressler thought they'd have a better chance if they concealed themselves.

The headmaster pulled in next to the graffiti-sprayed Tahoe belonging to Duane's father. As before, concert music was coming from the windows: Beethoven, this time, not Bach. Reluctantly, Dr. Dressler got out of the car and trudged up the steps and rapped on the screen door.

The stereo cut off and a raspy voice yelled, "Come in! Make it quick!"

"Mr. Scrod?"

Cautiously the headmaster stepped inside. Duane Scrod Sr. was reclining in a Naugahyde lounger in front of the TV set. The picture was on, but the volume was turned down. Duane Sr.'s cap was propped crookedly on his head, and his faded shirt was unbuttoned to the waist. Perched on the threadbare arm of his chair was the enormous blue-and-gold macaw.

"I 'member you," Duane Scrod Sr. said groggily to Dr. Dressler. "So does Nadine."

"May I sit down?"

"Nope. State your business and be on your way. I already had too many visitors today." Duane Sr. didn't take his eyes off the television screen. The bird, too, seemed entranced.

"What are you watching?" Dr. Dressler asked.

"A cookin' show. From France."

That wouldn't have been the headmaster's first guess. Based on Duane Sr.'s rough appearance, Dr. Dressler would have expected to find him tuned to pro wrestling or maybe a demolition derby on a Saturday morning. But you can't judge a book by its cover, Dr. Dressler reminded himself. After all, the man was into classical music.

Duane Sr. took a slug of Mountain Dew and said, "Junior's mom lives in Paris. We were thinkin' she might turn up on this TV show, when they get to the part of the recipe where they put in the cheese. She has a shop, that's all she sells — fancy cheese! You imagine?"

Dr. Dressler didn't know what to say. He reached in his coat and took out two packets of onion crackers from the school cafeteria. "I brought these for Nadine."

In a flash the bird swooped across the room and snatched the treat from his hand, then flew back to the chair.

Duane Scrod Sr. scolded the macaw for bad manners. "What do you say to the man,

311

Nadine?"

"Thanks a million!" the bird screaked. *"Danke schön! Merci beaucoup!"*

Dr. Dressler pressed onward. "I came to talk to you about Duane Jr.," he said. "After everything that's happened, I'm afraid we have to suspend him from school."

Duane Scrod Sr. finally turned and stared directly at the headmaster. "I sure don't wanna be the one to tell his granny."

"No, sir, that's my job. Did you see the news?"

"Yeah. Least they left his name out of it."

"The situation is very serious," Dr. Dressler said.

Duane Sr. agreed. "It's a shame, too. Past few days, D.J.'s been hittin' the books pretty hard. Then all this nonsense had to break loose." He brushed a piece of cracker off his sleeve and said, "Nadine, you eat like a pig."

He and the bird returned their attention to the French cooking program. Dr. Dressler stood there, feeling out of place and unsure what to do next. As headmaster of the Truman School, he had a duty in such troubled moments to say something wise and helpful to parents, but never before had he dealt with a character like Duane Scrod Sr.

"Can I say one more thing?" Dr. Dressler asked.

"All right, but only 'cause you brought crackers."

"The best thing your son can do is turn himself in to the police, as soon as possible."

Duane Sr. scratched his cap. "You might be right, but what if you're not? What happens to Junior then?"

"Mr. Scrod, they'll catch up with him eventually," Dr. Dressler said, "and when they do, they'll come down twice as hard. If you see Duane, please tell him."

"Heck, tell him yourself. Hey, Junior?" Duane Scrod Sr. sat forward and raised his voice. "D.J., come on out here!"

Dr. Dressler heard a door creak, followed by footsteps in the hallway. Duane Scrod Jr. appeared, looking calm but serious. He wore camouflage hunting-style clothes and carried his motorcycle helmet under one arm.

The headmaster, who'd never been in the presence of a fugitive, was more nervous than Duane Jr. "What are you doing here?" he asked the boy.

"My laundry," Duane Jr. replied matter-of-factly.

"But the police are staked out at both ends of the street!"

"I came in the back way," the boy explained, "through the neighbors' yard. They're at the rodeo in Zolfo Springs."

Duane Sr. spoke up: "Junior, the man says you're suspended from school."

"Duh."

"He also says you should give yourself up."

"Yeah, right," said Duane Jr.

The bird screaked, rose from the chair, and buzzed Dr. Dressler in search of more crackers. The headmaster ducked, to no avail. The macaw landed squarely on his neck and began poking its gnarly beak through his hair.

"Nadine!" barked Duane Scrod Sr.

"Help me," Dr. Dressler whimpered.

Duane Jr. grabbed the bird and launched it out the front door. His father sighed and sat back to watch the cooking program. Dr. Dressler gingerly probed the collar of his shirt to make sure that Nadine hadn't left him a nasty little present.

"That bird's a royal pain," Duane Jr. muttered, wiping his hands on his trousers.

"Am I bleeding?" Dr. Dressler asked.

"Just a scratch. Wash it out real good when you get home."

The headmaster weighed his next words carefully. "Duane, you can't keep running forever."

"I don't plan to."

"If you had a lawyer, he'd advise you to surrender to the police immediately."

"And I'd tell him the same thing I'm tellin' you," Duane Jr. said. "I can't prove I'm innocent if I'm locked up in jail."

"Duane, just listen —"

"No, you listen. I didn't set that fire, and I'm not takin' the fall."

Duane Jr. looked angry, and it didn't seem like an act. Over the years, the headmaster had heard many lame lies and invented stories from students who'd gotten into trouble, and he regarded himself as a hard man to fool. Now, as he looked into Duane Scrod Jr.'s eyes, it occurred to Dr. Dressler that the boy might be telling the truth.

"If you aren't the arsonist, who is?"

"No idea," Duane Jr. said.

"How'd your book bag end up in the swamp?"

Duane Jr. glanced over at his father and lowered his voice. "Pop says a tax man came here and stole it, but who knows. Some days, he's all over the map."

They heard a loud *thwap* and turned to see Nadine hanging like a giant moth on the screen door. Duane Sr. looked up from the TV and shook a fist. "Don't you dare let her back in till she says she's sorry! In all three languages, too!"

Duane Jr. paid no attention. To Dr. Dressler he said: "Now I got a question for you."

"Certainly." The headmaster was eager to offer some sensible guidance, but that was not what the young man wanted.

"Be straight up with me," he said. "After you leave this house, are you gonna run and tell those cops I'm here?"

Dr. Dressler hesitated, yet only for a moment. He was startled to hear himself say, "No, Duane, I won't breathe a word. That's a promise."

"Thanks, dude," said the boy called Smoke, and disappeared down the hall.

Mrs. Starch came out of the tent cradling her straw hat, with the crown facedown. The hat seemed to be crying.

"Hush now," said Mrs. Starch. Then, very quietly, to Marta: "There's a cooler full of milk bottles under the tarp. Would you please get me one?"

Mrs. Starch sat cross-legged at the base of a cypress tree with the hat in her lap. She warmed the bottle in her hands, uncapped it, and attached a rubber nipple. Nick and Marta knelt in front of her. Peeking inside the hat, they saw a squirming ball of honey-colored fur.

It was a kitten unlike any they'd ever seen.

"We call him Squirt," Mrs. Starch said, "because he pees all day long."

The little cat lunged for the bottle and began to suck noisily. When Marta reached to pet it, Mrs. Starch stopped her. "Rule number one: No cuddling," she said.

"He's so awesome," Marta whispered, edging as close as Mrs. Starch would allow. "What is it?"

"I bet Nick knows."

He said, "It's a baby panther."

A smaller, living-and-breathing version of the stuffed one that he'd seen in Mrs. Starch's house.

The teacher smiled. "That's correct. A Florida panther. Scientific name?"

"Puma concolor coryi."

"Correct again. Somebody's actually read the class syllabus!" Mrs. Starch said. "The other acceptable answer would be *Felis concolor coryi,* although *Puma* is more poetic. In parts of South America, the word means 'mighty magic animal.' "

To Nick, the kitten was a thing of unreal beauty, exotic yet delicate. Its pelt was dappled with spots that would fade over time, and its long tawny tail bent upward at the end but was ringed, almost like a leopard's. Oversized and pointy, the ears were woolly and as white as cotton on the inside.

The panther's muzzle was framed by bands of coal-black fur, now dribbled with milk, that gave the appearance of an outlaw-style mustache. Its eyes, barely open, were a creamy shade of blue. Soon they would turn brown and eventually pale gold, Nick remembered from his reading. The front paws, already larger than a tomcat's, were clasped around the rim of the nursing bottle.

And what a powerful motor for such a pint-sized critter — more rumble than purr.

"Where's the momma?" Marta wanted to know.

"Not so loud, dear," Mrs. Starch said.

"Is the mother cat dead?" Nick asked, fearing the worst. There were so few panthers left in the wild that hardly anybody ever laid eyes on one.

"No, the mother's alive," Mrs. Starch said. "At least that's what Mr. Spree believes, and he fancies himself the expert."

The kitten abruptly spit out the nipple and emitted a lion-sized burp. Mrs. Starch laughed, an uncommon sight.

To Nick and Marta she said: "You two have lots of questions, and I'll get to all of them in due time. But right now, little Sir

Squirt needs to finish his lunch — don't you, baby?"

As if on cue, the cat mewed for more formula.

Mrs. Starch gently lifted the bottle to the kitten's mouth and began humming a lullaby. The tune was surprisingly soothing and pretty. Marta and Nick were stunned; this was a side of their teacher that they'd never observed, or had even imagined to be part of her buzz-saw personality.

So, for a while, they sat peacefully in the swamp, listening to Mrs. Starch hum while the little panther slurped happily and the emerald leaves overhead shimmied and shook in the sunlight.

The cool breeze felt good. Nick reached for Marta's hand.

Twenty

On his search for the missing panther, Twilly Spree had crisscrossed hundreds of acres in the Black Vine Swamp. The quest was slow and often tedious, and on this day it led him toward an impressive cypress stand that he'd not yet explored.

Neck bent, eyes bolted to the ground, he moved ahead with measured, deliberate steps. In thick cover, panther poop wasn't always easy to see.

A flash of pink caught his attention, and at first it looked like the petal of a morning glory. Yet when Twilly picked it up, he found himself holding a small flag attached to a wire stem. Then he spotted another flag, and then another and still more, planted in a perfectly straight line.

Twilly's stride quickened. He followed the markers to the edge of the cypress, where he came upon a mucky area that appeared to have been flattened by all-terrain vehicles turning around, backing up, braking, spinning their fat wheels. . . .

He moved along, uprooting each plastic flag he saw. The trail took him under the lush canopy and into a wide clearing so sheltered by trees that it was virtually capped off from the sun and the sky.

The centerpiece was a man-made rectangular pit. Nearby loomed a stack of black iron pipes twice as tall as Twilly Spree and of the same eight-inch diameter as those he'd confiscated on the oil company's property and donated to Haiti. There were also four pallets of two-by-fours, a circular water tank (empty), and a fuel tank (full). On the opposite side of the clearing sat several crates bearing shipping labels from equipment companies in Texas and Oklahoma. The labels were all addressed to "J. L. Bayliss d/b/a Red Diamond." Twilly pried the lid off one bulky container, revealing a new diesel engine that he assumed would be used to power the drill.

He walked to the rim of the mud pit, which had partially filled with groundwater. To clear and dig out such a site in secrecy would have required careful timing and a small work crew. The project was ambitious, expensive — and highly illegal. From the research gathered by his private investigators, Twilly knew that Red Diamond didn't own or lease this particular section of land; it was part of a wildlife preserve that belonged to the state of Florida.

In the cool dome of shade, Twilly Spree sat down on a crate to ponder what he should do next. He stroked the brittle old buzzard beaks that dangled from his neck in case they might hold a trace of native magic.

Or any magic at all.

As soon as the cat-in-the-hat fell asleep, Mrs. Starch took it back to the tent. When she emerged, she said, "Now, where's that delicious cold pizza?"

Nick brought her the boxes. Mrs. Starch wolfed down four slices without pausing.

Marta said, "How old is the kitten?"

"Only a few weeks, according to Mr. Spree. Pardon my manners — we're short of napkins." Mrs. Starch wiped her sleeve across her lips. "Squirt needs momma's milk. For now, we're feeding him a special formula prepared by a friend of Mr. Spree who works at the Metrozoo. The bottles are delivered every Tuesday and Friday by private helicopter, which gives you an idea of Mr. Spree's resources."

"You mean he's, like, rich?" Marta said.

"He so doesn't look it."

Mrs. Starch said, "The cub is too young. Without his mother, he's not going to make it. Even if I spend the next year of my life out here in the boonies taking care of him, I can't teach him how to hunt."

"What about giving him to the zoo?" Marta asked.

"Mr. Spree says no. He says the subject is closed."

Nick asked Mrs. Starch to start at the beginning. "On the field trip," he said, "when the fire broke out."

"Yes indeed."

"And you went back into the woods for Libby's medicine."

Marta said, "Yeah, that was very . . . uh . . ."

Mrs. Starch arched an eyebrow. "Very what?"

"Brave." Marta flinched with guilt.

Nick knew she felt bad because of all the mean things she'd said about Mrs. Starch.

The teacher said, "Sorry to disappoint you, but I'm *not* a witch."

Marta's face reddened. "How did you know I called you that?"

"I wear a hearing aid in class. I don't really need one, but I do enjoy eavesdropping when you kids start to whisper." Mrs. Starch smiled slyly. "It's no bigger than a button. You probably never noticed."

Marta looked mortified.

"Oh, you aren't the first student to call me a witch," Mrs. Starch said, "or to use a cruder word that rhymes."

All Marta could say was, "I didn't mean it."

"Yes, you did. But that's all right." Mrs. Starch didn't sound angry or resentful. "Look, my job is to fill young minds with knowledge, and certain fields of knowledge can be boring at times. *Really* boring. Which means I have to be tough in order to keep my students focused. I don't expect to win any popularity contests, but at least you'll be able to write five hundred intelligent words about the Calvin cycle when you finish my course."

She opened a different cooler and took out three bottles of cold water, keeping one for herself and handing the others to Nick and Marta.

"Getting back to the fire," she said, "it took me a while to locate the spot where Libby dropped her asthma inhaler. The smoke was heavy and I started to cough. My lungs burned, my eyes stung, and before long I lost my way back to the boardwalk. Simply could not find it. In fact, I could hardly see the nose in front of my face — and it's not a nose that's easy to miss, as you've undoubtedly noticed."

"What did you do?" Nick asked.

"Freaked out, of course," Mrs. Starch said.

Marta stifled a giggle.

"I babbled, blubbered, yelled for help," the teacher went on. "I honestly thought I might burn to death in the middle of this swamp. Then, out of nowhere, somebody runs up from behind."

"Twilly?" Marta guessed.

"Correct. He grabs my hand and practically drags me all the way to this camp. Doesn't ask who I am, or even if I'm hurt. All he says is: 'I need your help.' "

Nick was trying to visualize the scene. Twilly could make a strong first impression. "Weren't you scared of him?"

"I was more scared of the fire," Mrs. Starch said. "Mr. Spree washed out my eyes with distilled water and gave me a warm beer to drink, which I declined. Then he showed me that exquisite, glorious little feline. . . ."

Her voice trailed off as she looked sadly toward the tent.

"Did you know what it was?" Marta asked.

"Of course. I know every endangered species in Florida — and you should, too."

"Right. I'm working on it," said Marta.

"Mr. Spree told me that the mother panther had been scared off by some jerk with a gun. He'd found the kitten crying in the woods — it was so tiny, its eyes weren't even open. Next thing I know, he places it in my arms and gives me a baby bottle and says, 'If you don't feed it, it's going to die. And it might die anyway, if we can't find its momma soon.' So here I am."

"A substitute," Nick said. This was the "family emergency" that was keeping Mrs. Starch out of school.

"Nursemaid. Surrogate. Cat-sitter. I had no choice but to step up," she said. "Mr. Spree couldn't take care of Squirt if he was gone all day trying to track down the mother. So I arranged to take my first and only leave of absence from the Truman School in eighteen years. My one regret is that you students were subjected to Dr. Waxmo, who, frankly, belongs in a different profession — the circus, perhaps."

Marta let out a groan. "That man's a total nightmare."

"Oh, I know," Mrs. Starch said ruefully. "Duane gave me a full report on Wendell. I sent Mr. Spree to chat with him, and he took ill shortly thereafter. Anyway, the new substitute, Mrs. Robertson, is a very able teacher —"

"Wait a minute. How does Duane fit into this whole picture?" Nick asked.

"I'm getting to that part. Be patient."

"The police are after him! They think he set the fire to get back at you for what happened in school, but he told me he didn't do it. Somebody stole his book bag and planted it out here to get him in trouble."

Mrs. Starch took a long, leisurely drink from the water bottle. She said, "According to the newspaper, a butane torch was also found. That looks mighty suspicious."

Nick heard his voice rise. "But I know Duane's telling the truth about his backpack getting ripped off because he came over to borrow my biology book —"

"Yeah, to study for an imaginary test," Marta cut in skeptically.

Mrs. Starch raised a hand. "It wasn't imaginary — I wrote up a test especially for Duane. I've been privately tutoring him in several subjects, academic and otherwise. You might have noticed a change in his punctuality and neatness at school. Even his acne has improved, thanks to good old-fashioned soap and water."

Nick thought: *That explains Smoke's mysterious transformation.* It was Mrs. Starch who created the new Duane Scrod Jr.

"And by the way," she added, "you're right: the young man *is* completely innocent of that arson. Now please don't interrupt me again."

Her tone was one that Nick and Marta remembered all too well from class. They fell silent and listened.

"It might seem strange that Duane and I are part of the same 'team,' " said Mrs. Starch, "but we've got more in common than you think."

Nick couldn't imagine what that could be.

"For one thing, we both love the wilderness," she went on. "Duane is happiest when he's out fishing or camping, or scouting for bears and deer. My own interest is endangered wildlife, as you surely figured out after sneaking into my house. Each of those mounted birds and reptiles and mammals that you saw was killed on the highway or in a storm, or shot."

"The young panther, too?" Nick asked.

"Sadly, yes. Struck by a car on the Tamiami Trail. I saw the body one afternoon while driving home from Miami, and I brought it to a taxidermist here in town, an old friend."

With her usual bluntness, Marta said, "There's more dead animals in your house than I ever saw before, except in a museum."

Mrs. Starch explained that she'd had the mounts made because she believed she would never get a glimpse of those species free in the wild: "Tragically, there are too few left." She went to check on the panther cub and returned with a bag of trail mix.

Nick and Marta weren't hungry; they were too caught up in her story.

Munching away, Mrs. Starch continued: "Here's something else that Duane and I share: we both know what it's like to be abandoned. 'Dumped,' in the current jargon. One day, Duane's mother just lit out for France without even telling him. My husband did the same thing — not to Paris, but to Plano, Texas, which is more his speed. I don't know why he walked out on me, but it hurt. Still does."

Marta squirmed, which meant she'd thought of something else to ask. Nick knew what was coming.

"There's a rumor that something bad happened to Mr. Starch," Marta said. "That he's, like, dead and stuffed like a moose."

"It would be better than he deserves," Mrs. Starch remarked dryly. "No, Stanley Starch is very much alive and kicking. Every April I get a birthday card telling me about his latest girlfriend. Is there any other ugly gossip I should know about?"

"Snakes — they say you keep poisonous snakes in your basement, rattlers and moccasins and copperheads." Marta was on a roll, and Nick couldn't do anything about it.

"Also untrue," Mrs. Starch said. "For a while I was lucky enough to have a pair of eastern indigo snakes, which were rescued from a construction site by one of my students. The indigo is absolutely gorgeous, totally harmless, and nearly extinct. I released mine far out in the Fakahatchee, where I hope they found true snake love and made lots of babies. Anything else?"

"No," said Nick quickly.

"Yes," said Marta. *"That."* She touched a finger to her chin.

"Ah. The scar." Far from annoyed, Mrs. Starch seemed amused by Marta's boldness.

Apologetically, Nick said, "It's none of our business."

"That's right, but I'll tell you anyway," Mrs. Starch said. "It happened when I was about your age. An osprey chick fell out of its nest, and being young and fearless, I decided to climb all the way up and put the little fella back with his brother and sister. The nest was high on a utility pole and the wind was howling, but somehow I made it to the top."

Marta asked, "So what happened — did the birds bite your face or something?"

"Heavens, no! They were timid as they could be. Halfway down the pole, one of my sandals slipped off the pegs and I dropped about twenty feet — I believe the term is 'face-plant' — onto a glass soda bottle that a litterbug had tossed by the side of the road." Mrs. Starch tapped her scar. "Some people say it's the shape of an anvil, some say an hourglass. But no, Marta, it's *not* the mark of the devil. It's the mark of the Pepsi-Cola company."

"How many stitches?"

"Foolishly, I refused to go to the hospital. Thus the unsightly result." Mrs. Starch stretched her arms. She said she was tired and needed a nap. "Wait here for Mr. Spree. He'll drive you back to town. And remember, you're both sworn to secrecy."

"You haven't gone home since the fire?" Nick asked.

"No, I've stayed right here, day and night. Mr. Spree has been good enough to run all my errands, beginning with the return of Libby's asthma medicine. He even got the tires rotated on my car."

Marta sat upright. "Listen!"

It was the faraway whine of a high-pitched engine, gears shifting.

Mrs. Starch looked anything but worried. "A friendly," she said. "One of us."

"Is it Duane?" Nick asked.

"Correct."

"Here's what I don't understand: How did you get him to help? That day he bit your pencil in half — he was seriously ticked off about the pimple paper," Nick said.

"Oh, I never asked Duane to get involved in this project. Wouldn't have dreamed of it!" Mrs. Starch asserted. "Believe me, that boy was *número uno* on my list of trouble-makers. It was Mr. Spree who recruited him. They knew each other from a past adventure."

Marta said, "That figures."

"Yes, it's a small world. Imagine my shock when Duane strolled into camp one morning."

Imagine his *shock,* thought Nick.

The motorcycle, much closer and noisier than before, suddenly spluttered to a stop. "He'll hide the bike in the woods and hike in from the south," Mrs. Starch explained. "Usually takes him another half hour or so."

Nick's head was pounding as he struggled to absorb everything the teacher had told them. "But how did Twilly meet Duane?" he asked. "What kind of adventure are you talking about?"

"That I cannot answer. Speak to Mr. Spree." Mrs. Starch yawned and said, "Marta, may I have a word with Nick privately in my tent?"

Marta looked around dubiously. "What'm I supposed to do out here all by myself?"

"Listen to the birds."

Nick got down and followed Mrs. Starch into the tent. Crawling wasn't easy with his right arm bound; he hopped like a three-legged dog. He managed to fit himself cross-legged on the ground beside her sleeping bag. Arranged neatly on a square of cardboard were a few basic items: flashlight, toothbrush, mouthwash, hairbrush, a bottle of aspirin, a bar of soap, and some note-sized lavender envelopes. There was also a small manual typewriter. Nick felt uneasy in her personal space.

"Here." She handed him the straw hat, which he held in the crook of his left arm.

The kitten was dozing in the shape of a fuzzy, plump comma. Its padded paws covered its face, muffling a muscular snore.

Mrs. Starch dropped her voice. "Nick, do you want to be part of this — and help your friend Duane at the same time?"

Nick couldn't take his eyes off the cat. It was astonishing to think that he was holding one of the last panthers on earth.

"Are you in, or out?" Mrs. Starch asked.

"In."

"You must be certain."

"I am."

"Excellent." She took the hat with the kitten and positioned it carefully on the soft flannel flap of her sleeping bag. "Nick, I'm going to ask you to do something."

"Sure."

"Take off that sling."

He was caught by surprise. "How come?"

Mrs. Starch said, "I know why you're wearing it — Duane told us what happened to your father, and I admire your devotion. But here's the present situation in the Black Vine Swamp: for what lies ahead, each of us will require a strong heart and two good arms. We need one hundred percent of you."

Nick hesitated.

"Your dad would understand," she said.

He removed his shirt and she helped unwrap the Ace bandage from his shoulder and armpit. Once his right arm was unbound, he flexed his elbow and made a fist with his hand to get the circulation flowing.

"What if Twilly can't find the mother panther?" he asked Mrs. Starch. "Or what if she won't take back her cub?"

"Hope springs eternal, Nick."

Again they heard an engine in the distance. Mrs. Starch frowned, tilting an ear toward the sound.

"That's not a motorcycle," she said. "That's a helicopter."

"Friendly?"

"I seriously doubt it."

TWENTY-ONE

Jimmy Lee Bayliss held the gun across his lap, which made the chopper pilot nervous.

"Relax. I know what I'm doin'," Jimmy Lee Bayliss said, which wasn't altogether true.

He'd never been a very good shot. Any target, moving or nonmoving, presented a challenge. His buddies back in Texas invited him along on hunting trips mostly out of pity.

The deer rifle in his hands had never killed a deer, or even come close, though it had frightened many. That's all Jimmy Lee Bayliss aimed to do if he came across the trespassers who were hassling Melton and messing with Red Diamond's gear — scare 'em off by firing a couple of rounds over their sneaky heads.

Same as he'd done to that panther.

The pilot said, "You got the safety on, right?"

"Gimme a break." Jimmy Lee Bayliss peeked at the safety button above the trigger. He was relieved to see that it was, in fact, on.

"Got any Tums?" he asked the pilot.

"No, I don't."

"Rolaids?"

"Sorry."

"Maalox?"

"Do you want me to set her down so you can make a potty stop?"

"Naw."

Jimmy Lee Bayliss wondered if his boss was feeling better. The nurses had been taping Drake McBride's ribs when Jimmy Lee Bayliss had left him at the hospital, cussing and whining and making a nuisance of himself.

The pilot said, "How low do you want to go?"

"Two hundred feet, give or take."

They circled Section 21 for fifteen minutes and saw no life on the ground except for a pair of wild boars. Jimmy Lee Bayliss decided to shoot at them for target practice. However, the pilot took his sweet time setting the helicopter in a hover, and the pigs trotted safely into the scrub.

"Nice work," Jimmy Lee Bayliss grumbled.

"Where to now?"

"The usual."

Section 22 appeared quiet, too. Jimmy Lee Bayliss ordered the pilot to take an extra-slow pass to make sure that Red Diamond's pirate well was still invisible from the air. A person looking hard enough might have noticed ATV tracks at the off-loading site, but the natural suspects would be deer poachers, not oil drillers.

As the chopper climbed to five hundred feet and angled slowly back toward the coast, the pilot pointed out his window and said, "Hey, check it out!"

At first Jimmy Lee Bayliss couldn't see what he was talking about. Then, as the nose of the aircraft tipped, the scene came into full view. His mouth went dry and his ears got hot.

"Hold it here!" he barked at the pilot. "Now!"

"Ten-four."

"Why are you laughin'?"

"Because it's funny," the pilot said.

"Not to me, it ain't. Not to Mr. McBride, either, the man who's payin' for this whirly-bird!"

"Okay, fine. It's not funny."

"Damn right it's not." Jimmy Lee Bayliss was steaming mad.

All the pink flags — once laid out so precisely with the eye of a surveyor, marking the future path of the illegal pipeline from Section 22 to Section 21 — had been yanked from their holes, uprooted by an unknown hand.

A criminal's hand it was, too: some warped outlaw, some lame excuse for a comedian who had replanted them on their stems, all those little pink flags, brightening a patch of parched prairie like candles on cornbread.

Rearranged in such an obvious way that anyone flying low enough in a helicopter couldn't help but see the double-edged insult.

"S-C-A-T," the flags sneered in fluttering capital letters, as cheery as confetti. SCAT.

"Either he's telling you to go away," the pilot mused, "or he's calling you a name."

Or both, thought Jimmy Lee Bayliss with disgust.

Still shading a grin, the pilot said, "You want me to land so you can look around?"

"No, sir," Jimmy Lee Bayliss said gravely. "I want you to find out where I can rent me some bloodhounds."

They heard Smoke's motorcycle crank up and speed off.

Mrs. Starch said, "The helicopter must've spooked him."

Nick peered up through the thick branches at a blue pane of sky. "Was it the sheriff?"

"I don't believe so."

Marta was dejectedly examining her waterlogged sneakers. "We need to go," she said. "Is it safe yet?"

"Not without Mr. Spree." Mrs. Starch opened the second pizza box. "Anybody care for a slice?"

Nick said, "So, what exactly is the master plan?"

Marta jerked on his right sleeve. "If I don't get home soon, I'm gonna be grounded until I'm, like, a hundred. Hey, your arm grew back!"

"Teacher's orders," said Mrs. Starch, gnawing on a slice of pepperoni. "Is it Saturday or Sunday? I lose track of time out here."

Nick told her it was Saturday. Her brow furrowed, but she continued to eat. Marta reached over and flicked a fat red ant off her pants.

"The plan," said Mrs. Starch, "is to get that kitten back with his momma as soon as possible. The longer they're apart, the harder it's going to be. There will come a day, sadly, when the mother cat simply gives up and moves on. . . ."

"Okay, what can *we* do?" Nick asked.

"Number one: Stay close to Duane. Make sure he doesn't try anything crazy."

Marta rolled her eyes. "You mean like running from the cops? Gee, that's not crazy at all."

Nick said, "Mrs. Starch, nobody gets close to Smoke."

"And what does that have to do with the panthers, anyway?" Marta asked.

Patiently, Mrs. Starch explained: "Your friend Duane has a special talent that's crucial to this mission. There's no chance of succeeding without him."

Nick was intrigued. "What kind of talent?"

Exasperated, Marta said, "He's a fugitive! If we help him, we're breaking the law."

But he's also innocent, Nick thought. Another heavy decision.

"Watch after Duane, please," Mrs. Starch urged. "If you don't, Squirt might die out here in my arms. So watch after Duane."

A sharp, familiar whistle rose from fifty yards away. Mrs. Starch smiled and glanced at the watch on her wrist.

Twilly Spree entered the campsite at a dead run. He was panting hard and slick with sweat.

"Let's move!" he snapped, beckoning to

Marta and Nick.

"Finally," Marta said, and sprang to her feet.

Nick asked Twilly what was wrong.

"Just follow me, and stay quiet," he said.

Mrs. Starch stood up. "Hold on. What happened?"

"I'll tell you later."

The teacher folded her arms rigidly, as if addressing a wayward pupil. "What did you do now, Mr. Spree?"

"I left 'em a message. They deserved it."

"What sort of message?"

"The four-letter sort."

"Oh Lord," said Mrs. Starch. "Don't bother sharing it, please."

"I couldn't resist."

"Take these young people back to town immediately, and try not to corrupt them on the way."

The jog to the car was tense and hurried, Twilly keeping well ahead of Nick and Marta as he bulled through the hammocks and bounded across the flatlands and vaulted over the saw palmettos. Nick was glad to have both arms free to shield his face from the whippy twigs, ropy vines, and gluey spiderwebs. Marta struggled to stay close and, as instructed by Twilly, said nothing. It was an ordeal for her to remain quiet for more than a few minutes, and Nick was impressed by her self-restraint.

The Prius was barreling down the rutted farm road — Nick and Marta bouncing against their seat belts — when Twilly finally spoke.

"How much did Aunt Bunny tell you?" he asked.

"Everything except the part about how Smoke got involved," Nick said.

"I see."

"It would be good to know."

"Good for whom?" said Twilly. He put on his ski beanie and black wraparound sunglasses.

Marta sat forward. "You trust us. Stop pretending that you don't."

"Ha!"

But a few minutes later, Twilly grudgingly opened up: "A couple of years ago, I was driving from Tallahassee to Chokoloskee, nonstop, and don't ask why. After about seventeen cups of coffee, I pulled off the interstate to answer the call of nature."

"Where?" Nick asked.

"Right here in Naples. Beautiful Exit 101," Twilly said. "Four in the morning, fog thicker than clam chowder, and I'm standing there watering the weeds under some billboard when I smell smoke — and I don't mean your friend. I mean smoke, as in *fire*. I look up through the mist and see flames. The billboard is definitely burning."

"It was Duane being a pyro, right?" Marta said.

"I took off from one way and he took off from another, and we literally ran smack into each other," Twilly recalled. "First thing out of his mouth: 'I'm the one who did it!' As if I hadn't figured that out, him with his jerry can of gasoline and burned mops. I asked him why and he told me. I asked his name and he told me that, too. Then we heard the sirens and I promptly hauled butt. Duane, he stayed behind and gave himself up."

Marta asked why Smoke hadn't escaped while he had the chance.

Twilly said he didn't know. "But I'll tell you what was on that billboard he torched: a big ad for American Airlines. They were running a winter special — Miami to Paris for three hundred and ninety-five dollars."

"Paris?" Nick said. Now it made sense. "Mrs. Starch told us about Duane's mom."

"Yeah. A tough deal." Twilly shook his head ruefully.

"Was that the same flight she took?" Marta asked.

"Never even said goodbye."

"That sucks," Nick said.

"Big-time. I felt bad for the kid," said Twilly. "Offered to find him a good defense lawyer, but his granny took care of all that. He ended up getting probation for torching the billboard."

"But you stayed in touch," Marta said.

"We go fishing now and then."

Nick couldn't wait any longer to ask: "Why do you need Smoke's help to save the baby panther? What's his 'special talent' that Mrs. Starch was talking about?"

"Simple: the boy's a born tracker. Anybody can find the mother cat, it's him."

Twilly told them about a camping trip to Highlands County when Duane Scrod Jr. dogged the trail of a black bear for miles at night in a driving rain, across two muddy creeks and three county roads, all the way to the animal's den tree. Then he carved his initials in the trunk, turned around, and hiked back through the storm, as giddy as a child on Christmas morning.

"It's a gift. Even the old Seminoles aren't sure how he does it," Twilly said. "So the plan is for me to find the scat and then put Duane on the trail of the panther. Once we know where she is, we turn the cub loose nearby. After that, there's nothing left to do but pray they find each other before a bobcat or a coyote gobbles the little one."

Marta shuddered at the thought. "Have you seen any, you know . . . ?"

"Panther poop? Yes, ma'am, I hit the jackpot yesterday. Whether it was left by Squirt's mother or not, I couldn't say." The car struck a pothole and Twilly grunted.

"There's an oil company out here that's up to no good," he said. "They don't want anybody snooping around, especially game wardens on the lookout for endangered critters."

For Nick, the threads of the story were coming together at last. "That's who started the fire at the Black Vine Swamp, isn't it? The oil guys. That's who framed Smoke."

"Yeah, and that's who scared off the momma panther," Twilly added, "with a gun. The Red Diamond Energy Corporation."

Marta was outraged. "How do we stop 'em? What can we do?"

"They've had a few problems finishing their project. They're about to have more."

Nick said, "Are you a monkey wrencher?"

In the rearview mirror he could see Twilly react with a curious smile.

"Well, are you?" Nick asked. "In that book I'm reading, this crazy gang is running around the desert, blowing up bridges, wrecking bulldozers. . . ."

"Burning billboards," Twilly added with a wink. "Acts of crime, each and every one. Although it's hard not to root for those folks, isn't it? Fighting to save a place they love."

To Nick, Marta whispered, "I guess that answers your question."

Twilly said, "There's some rough language in that book. Maybe you should put it down until you're older."

"Tell the truth. Are you trying to be Hayduke?" Nick was referring to the fictional leader of the Monkey Wrench Gang.

When Twilly spoke again, he sounded tired and impatient. "Do you remember that panther screaming on the day of the fire?"

"I'll never forget it," Nick said.

Marta shuddered. "Me neither."

"Well, that was the cat I've been hunting for. I'd come across her tracks near the road where your school bus was parked, so I knew she was close, hunkered down and waiting for dusk — probably waiting to come search for her baby."

Twilly drummed his fingers on the steering wheel. "Then the fire started. Or, I should say, the arson."

"She took off again?" Nick said.

Twilly nodded grimly. "Most wild animals,

they run at the first whiff of smoke," he said. "But there's a chance she's back. The scat I found yesterday was fresh."

They reached the intersection at Route 29, where Twilly turned south and ended up behind a line of vegetable trucks.

"How long until she forgets about the cub?" Nick asked.

"Each day, the odds get worse."

A sheriff's car sped by, going the opposite direction. Nick noticed that Twilly was driving five miles below the speed limit and was dutifully wearing his seat belt.

"What the heck were you doing out in that swamp when you found the kitten?" Marta asked.

"Minding my own business," Twilly replied. "You should try it sometime."

"Mrs. Starch says you're rich."

"Just born lucky."

Nick said, "Definitely not Hayduke."

Twilly steered the car off the pavement and parked near a row of newspaper racks. He snatched the ski beanie from his head, rubbed his brow, and then suddenly slugged the dashboard so hard that Nick and Marta jumped.

Turning in his seat, Twilly raised his sunglasses and fixed the kids with a raw, pained stare.

"Let me tell you something even dear Aunt Bunny doesn't know," he said. "After that, don't ever ask again about who I am or am not, or why a man like me lives in a tent. I've got a gutful of anger about what's happening to this land and everything that lives out here. That's all you need to know."

He sounded more sorrowful than angry. "Some days are worse than others," he said.

Nick and Marta weren't sure how to react.

Twilly raised two fingers. "That's how many there were."

"How many what?" Marta asked, puzzled.

"Panther cubs," he said. "That's how many I found. The mother cat had two."

Nick closed his eyes.

"One of them died," Twilly said. "I tried everything, but the smaller one didn't make it through the first night. I never told Bunny or Duane. Never told anybody."

Marta covered her face.

Twilly lowered his glasses. "Any more questions?"

"No," said Nick quietly. "No more."

TWENTY-TWO

On Sunday morning, Duane Scrod Sr. dragged himself out of bed and stumbled to the front door.

"How'd you get here so fast?" he asked Millicent Winship.

"Chartered a jet plane. Now open the door."

With fake cheer, Duane Scrod Sr. welcomed his mother-in-law into the house. She almost knocked him down as she whisked past. There was not a wrinkle to be seen in her elegant gray pants suit, nor one silver hair out of place on her head.

"Did you sleep in that stupid hat?" she asked.

"I guess." Duane Sr. was more worried about her reaction to his NASCAR boxer shorts.

Mrs. Winship scowled and looked away. "Go put on some pants, for heaven's sake. And keep that awful parrot away from me or I'll pluck her bald."

"Millie, she's not a parrot. She's a macaw."

"A nuisance is what she is. Hurry up."

Duane Scrod Sr. pulled on some blue jeans and wrestled Nadine into her cage. When he returned to the living room, Mrs. Winship was waiting with folded arms.

"So my grandson is now a fugitive," she said. "I got the whole ugly story from the headmaster. D.J.'s been suspended from Truman as well, but I suppose that's the least of our problems."

"The cops are makin' a big mistake."

"Where is he now?"

"I don't honestly know," Duane Sr. said. "He comes and goes like some sorta ghost."

"And you have no way of reaching him? What about the cell phone I bought him?"

"He never picks up, Millie. Did you tell his mom about this mess?"

"Of course. I phoned her right away."

"Is she coming back?"

"No, Duane. What good would that do?" Mrs. Winship brushed the stale cracker crumbs off a chair and sat down. Her daughter had offered to call the boy and urge him to surrender, but she had not offered to come home and see him.

Duane Sr. said, "It's not cheap, I guess, flying all the way from France."

"Money has nothing to do with it. I would have bought her a first-class ticket."

"Then what?"

The only time that Mrs. Winship felt old was when she had to talk about her daughter. "Whitney says she has to stay and take care of the shop. She says it's the busy season."

Duane Sr. gazed drearily at the floor. "In other words, cheese is more important than her own flesh and blood."

"I'm sorry, Duane. Truly I am."

"What's gonna happen to Junior?"

"I've contacted a lawyer. Where do you think he's hiding?"

"Somewhere out there in the boonies." Duane Sr. motioned with a limp wave.

"That's very helpful," Mrs. Winship muttered. "Narrows it down to about two million acres."

She stood up, smoothed her slacks, and slung her purse over one shoulder. "Next time you see your son, please inform him that his grandmother strongly suggests that he turn himself in to the police as soon as possible. Tell him that's the only way I can help him out of this mess."

"I will, Millie, but D.J. listens to me about as good as Whitney listens to you."

Mrs. Winship let the remark slide. Duane

Sr. had a right to be bitter. He loved Whitney, but she'd left him anyway.

"According to the newspapers, Duane's book bag was found at the scene of the arson," Mrs. Winship said. "How could that possibly be true, if he's innocent?"

Duane Sr. spilled out his jumbled theory about the government tax collector stealing Junior's backpack from the house. Mrs. Winship looked doubtful.

"Well, we've certainly got our work cut out for us," she said, shouldering past Duane Sr. on her way out the door.

"Thank you, Millie," he called after her.

She spun around on the steps. "Thanks for what?"

"Caring so much about the boy."

"Believe it or not, I care about both of you," Mrs. Winship said gruffly. "Now go play with your parrot."

Drake McBride went straight from the hospital to a suite at the swanky Ritz-Carlton Hotel so he could recuperate in high style. Jimmy Lee Bayliss, following orders, brought the man with the bloodhound up to the room.

The dog's name was Horace. It had humongous flappy ears and rubbery wet jowls and a nose like a loaf of gingerbread. It promptly lay down on the floor and dozed off in a puddle of drool.

"Horace is tired," explained the handler.

"Is this all you got? We need more than one hound," Drake McBride complained.

"No, you don't," said the handler.

"They hunt better alone. I checked it out with my buddies back in Houston," Jimmy Lee Bayliss said.

Drake McBride, still sprawled in bed, insisted they needed a whole pack of dogs. "That's how they catch bears, right?"

The handler said, "I didn't know you was after bears. I thought you was after humans."

"We are," Jimmy Lee Bayliss said. His stomach felt like he'd swallowed a handful of hot barbecue coals. He explained to his boss that Horace was a world-class man-hunter. "They use him to track down missing persons, lost hikers, escaped convicts. Twice he was on *America's Most Wanted*."

"All he needs is a scent," the handler said.

"Do we have a scent?" Drake McBride asked grumpily.

Jimmy Lee Bayliss said, "We do." The culprit's odor was on dozens of pink flags that he'd touched while rearranging them.

When Drake McBride reached for a glass of water on the nightstand, he let out a yelp of pain, which caused Horace briefly to open his watery brown eyes and blink.

"Mr. McBride got thrown from a horse and busted some ribs," Jimmy Lee Bayliss informed the dog handler.

"Got me a concussion, too," Drake McBride added. "Hey, pardner, you know anybody who wants to buy a Thoroughbred real cheap?"

The handler said no.

"Can you get started today?" Jimmy Lee Bayliss asked. "We'll take you out there by helicopter."

"That's fine."

"And you're sure this dog can follow the smell of a person through a tropical swamp?"

"He can follow the smell of a person through a vinegar factory," the handler said.

Drake McBride pointed at the bloodhound, whose eyelids had once again sagged shut. "When will ol' Horace be done with his nap?"

"Whenever I say so."

"How about right now? Because I gotta talk to Mr. Bayliss in private." Drake McBride clapped his hands three times loudly. "Horace, wake up! Horace!"

The dog did not stir, much to Jimmy Lee Bayliss's dismay.

Drake McBride scratched his unshaven cheeks. "Well, I ain't impressed. Let's find us another mutt, Jimmy Lee."

The bloodhound handler softly clicked his tongue. Horace sprang up from the floor as if electrified, nostrils in the air, tail erect, eyes wide and shining.

"Don't call him a mutt," the handler said.

Drake McBride chuckled. "Sorry, Horace. Now will you two excuse us, please?"

Jimmy Lee Bayliss led the bloodhound and the handler to the door of the suite, and said he'd meet them in the lobby in ten minutes. When he returned to the bedroom, he found Drake McBride upright, massaging his head. His pajama shirt was unbuttoned, exposing his heavily taped chest.

"My old man called last night," he said unhappily. "I lied and told him everything down here was goin' smooth as silk."

"And it will be, once we get rid of our problem." Jimmy Lee Bayliss was well aware that the Red Diamond Energy Corporation wouldn't exist if it weren't for Drake McBride's rich father. He was also aware that Drake McBride's father had dwindling patience with Drake McBride. "Sir, once that bloodhound hunts down this guy on the property —"

"Or guys," Drake McBride said. "Whoever's messin' with our stuff."

"Right. But after we catch 'em, what do we do with 'em?" Jimmy Lee Bayliss asked. "What if they already found the pirate well? We can't call the cops on 'em, because they'll just rat us out. Then you and me are the ones who get hauled off to jail."

"No, we can't call the cops. Definitely not," agreed Drake McBride.

"So what are we s'posed to do with these vandals? If they already know about Section 22, I mean."

There was a pause that got heavier with each passing second.

"I haven't worked out all the details," Drake McBride said finally, "but we'll do whatever it takes to protect this project. You understand, pardner? Whatever it takes."

It was not an answer that made Jimmy Lee Bayliss's belly stop burning.

The digital clock by Nick's bed said 9:15, which was odd. On most Sunday mornings, his mother awoke him at eight sharp so they could make buttermilk pancakes and bacon.

He rolled out of bed and put on a robe. From down the hall came the sound of muffled voices; a discussion was under way. Through the window he saw a gray U.S. Army van parked in the driveway.

Nick ran to the living room just as his father was being helped into a wheelchair by two young soldiers. His mother stood stiffly by the door, the knuckles of one hand pressed to her chin.

"What's going on?" Nick asked.

"Minor setback," his father said hoarsely. "They miss me up at Walter Reed, I guess." His face looked feverish, and his eyes were red with fatigue.

Nick turned to his mom. "Did the infection come back?"

"It never went away."

One of the soldiers rolled the wheelchair out to the van, which had a ramp that elevated Nick's dad to the side door. The other soldier carried a small nylon suitcase that Nick's mother had packed, and he placed it in the van beside the wheelchair. Capt. Gregory Waters kicked a woolen blanket off his legs and said, "I'm not eighty years old!"

Nick's mother kissed his father goodbye and said, "I'll come up and see you in a day or two."

"Me, too," Nick said.

"No, sir, you're not missing one more day of school," his father told him.

"But, Dad —"

"That's enough. I'll be home again before

you know it."

He squeezed Nick's right arm. "Hey, are you keeping the sling off? Don't tell me you're giving up the southpaw life."

"Just wait. By the time you get back I'll be a total hard-core lefty."

His father managed a smile, but Nick could see the pain in his face. "Yeah, Nicky, we'll go fly-fishing down in Everglades City, just the two of us."

Nick and his mother waved as the van pulled out of the driveway, and they continued waving long after Capt. Gregory Waters could no longer see them. Nick was dazed; the whole scene seemed like a terrible dream. His dad had seemed okay the night before.

"What's going on, Mom? Tell me!"

"After breakfast," she said crossly.

"I'm not hungry."

"Well, I am."

She was, too: three pancakes, two strips of bacon, a banana, a half-cup of blueberries, and a tall glass of fresh-squeezed orange juice.

Nick picked at a bowl of dry granola. He waited, fidgeting, until his mother finished eating. There was no point in nagging her.

After pouring herself a cup of coffee, she settled in and told him what had happened.

"Remember when you tried to call your dad at the hospital but he was gone?"

"Sure. That was the day he came home."

"Yes, he came home," Nick's mother said. "He came home without telling his doctors. Strolled out of Walter Reed at four-thirty in the morning, grabbed a cab, and went straight to the airport."

"No way!"

"It was a foolish thing to do. He wasn't ready, Nicky."

"So he lied?"

"He didn't want us to worry."

"Is he crazy, or what?" Nick said angrily.

"Your dad wanted to be here more than anything. He was sure he'd get better faster if he was home with you and me."

"But he didn't get better," Nick said bleakly. "He got worse."

His mother was staring at her coffee, stirring it slowly with the wrong end of a spoon. She said, "Last night he woke up with chills and a 104-degree fever, so I knew the infection wasn't gone. He was so miserable that he finally admitted the truth — he's still got shrapnel from that rocket in his shoulder. He needs more surgery."

"Oh no." Nick sagged in the chair.

"Your dad's a tough customer. He'll be all right."

360

"What about you, Mom?"

"I'm pretty darn tough myself, in case you hadn't noticed. Now," she said, rising, "I'd better go pack. I'm flying up to be with your father."

Nick held her tight. "I can't believe he bailed out of the hospital. If I ever did something like that, I'd be grounded for a year."

"It wasn't the brainiest move," Nick's mother agreed, "but he missed us, Nicky, that's all. Let's just be thankful he's not in Iraq anymore. As soon as the doctors in Washington finish fixing him, he'll be home for good."

After his mom left, Nick tried to keep busy and not worry about his dad. He cleaned the kitchen sink and loaded his dirty laundry into the washing machine and worked some algebra problems and rewrote the outline for an English essay that wasn't due for two weeks.

Marta called twice, but Nick didn't answer the phone. He wasn't in the mood to talk with any of his friends. For lunch he fixed a peanut butter sandwich, but he took only three bites; he had absolutely no appetite, and too much nervous energy.

So he put on a Red Sox cap and went out to the backyard and threw baseballs left-

361

handed at the pitching net until his elbow throbbed. There was so much he'd wanted to talk to his father about, yet he understood that this was no time to be selfish. It was essential for his dad to return to the hospital and get the operation he needed.

After retrieving· the balls from the net, Nick lugged the bucket back to the home-made pitching mound and resumed throwing again, as hard as he could, despite the burning ache.

In the middle of a windup, a voice from behind said, "You're gonna wreck your arm, dude."

Nick spun and saw Smoke walking his motorcycle around the corner of the house.

"What're you doing here?" Nick asked.

Duane Scrod Jr. leaned the bike against the wall and said, "You gotta help me. They turned a manhunter dog loose out there near the camp."

"Who did?"

"The oil company."

"Where's Twilly?"

"Running like crazy. He's the one told me to come see you." Smoke looked around nervously. "I can't hide out at home 'cause of the cops. Now they got a squad car parked right in front of the house!"

"What about Mrs. Starch and the baby

panther?" Nick said.

"They're okay, so far. But that dog is good, man. That dog is a pro."

"How can I help?" asked Nick, knowing what the answer would be.

"I need a place to stay," Smoke said, "just for a while."

"Sure."

Nick dropped the baseball into the bucket. He wondered how, or even if, he should tell his mom. It would probably be the first time she had a fugitive as a houseguest.

TWENTY-THREE

Detective Jason Marshall didn't usually work on Sundays, but he wasn't going to relax until he tracked down Duane Scrod Jr., the missing arson suspect. It didn't help that the other detectives kept needling him because the kid had dashed away before he could snap on the handcuffs, and then had easily outrun him.

Every night Jason Marshall took two aspirins and pressed a heating pad against his sore hamstring muscle and drifted off into a fitful sleep, wondering where Duane Jr. was hiding.

And every morning Jason Marshall woke up thinking of evidence to follow that might lead him to the boy, or at least lock up the arson case. On this particular day, the detective decided to skip church and do some Internet research on handheld butane torches.

The brand found in Duane Scrod Jr.'s

book bag was called The Ultra Igniter, and the company's Web site helpfully provided a list of retail outlets that sold its products in Collier County. There were only three, all hardware stores.

One had gone out of business, and Jason Marshall figured the other two would be closed on a Sunday, but he was wrong. The store on the east side of Naples was open.

The detective drove there, bringing a photograph of Duane Scrod Jr. that had been taken after his arrest for setting fire to the billboard. The owner of the hardware store swore he'd never seen the kid before.

"Do you sell lots of those Igniter torches?" the detective asked.

"Not many," the store owner replied. "I can look it up on the computer and tell you the exact number."

The store had sold only two Ultra Igniters during the past thirty days. Jason Marshall wrote down the dates.

"You wouldn't happen to have the names of the customers, I suppose," the detective said.

"Nope. All I can tell you is that both items were bought with a credit card."

"You sure about that?"

"Yup. Our inventory software keeps track of whether it's a cash purchase or plastic," the store owner explained.

Jason Marshall thought it was highly unlikely that Duane Scrod Jr. would be using a credit card, unless it belonged to his father or he'd stolen it.

"I notice you've got security cameras," the detective said.

"Doesn't everybody, these days?"

"Do you still have the videotapes from the dates that you sold the Ultra Igniters?"

"I doubt it," the store owner replied, which was a lie. He saved all the security videotapes for six months, in case they were needed to prosecute shoplifters. On this particular day he just didn't feel like sifting through hours of videos.

"Let's take a look," Jason Marshall said.

"Actually, I'm sorta busy right now. Maybe you could stop by another time."

"I'm pretty busy myself," said Jason Marshall. "So let's see those tapes."

It didn't take very long to review the surveillance film, and the detective found both sales transactions that he was looking for. He informed the store owner that he was keeping the tapes as evidence.

"What's this all about?" the man asked worriedly. "Am I in trouble or something?"

"Not at all," Jason Marshall said.

Driving back to the sheriff's office, he

phoned Torkelsen, the arson investigator with the fire department. He told him he'd located a store that had sold two butane torches identical to the one found in the backpack of Duane Scrod Jr.

"One was bought on the day before the fire at the swamp," the detective said.

"Good work!"

"But the second torch was purchased only three days ago."

The arson investigator said, "I don't care about that one."

"Well, you should," Jason Marshall said, "because the same guy bought both of them — and it wasn't the Scrod kid."

"How do you know?"

"The hardware store has security cameras. I got the tapes."

There was an edgy silence on the other end: Torkelsen, trying to figure out what this information could mean.

"Maybe the boy has an accomplice. Maybe they bought the second torch because they're planning another fire," he said finally. "How old is that customer on the video?"

"Between fifty-five and sixty, I'd say."

"Oh," said Torkelsen. "So it's not the boy's father."

"Nope."

"Well, there's got to be an explanation."

"I can think of one," the detective said.

"Let's hear it."

"Maybe we're after the wrong guy."

After another uneasy pause, the arson investigator said, "I need to see those tapes."

"Yes, you do," agreed Jason Marshall.

The oak tree was forty feet high and dead as a doornail, killed years earlier by a lightning strike. Way up high was a hole in the trunk where a female raccoon was living with three little ones.

One day a huge backhoe arrived on the lot and started smashing down trees. The boy, who'd been spying on the raccoon family for weeks, jumped off his bicycle and shouted at the driver of the backhoe to steer clear of the dead oak.

But the driver never heard him. He just waved the boy away, revved the big machine, and flattened the den tree, killing all the raccoons, including the mother. The boy could do nothing but watch from a distance, and sob.

The construction company that owned the backhoe was clearing the property to make way for a patio-furniture warehouse. Two days after all the trees were demolished, the company set up a shiny double-wide office trailer with a bright banner heralding the new project. That same night, the boy rode his bike out to the property and set fire to the double-wide, which burned to a rather immense and twisted cinder. Nobody was inside at the time.

"I made sure of that," Smoke assured Nick, who'd listened to the entire arson story without interrupting.

"See, I'm not a true pyro," Smoke added. "I didn't do it for kicks. I was just mad."

"Still, that's . . ."

" 'Dumb' is the word. Same with torching the billboard," Smoke said. "My mom had just taken off for Paris and I was all messed up. When I saw that big sign for the airline, I flipped out. You wouldn't understand, dude. Nobody does."

Nick didn't say a thing. It was impossible for him to envision his own mother getting on a plane and flying away forever without even saying goodbye. Such heartbreak was beyond Nick's experience.

Smoke chuckled bitterly. "They built that stupid furniture warehouse anyway. Just like they put up a brand-new billboard in the same spot as the other one."

"Did you set any other fires?" Nick asked.

"Never."

"So why do you want people to call you

Smoke?"

"Because it sounds a lot cooler than Duane."

They were sitting on the floor in Nick's bedroom. The shades were drawn and the door was locked.

"Twilly says you're a tracker," Nick said.

"It's the one thing I'm good at, I guess."

"He says that if anybody can find that mother panther, it's you."

"I sure aim to try." Smoke spoke with determination.

"Mrs. Starch says there's not much time."

"She's right. And this bloodhound sniffin' all over the place doesn't make the job any easier," Smoke said. "Wild cats run like crazy from dogs."

Nick had to ask. "What's the deal with you and her?"

"Mrs. Starch? She's not so bad."

"Everybody thought you hated her guts after what happened in class."

Smoke grinned. "For sure I did. But come to find out she's not as mean as she acts. Hey, I heard a car pull up!"

Moments later, the front door opened and Nick's mother began calling his name. Smoke grabbed him by the shoulders. "Don't say a word about me!"

"But I can't lie," Nick whispered.

"Listen, bro. Once she knows I'm hidin' here, she's gotta tell the cops or else she can go to jail."

"What're you talking about?"

"Harboring a fugitive is what I'm talkin' about," Smoke said. "If you tell your mom I'm here, you're draggin' her into the middle of this whole mess. Is that what you want?"

From down the hall: "Nicky? Where are you?"

"I'll be right out, Mom!"

Smoke edged himself sideways into Nick's bedroom closet. "Go!" he said to Nick. "Act like nuthin's wrong."

Nick slipped out the door and closed it behind him. He walked down the hall to the living room, where he was surprised to see that his mother wasn't alone.

"Nicky, you remember Peyton?"

"Sure," he said.

Peyton Lynch had been one of Nick's regular babysitters back when he was in elementary school and she was in high school. Now she attended junior college and worked part-time at a sandal shop.

"Hey, Nicky," she smacked through a cheekful of bubble gum.

Nick's mother said Peyton would be staying at the house for a few days while she went to be with his father. "There's a flight out of Fort Myers late this afternoon that connects to Washington."

"That's good," Nick said.

And it *was* good — for Nick's dad, and also for Nick. Peyton Lynch was a nice girl, but she wasn't the sharpest knife in the drawer, as Mrs. Starch might say.

When Nick was little, he'd done pretty much whatever he'd pleased while Peyton was there, because she was usually yakking on the phone or painting her toenails blue or staring at MTV. She was the ideal baby-sitter — clueless.

One time, when Nick was nine years old, he'd accidentally bounced a golf ball through the screen of his desktop computer. Peyton hadn't heard the tube explode because her headphones were turned up so loud. Nor had she shown the slightest spark of curiosity when Nick had emerged from his room carrying a box full of broken glass.

Nick's mother said, "Make yourself at home, Peyton. I'll go finish packing."

Peyton dropped her travel bag on the rug and plopped down on the sofa. "So, how's school, Nicky?"

"It's okay," he said.

"Hey, you guys got any Diet Snapple?"

"I don't think so."

"Green tea?" she asked, plugging the iPod buds into her ears. "Tofu burgers? Spring rolls?"

"I'll check the fridge," said Nick, smiling to himself.

Peyton Lynch would never notice that Duane Scrod Jr. was staying at the house as long as he didn't park his motorcycle in the kitchen.

Drake McBride was extremely annoyed.

With a groan, he pushed himself out of bed and hobbled after Jimmy Lee Bayliss to the sitting room, where the dog handler waited somberly.

"What happened?" Drake McBride demanded, with no trace of sympathy.

The dog handler said, "You owe me two thousand dollars."

"Because your dumbass dog got lost? You outta your mind?"

"Horace didn't get lost," the man said flatly. "I ain't leavin' here till I get my money."

Jimmy Lee Bayliss bit his lip. He'd strongly urged his boss to pay the man and be done with it, but Drake McBride said no way, pardner, not one red cent.

"Here's what I think," Drake McBride said, buttoning his purple pajama top. "I think you tried to scam us with a defective hound dog. I think ol' Horace couldn't find his own butt in a breadbox."

The handler wasn't as tall as Drake McBride, but he was wiry and tough. Jimmy Lee Bayliss knew the type.

"Look, whatever happened out there, the man's dog is gone," Jimmy Lee Bayliss said to his boss, "and we need to reach some sort of agreement."

"Horace was a champion tracker," the handler stated proudly. "Horace was the best."

"Horace was a dud!" Drake McBride cackled. "Whoever heard of a champion bloodhound gettin' lost?"

At that point Jimmy Lee Bayliss realized that nothing could be done to save Drake McBride from his own big mouth. The president of the Red Diamond Energy Corporation was now pinned against the wall of the hotel room, his face turning the same color as his ridiculous pajamas.

"Horace did *not* get hisself lost. He got kilt!" the dog handler said, squeezing. "And he got et!"

Jimmy Lee Bayliss attempted to pry the man's hands from Drake McBride's neck, but the handler was very strong and very angry. Drake McBride's eyeballs were bulging and his arms were flapping, and mousy little squeaks were leaking out of his lungs.

"Let go of him, please!" Jimmy Lee Bayliss implored. "He'll pay you the two grand."

"And 'pologize for what he said about Horace?"

"He'll take out an ad in the paper, if you want."

The dog handler released his hold on Drake McBride, who crumpled to his knees on the carpet. After five solid minutes of hacking and wheezing, he finally recaptured his breath and said he was sorry.

"Gimme my money," the handler said.

"You say your dog was eaten?"

"Bet on it."

"Eaten by what, if I might ask?"

"Like you don't know," the man said coldly.

Drake McBride looked quizzically at Jimmy Lee Bayliss. "What's he talkin' about now?"

To himself, Jimmy Lee Bayliss thought: *I'm employed by a total moron.*

"He's talking about a panther, sir."

"Ha! Ain't no panthers out there!" Drake McBride declared, but it was all bluster. His face was a pale mask of anxiety.

The dog handler said, "I saw the scat

myself."

"You're mistaken, pal. It was most likely a bobcat."

"Yeah?" The man yanked Drake McBride to his feet and then shoved him into an armchair. "I know bobcat scat from panther scat, and what I saw didn't come from no puny bobcat."

In fear of another throttling, Drake McBride gave up the argument. "Whatever you say; you're the expert."

"That I am," the handler said.

To bring the conversation to a peaceful end, Jimmy Lee Bayliss explained to Drake McBride that the handler would never have allowed Horace to track a scent through the Black Vine Swamp if he'd known a panther was lurking in the area.

"The dog's purely a human hunter, not a cat hunter," Jimmy Lee Bayliss said. "I believe we've got an obligation to compensate this man for his loss."

"All right, all right," Drake McBride mumbled, and limped to the bedroom to get his checkbook.

The handler said, "Out west they use special cat hounds for huntin' cougars. But Horace, he wasn't schooled for that. He probably just run up on that ol' panther without even barkin' and got hisself kilt and et. Thing is, I had a fondness for that ol' fella."

"We're very sorry this happened. Deeply sorry," Jimmy Lee Bayliss said in his most sincere-sounding voice.

"You oughta be," said the handler.

"Mr. McBride and I had no idea there was a dangerous panther on our land."

"Know what? I think you're both fulla crap."

Jimmy Lee Bayliss didn't dispute the point. His boss returned and slumped into the armchair, a ballpoint pen in one hand and a checkbook open on his lap.

With forced politeness he said, "Two thousand even, right?"

The dog handler rubbed his leathery chin in a pondering way that caused Jimmy Lee Bayliss to grope for his Tums.

"Right 'fore Horace disappeared, he struck a red-hot trail," the handler recalled. "It led us off your company's land all the way over to the next section, where you can't believe what I found — or maybe you can."

Jimmy Lee Bayliss swallowed a sour burp. Drake McBride's shoulders drooped.

"There was a big ol' stack of pipes and boxes of drillin' gear," the dog handler went on, "like somebody was fixin' to sink an oil well on state property! You can't never guess what name was on the labels of them crates — or maybe you can. It was 'Red Diamond Energy,' same as your outfit. Ain't that odd?"

Drake McBride looked up and croaked, "What exactly do you want from me, mister?"

The handler gave a long, phony sigh. "I sure do miss my hound dog."

Jimmy Lee Bayliss said, "Let's cut to the chase — how does five thousand bucks sound?"

"Real fine is how it sounds to me."

"But if anyone ever asks, you never set foot in Section 22, did you? You didn't see no mud pit or drillin' equipment or nuthin'."

"No, sir," the handler said. "The only one who knows different is Horace, and he ain't here to spill the beans, God rest his soul."

Drake McBride scowled. "Stop. You're gonna make me cry."

He scribbled a check for five thousand dollars and handed it to the handler. "Here, go buy yourself another mutt," he said, and staggered back to bed.

TWENTY-FOUR

Nick felt himself being shaken roughly. He hoped it was a dream, because he wasn't ready to wake up.

"Move it!" a hushed voice commanded.

Nick opened one eye and saw Duane Scrod Jr. standing over him, dressed in hunting camo. "Twilly just called," said the kid, holding up his cell phone. "We gotta go."

"Where?"

"There."

"But what about school?" Nick asked.

Smoke grabbed his ankles and hauled him out of the sheets. "Go write a note to your babysitter."

"She's not my babysitter!"

"Whatever. Put a note in the kitchen — tell her you caught a ride to Truman with one of the seniors."

"But it's still nighttime," Nick said.

"No, dude, that's fog."

Nick dressed in his regular school outfit, including a necktie and blazer, in case Peyton Lynch woke up and saw him leaving. He didn't know that she was in a deep, bearlike sleep, having been up until 3 a.m. texting back and forth with girlfriends who were on a trip to Hong Kong.

Together, Nick and Smoke slipped out the front door.

"Are we taking the motorcycle?" Nick asked, wondering if he'd dressed warmly enough for an open ride.

"Twilly said no, the muffler's too noisy," Smoke said. "Today we need to be quiet."

At the end of the block they came upon the blue Prius, parked with its headlights on. Although the windshield was glossy with dew, Nick could make out two upright shapes inside the car. He assumed it was Twilly and Mrs. Starch, and he was half right.

The driver's window rolled down, and Twilly told Nick and Smoke to get in the backseat. Once they were buckled in, Twilly pointed at his four-legged passenger.

"Say hello to Horace."

With droopy eyelids the bloodhound turned toward the boys, a string of pearly drool unspooling from its lower lip.

Smoke crowed delightedly. "Is that the

same one that was chasing us?"

"All is forgiven," Twilly said from behind his black sunglasses.

Nick stroked the dog's silky ears. "Don't tell me he fell for the old raw-hamburger trick."

"Naw, it was steak," Twilly said. "One sniff and Horace decided I was his new best friend. Turns out he's pretty good company. Doesn't ask lots of nosy questions."

"How do you know his name's Horace?"

"Because that's what his boss man was hollering all over the woods after he lost him. By the way," Twilly said, eyeing Nick in the rearview, "why are you dressed like an usher? Or is that what you usually wear on a hike through the swamp?"

"Uh, no. I had to look like I was on my way to school," Nick said, reddening. He shed his Truman blazer and yanked off his tie. "So, why are *you* wearing shades?" he said sharply to Twilly. "It's practically dark out."

"Not to me."

Smoke asked, "Did you find some more you-know-what?"

"Yup," Twilly said.

"How fresh?"

"Two hours, tops."

Nick sat forward excitedly. "Panther scat?"

381

"Right," said Twilly.

Smoke looked out the window of the car. "Awesome," he murmured.

Nick borrowed Smoke's cell phone to call Marta, who begged to come along. At first Twilly balked, but Smoke spoke up and said it couldn't hurt to have an extra set of eyes and ears on the hunt. Nick instructed Marta to meet them at the mailbox near the bus stop, and she was waiting in jeans and a hooded sweatshirt when the car pulled up.

She was so excited that she practically hurled herself into the backseat. It took a few moments before she noticed the large, slobbering dog in the front. "What's the deal with *him?*" she said.

"That's just Horace," said Nick.

"He's a bloodhound," Smoke added. "A good one."

Horace yawned at the compliment.

Marta said, "Oh, I get it. He's gonna help track down the momma panther."

Twilly made a noise like a game-show buzzer. "Wrong," he said. "Horace will soon be tied under a tree, snoring like a train. He doesn't do cats."

"He's a trained manhunter," Smoke explained.

"Where'd he come from?" Marta asked.

Nick said, "Twilly dognapped him."

"Not true. I bribed him with a T-bone, that's all," said Twilly.

He drove slower than normal because of the soupy fog, so it took a while to reach the dirt road leading to the Black Vine Swamp. Along the way he pulled over briefly to snug the seat belt around Horace, which Nick thought was a good idea. A bouncy ride could cause unpleasant problems for a big dog with a full stomach, and also for the other passengers.

They concealed Mrs. Starch's car in the same place as before, beneath the same strangler fig, and set out on foot. Twilly led Horace on a rope leash, and Smoke followed next. Nick and Marta stayed close so that they wouldn't get left behind in the fog, which hung like a wet woolen shroud over the marsh and tree islands.

A small fire was burning at Twilly's camp. Smoke joined Marta and Nick as they stood beside it, the heat feeling glorious on their cheeks. Twilly tied the hound to a cabbage palm and set out a bowl of water, which was loudly slurped up.

Afterward Twilly made a pot of coffee and everybody had a cup. Twilly told them to drink up quickly. Nick wasn't crazy about the taste, but he was grateful for the warm rush.

Mrs. Starch came out of her tent holding the straw hat. The baby panther popped its head up and cried plaintively.

"Patience, dear Squirt," Mrs. Starch said to the kitten.

The three kids gathered around to look. As adorable as it was, the cat was restless and squirmy and not very huggable. Nick noticed long, nasty scratch marks on Mrs. Starch's arms. Meanwhile, Horace the bloodhound had already dozed off under the palm tree.

Twilly stood away from the fire, pressing buttons on his handheld GPS. He said, "The good news is, they won't be using helicopters to hunt for us — not in this weather. The bad news is, it's gonna be twice as hard for us to find this little guy's mother."

Mrs. Starch fixed an iron gaze on Nick and Marta. "Silence on the trail is absolutely essential," she told them. "One tiny human sneeze could scare the momma cat away for good. That would be a death sentence for Squirt, do you understand? He can't live on zoo milk forever."

Marta and Nick nodded soberly. Both were thinking of the other panther cub, the one that had died.

"Time to go," Smoke said.

Twilly ducked into his tent and emerged with a rifle.

"What's *that* for?" Marta asked nervously.

"Peace of mind." Twilly checked his ammo belt to make sure that the bullet sleeves were full. "Everybody ready?"

The miniature panther growled impatiently inside the straw hat, and even Twilly laughed. They filed out of the clearing and into the misted woods, Twilly leading the way, followed by Duane Scrod Jr., Nick, Marta, and lastly Mrs. Starch, pressing a bottle of formula to the hungry cub's mouth.

For almost half an hour they hiked briskly yet quietly through cypress woods, flatlands, hammocks, and then more pines and palmetto scrub. The fog only seemed to get thicker, wetter, colder.

Twilly was using the GPS unit to retrace his earlier steps; without it, Nick knew, they'd never find what they were looking for. Not a word was spoken, even by Marta when she briefly lost a sneaker in the muck. Likewise, Mrs. Starch didn't utter the faintest cry when the panther kitten, miffed because the milk had run out, swatted her nose with an oversized paw, drawing blood.

At last Twilly motioned for the search party to halt and gather around him. He bent down and carefully lifted a palmetto frond, revealing on the ground a dark greenish pile of unmistakable origin, containing tufts of deer hair, bits of bones, and wisps of white egret feathers.

Marta pointed at the smelly lump and silently mouthed the words "Panther poop?"

Twilly made a thumbs-up sign. Duane Scrod Jr. dropped to one knee and began examining the scat. The only extraordinary sound in the swamp was that of the baby panther, rumbling inside Mrs. Starch's straw hat. Nick felt Marta gently take hold of his shirttail.

After a few moments, Smoke rose and began to move stealthily in small, weightless steps along a tangled trail that he alone could detect.

The others followed, their hearts hammering with anticipation.

Jimmy Lee Bayliss thought it would be best if he spoke to the game warden alone, but Drake McBride insisted on coming along. Jimmy Lee Bayliss had already told Melton and the rest of the crew to take the morning off, in order to avert any risk of the federal officer overhearing Red Diamond's machinery at work in Section 22.

The jostling drive to the Black Vine

Swamp was murder on Drake McBride's fractured ribs, and he groaned and cussed the whole time. Jimmy Lee Bayliss stopped the company truck near the entrance to the public boardwalk; he'd never seen fog so thick. It was like a cold, clinging smoke.

Drake McBride got out, rubbing his bandaged midsection. He was still mad about the five thousand dollars he'd given to the owner of the missing bloodhound.

"You think a panther really snacked on that dog? No way, pardner."

"Doesn't matter," Jimmy Lee Bayliss said. "We had no choice but to pay the man off."

Drake McBride snorted scornfully. "He's nuthin' but a scammer."

"Whatever. He found the well pit in Section 22," Jimmy Lee Bayliss reminded his boss for the tenth time. "He would've ratted us out if we didn't give him some money."

"Man, I hate scammers," Drake McBride said.

Jimmy Lee Bayliss laughed. He couldn't help it. He completely understood why Drake McBride's father thought his son was a boob.

A green pickup rolled out of the haze and stopped. On the side of the truck was the logo of the U.S. Fish and Wildlife Service.

Drake McBride said, "Let me deal with this punk, Jimmy Lee."

The "punk" turned out to be a good bit older than Drake McBride, though much more physically fit. He wore a badge and carried a gun on his hip, and he introduced himself as Special Agent Conway.

" 'Special agent'?" Drake McBride smirked. "So you're, like, James Bond of the boonies?"

"And who would you be?" Conway said.

"Drake McBride. I'm the president of Red Diamond Energy."

"Right." Conway looked at Jimmy Lee Bayliss. "And you?"

"He's my project manager," Drake McBride said. "Mr. Bayliss is his name. Lemme save all of us from wastin' one more second of our precious time — there's no panthers out here, okay? *Nada.* Somebody made a big mistake."

Conway smiled politely. "We received a report from a citizen who was quite certain he saw one in this area, so we're required to check it out. But not today, gentleman. Not in this heavy fog."

Jimmy Lee Bayliss quietly exhaled in relief. Drake McBride simmered.

"Where does the boundary of your oil lease start?" Conway asked.

"Three-quarter mile down the road," Jimmy Lee Bayliss said, pointing. "There's a sign and a metal gate."

"Leave it unlocked tomorrow morning," the Fish and Wildlife agent advised. "If there's no weather, I'll be back with a couple of other officers and a tracking dog."

"Oh, great," muttered Drake McBride under his breath. "Another mutt."

"Excuse me?"

"Nuthin'."

Jimmy Lee Bayliss quickly cut in. "We'll cooperate totally, Agent Conway. Whatever you need us to do, consider it done."

"Good." The officer took off his wire-rimmed eyeglasses and wiped the condensation from the lenses. "Hardly any animal on earth is more endangered than the Florida panther — are you aware of that? There's somewhere between sixty and a hundred left, that's all, and our job is to try and save 'em from extinction. That's why we follow up on possible sightings."

"But I told you, there can't possibly be a sighting out here, because there ain't no damn panthers!" Drake McBride protested.

The officer said, "They're really quite beautiful. Ever seen a picture?"

"No, but I've seen cougars out west, shot dead and skinned where it's all proper and legal. Basically the same varmint."

Conway put on his glasses and turned his back on the president of the Red Diamond Energy Corporation. "Make sure you leave that gate unlocked," he said to Jimmy Lee Bayliss.

"Yes, sir. Can I ask who it was that called up and said they saw one of those cats around here?"

Conway walked to his truck and looked at his clipboard. "The name on the report is Hayduke," he said. "George W. Hayduke."

The name meant nothing to Jimmy Lee Bayliss or his boss, who hadn't finished a book since his junior year of college.

"He gave a GPS waypoint, too," Conway added, "so we've got a good place to start."

"Really?" Jimmy Lee Bayliss suddenly felt queasy.

Sulking, Drake McBride said, "So I guess any ol' crackpot can call up the U.S. government and say they saw a panther or a unicorn or even a UFO, and you guys put a posse together the next day. Is that how it works?"

Special Agent Conway got in his truck and rolled down the window. "Be careful in this fog," he said, and drove off.

Detective Jason Marshall had received two

unexpected phone calls that Monday morning. The first was from a man named Bernard Beanstoop III, otherwise known as Bernie the Bean, who was only the most famous and most expensive criminal defense lawyer in Tampa.

Bernie the Bean informed Jason Marshall that he'd been hired by the grandmother of Duane Scrod Jr. to represent the young man accused of arson. Bernie the Bean said he was currently working with the family to find Duane Jr. and persuade him to turn himself in. The attorney also stated that the boy was "one thousand percent innocent," and would fight all the charges pending against him.

"But he ran away from me," the detective pointed out. "That's resisting arrest."

"Extenuating circumstances," chirped Bernie the Bean. "The poor kid simply freaked. Anyway, if you should find Duane before we do, please inform him that his grandma already got him an attorney. And not just any attorney — the best!"

The conversation was not a bright spot for Jason Marshall, who'd been nursing doubts about the Black Vine Swamp case ever since visiting the hardware store where the butane torches had been sold.

No less troubling was the second phone

call of the day. It came from an eager state prosecutor who told the detective not to fret about the videotapes showing that the torches weren't purchased by Duane Scrod Jr. The fugitive teenager remained the prime suspect, the prosecutor asserted.

"The tapes don't prove that punk didn't set the fire," he added. "They just prove he didn't shop at that particular store. Heck, he could've bought the exact same brand of torch over the Internet!"

Which was probably true, the detective thought, yet still it seemed like a suspicious coincidence, given the timing of the arson.

"The only mystery in this case," the prosecutor went on, "is how a rotten apple like Scrod ever got into a private school as good as Truman. I mean, your daughter goes there, right, Jason?"

"She does," the detective said tightly.

"Well, if it were my kid, that would seriously sketch me out — guy with a rap sheet like Scrod's, walking the same halls."

"I'll let you know the minute we find him," the detective said, without much enthusiasm.

Torkelsen, the fire investigator, arrived at the sheriff's department at ten o'clock sharp. Jason Marshall took him to his office and shared his misgivings about the case.

Torkelsen listened thoughtfully, then said: "May I see the tapes?"

The detective cued up a VCR and sat down behind Torkelsen, who watched each of the two video loops, pausing repeatedly to study the features of the man popping antacid tablets at the cash register while waiting to pay for the Ultra Igniter butane torches.

"That's not the Scrod boy," Jason Marshall said.

"Obviously." The fire investigator hunched in front of the television screen, his knuckles propped beneath his chin.

"Well, what do you think?" Jason Marshall asked.

"I think our prosecutor friend is going to be extremely disappointed." Torkelsen punched the Pause button on the VCR, clicked open his briefcase, and removed a clear plastic bag, which he held up for the detective to see.

Inside the baggie was a cheap ballpoint pen stamped with the name of Red Diamond Energy.

Jason Marshall said, "I remember that pen. You found it near the flashpoint of the arson."

"That's right," said Torkelsen. "The man who lost it is the same one who later called

393

to say he'd found the boy's book bag at the scene."

The detective tightened his necktie. Smiling now, he said, "How about that? The same book bag with the butane torch hidden in the pocket."

"Yeah. How about that?" The fire investigator turned back to the TV screen, where the torch buyer's face was frozen in black and white; grainy, yet easily identified.

"His name is Jimmy Lee Bayliss," Torkelsen said. "He works for that oil company, Red Diamond."

Jason Marshall managed to appear calm and professional, although he was very excited. "So it went down like this: Bayliss goes to the hardware store and buys torch number one to start the fire with."

Torkelsen nodded. "Probably got rid of it the same day."

"But later, when he finds out that you know it was arson, he gets worried."

"More like panic-stricken."

"So he rushes out to the same store and buys another, identical torch," the detective said, "to frame the Scrod boy for the crime."

"That's how it adds up, doesn't it?" The fire investigator returned the incriminating ballpoint pen to his briefcase.

Jason Marshall stood up and checked the

back of his belt, to make sure he had the case containing his handcuffs. He said, "There's still one big piece of the puzzle missing: Why did Bayliss set fire to that swamp in the first place?"

Torkelsen popped the videotape out of the VCR. "Let's go ask him."

TWENTY-FIVE

It was like tiptoeing through clouds.

Moistened by the fog, Nick's shirt stuck to his chest. His skin felt slick, and tiny droplets of dew hung like silvery globes in his eyelashes. The swamp was bathed in a pale gray twilight; Nick could hardly believe that it was morning, and that somewhere high above hung the sun, blazing.

Smoke advanced steadily in pursuit of the mother panther, pausing now and then to point out a broken sprig, a flattened tuft of grass, or a partial paw print. With each step the searchers drew closer to the cat, yet she remained an unseen phantom, a vapor of imagination.

Was she running? Hiding in wait? Watching from the bough of an oak?

Twilly Spree had removed his lucky necklace because he feared the clicking of the dried buzzard beaks would alert the panther. He stayed at Smoke's heels, carrying his rifle by its stock, the bluish barrel pointed skyward. Marta had dropped back a couple of steps to walk with Mrs. Starch and to be near the sleeping kitten.

Nick marveled at how quietly the five of them had learned to move together through scratchy brush and sodden marsh — in fluid unison, like a centipede or the muscles of a snake. But he also knew that panthers possessed a keen sense of hearing, that a muffled cough or a slight clearing of the throat could spook the cat into flight and it might not settle down for miles.

Tracking such a wary animal required so much stealth and concentration that Nick's thoughts couldn't stray far, which was a good thing. It would have been a long, restless day at school, hour upon hour in which to worry about his father lying on the operating table at the military hospital. The cat hunt was a perfect distraction, physically and emotionally. Nick had never felt more focused, more absorbed.

He had no clue where they were, or even what direction they were heading, until the boardwalk appeared out of the mist. Smoke abruptly shrank to a crouch, and the others did the same. Twilly signaled urgently for Mrs. Starch to bring the cub to the front of the line.

Carrying her straw hat with both arms, as if it held some rare and fragile treasure, the gangly teacher moved forward with wavering, slow-motion steps. She reminded Nick of a stork sneaking up on a bug. He groped behind him for Marta's hand and tugged her close so that she could see better.

Smoke was up again, peering into the bank of fog. Twilly whispered to Mrs. Starch, and she removed the baby panther from the crown of her hat. The kitten stretched its stubby legs and yawned mightily. Then it began to squirm and writhe and thrash, the plump oversized claws raking Mrs. Starch's hands and forearms. Somehow she got the cat under control, but Nick and Marta were surprised to see so much power in such a small, cute-looking package.

Soon the kitten began to cry, which brought a fond smile to Mrs. Starch and affirming nods from Twilly and Smoke. The crying is what they hoped would draw the mother panther out of the woods, what they hoped would lead her to the cub.

But only if she heard it.

Smoke said something to Twilly, who stiffened and swung his rifle to a ready position. Nick felt Marta's breath on his neck.

"Somebody else is out here!"

"No way."

"Listen, Nick! Voices."

Smoke must have heard them, too, although Nick didn't. The only sounds that registered in his ears were the mewling of the kitten and the thump-thumping of his own heart.

When Mrs. Starch released the cub, it scampered a few yards to a small clearing and then sat down abruptly, wide-eyed and bewildered.

Twilly motioned for everyone to back away. They regrouped in a stand of young pines, where despite the fog they still had a view of Squirt — a spotted puff of fur on the ground. The little panther cried and cried, yet instinctively it knew not to move, for even a twitch might catch the attention of a hawk.

"Hurry, momma cat," Mrs. Starch murmured in an aching voice unfamiliar to Nick and Marta. This was not the same person who terrorized them in biology class.

"Did you actually see the panther?" Nick whispered to Smoke, who shook his head.

"But she's not far," he said.

"How do you know?" Marta asked.

"There was fresh pee on a resurrection fern."

"Lovely."

Nick asked Smoke if he, like Marta, had heard voices.

"Yeah, bro, I did," he said apprehensively.

Twilly wasn't watching the kitten; he was scanning the trees and thickets, the gun pulled tight against his chest. The cub's cries sounded pitiful and small in the great swamp, like squeaks from a stuffed nursery toy.

"Don't give up, little guy," Mrs. Starch said. She was clutching her straw hat so fiercely it had crumpled in her fists.

Marta shut her eyes. Nick figured she was saying a prayer for the baby cat; her family was very religious, and Marta never missed church on Sundays. Nick thought: *A prayer couldn't hurt.*

The seconds ticked by with agonizing slowness, and the sounds from the cub became weaker. The cat was getting tired of crying.

"Not good," Smoke said.

Twilly agreed. "Let's give it five more minutes."

The kitten must have heard their whispers, for it pricked its ears and turned its head toward their hiding place among the pines.

Mrs. Starch said, "This is breaking my heart."

From deep in the fog arose a high-pitched

400

scream, piercing and raw, like something from a slasher movie. Twilly froze, Mrs. Starch gasped, and Marta dug her fingernails into Nick's shoulder.

"Panther!" Smoke said triumphantly.

Then came the gunshots.

Long after Special Agent Conway's truck disappeared into the mist, Drake McBride and Jimmy Lee Bayliss paced back and forth on the dirt road. They were having an uncomfortable conversation about the future of the Section 22 oil scam.

"We're doomed," Drake McBride stated bitterly. "We're toast."

"Maybe not. Remember, it's the guv'ment," said Jimmy Lee Bayliss. "Half of everything they do is half-assed."

"No, you heard the man. They're gonna have rangers trompin' all over this swamp — plus a dog, too, probably a serious dog. They're bound to find our drill site, Jimmy Lee, and then we are *doomed!*"

Jimmy Lee Bayliss feared that, for once, his boss was right. The officers searching for the panther probably would find the pirate well first, and then Red Diamond Energy would be in deep trouble for trying to steal petroleum from land belonging to the good citizens of Florida.

"You got nuthin' else to say? That's it?" Drake McBride spluttered.

"I'm just thinkin'," Jimmy Lee Bayliss said.

"Thinkin' about what — which of us gets the top bunk in our prison cell?"

Actually, Jimmy Lee Bayliss was thinking about Mexico. On TV it looked like a warm and friendly place to live, where nobody asked too many questions. There had to be direct flights from Tampa, or maybe Orlando. The question was, had he left his passport back in Texas?

Drake McBride rubbed his sore ribs and griped about all the rotten luck that had befallen him. "I'd give anything to know who called the feds about that cat. Had to be the same joker's been messin' with Melton."

"No doubt," said Jimmy Lee Bayliss. His mind flashed back to the spectacle of all those little pink flags, mischievously rearranged to tell the Red Diamond helicopter to S-C-A-T. Jimmy Lee Bayliss hadn't shared that story with his boss, and he saw no reason to do so now.

"What'm I supposed to tell my old man?" Drake McBride lamented.

"Tell him to get you a lawyer."

"Oh, that's real funny."

Jimmy Lee Bayliss said, "I'm not jokin'."

Drake McBride kicked at a rock. "It just ain't fair."

"I told you this whole thing was a bad idea. I warned you, but you wouldn't listen," Jimmy Lee Bayliss groused.

"Is that right? Well, pardner, I recall your squinty li'l eyes lightin' up like the Fourth of July when you heard how many jillions of dollars we could make off this operation."

Jimmy Lee Bayliss leaned against the wet bumper of the truck and mulled the situation. Removing all of Red Diamond's pipes and equipment from Section 22 would take several days, and then the pit would have to be filled. There simply wasn't enough time. Reaching into the pockets of his pants, Jimmy Lee Bayliss was dismayed to discover that he was out of Tums again.

"Hey, we could always start another fire," Drake McBride suggested, "to stall the game wardens."

"Are you serious?"

"I'm talkin' about a big one this time. A real monster."

"No."

"A fire that would burn for weeks! We'll keep the flames a couple hundred yards downwind from the drill site, then sneak in Melton and the boys to clear out our gear

403

and bury the pit. Presto, we're out of the woods!" Drake McBride paused. "How come you're lookin' at me that way?"

"Because you just may be the biggest bonehead I ever met."

"What!"

"You heard me." In his own mind, Jimmy Lee Bayliss was no longer employed by Red Diamond Energy, and therefore he felt free to insult Drake McBride. Never again would he address this numskull as "sir."

"You want another wildfire, do it yourself," he hissed at his ex-boss.

Red as a tomato, Drake McBride balled his fists and stepped toward Jimmy Lee Bayliss, who rose up and prepared to re-fracture Drake McBride's ribs, if necessary.

The men stood inches apart, glowering at one another, when a blood-curdling yowl cut through the fog. It sounded almost human; a cry someone might make after falling into boiling water.

Jimmy Lee Bayliss felt the hair rise on the back of his neck. Drake McBride frantically reached into the bed of the pickup truck and grabbed the rifle, which he waggled recklessly at the curtain of haze.

"Gimme my gun," Jimmy Lee Bayliss said.

"Back off!" Drake McBride's eyes were gleaming. "That was a panther," he whispered hoarsely.

"Let's get outta here."

"No, it's our only chance."

"Don't make me hurt you," said Jimmy Lee Bayliss.

"We can be free of this mess right now — with one shot!"

With the rifle thrust forward, Drake McBride began creeping down the dirt road in the direction of the scream. Jimmy Lee Bayliss followed closely, planning to overpower his brainless ex-boss, snatch the gun, and flee the Black Vine Swamp forever. Surely an experienced oilman could find a decent job in Mexico.

"You see that?" Drake McBride stiffened, slowing his pace.

"What?"

"Somethin' moved up ahead of us, I swear."

Jimmy Lee Bayliss said, "I can't see nuthin'."

But Drake McBride was not imagining ghosts.

The fog parted and a tawny shape materialized, sleek and low-slung. It was poised on muscled haunches barely ten yards away, its pale gold eyes locked on the two startled men. The cat remained motionless except for a twitch of its long, kinked tail.

Jimmy Lee Bayliss held his breath. Never had he seen such an imperial predator up close, yet he was more amazed than afraid. The presence of the rare panther was so hypnotic that Jimmy Lee Bayliss failed to notice Drake McBride raising the rifle.

Instantly a palmetto exploded next to the cat, which snarled and made two great soaring leaps into the mist. Half-crazed with fear and fury, Drake McBride fired two more rounds.

Jimmy Lee Bayliss lunged for the gun, but Drake McBride jerked away, aiming blindly into the shrouded trees. By the time Jimmy Lee Bayliss was able to tackle him, Drake McBride had run out of bullets. A heavy, electric silence settled upon the swamp.

Twisting the rifle from his ex-boss's hands, Jimmy Lee Bayliss said, "I oughta leave you out here to rot."

"Did I hit the danged thing?" Drake McBride asked.

"You'd better hope not."

"What — you gonna turn me in? I don't think so," Drake McBride said with a smirk. "Now stop all this nonsense and help me up, pardner."

Both of them jumped at the sound of a metallic click, which was followed by a flat voice: "Drop the weapon and stand slowly with your hands over your head. I won't say it twice."

Two men stepped out of the fog. One wore a coat and tie, and he was pointing a cocked revolver at Jimmy Lee Bayliss. The other was dressed in a dark blue jumpsuit bearing the words "Collier County Fire Department." With despair, Jimmy Lee Bayliss recognized the second man immediately — it was Torkelsen, the arson investigator.

He said, "Mr. Bayliss, I would strongly advise you to do what Detective Marshall says."

Jimmy Lee Bayliss obediently stood up, dropping the rifle as if it were a hot poker. As he raised his hands, he kicked Drake McBride in the butt and growled, "You happy now, bozo?"

Drake McBride rose slowly, clutching his sides. If he'd been hoping for sympathy from the lawmen, he was disappointed.

"You're both under arrest," announced Detective Marshall.

"Hold on," Jimmy Lee Bayliss said. "I wanna make a deal."

Drake McBride glared at him. "I don't believe this — you're gonna try and hang it all on me?"

"With pleasure."

"Gentlemen, please," Torkelsen interjected. "Give Detective Marshall your full attention."

"No, sir! No, sir!" brayed Drake McBride, and he ran off crashing through the swamp.

The arson investigator and the detective traded shrugs, and they made no move to chase after the president of the Red Diamond Energy Corporation.

"Is he really that stupid?" Torkelsen asked.

"Times ten," said Jimmy Lee Bayliss, and held out his wrists for Jason Marshall to handcuff.

TWENTY-SIX

After the first gunshot, they dove to the ground and pressed themselves flat. Then came two other shots, followed shortly by more. Nick was sure he heard one of the bullets zing off a nearby tree.

When the firing stopped, Twilly got up pointing his own rifle. He was breathing hard, listening for human footfalls.

Smoke was the next to stand; then Nick and Marta, who was trembling badly.

"Everybody okay?" Twilly asked.

The kids nodded.

But everybody was not okay. Mrs. Starch was still down. Her face was pale and her eyes looked glassy, and a crimson stain was blooming on the side of her canvas trousers.

"Oh no," said Twilly. He put down the rifle and knelt beside her. Nick and Smoke helped turn her over while Marta stood back, sobbing softly.

Twilly hurriedly cut away the bloody pants leg to examine the bullet wound, which was serious. Nick felt light-headed and slightly sick. "She needs a doctor," he said.

"Is she gonna die?" Marta called tearfully.

Mrs. Starch lifted her head. "No, dear, I am *not* going to die."

Her voice was weak but firm.

"We're taking you to the hospital," Twilly said.

There was no debate, no argument. Because Mrs. Starch was a large person, Twilly and Duane Scrod Jr., the two strongest in the group, would attempt to carry her back to the car. It would be a long, difficult haul through the marsh and hammocks.

Without asking, Twilly tore a strip of fabric from Smoke's shirt to make a pressure bandage. "We don't have much time. You're bleeding like crazy."

"I'm aware of that," Mrs. Starch said. "Where's the kitten?"

At that very moment, something swift and heavy burst from a nearby thicket — a tan, snarling streak that passed within arm's reach of the fallen teacher and her helpers before bounding to the top of a craggy dead pine.

"It's her," Smoke said. He gazed up with pure awe at the mother panther, which was

410

panting hotly and still spooked from the gunfire.

"Where's the kitten?" Mrs. Starch whispered again.

Nick scanned the clearing and spotted the cub, a frightened lump huddled on a bed of pine straw.

"He's fine," Nick assured Mrs. Starch.

"Can you handle him? It's all up to you now," she said. "You and Marta."

"We can do it."

With grim efficiency, Twilly worked on Mrs. Starch's leg to stanch the bleeding. Smoke kept his eyes glued on the panther in the tree, while Nick and Marta watched the kitten on the ground. The two cats, mother and baby, remained unaware of each other.

After a few minutes, Twilly hoisted Mrs. Starch to her feet and instructed her how to hold on. Smoke got on the other side, and together he and Twilly formed a human crutch.

"If you hear somebody coming," Twilly said to Nick and Marta, "take off running. If you can't get away, then use that." He nodded toward his rifle, leaning against a stump.

Nick had never fired a real gun; his father didn't own one, though he'd become an expert marksman in the National Guard.

Marta said, "I've shot a .22 before. My cousins in Miami took me to a target range."

"This is different," Smoke told her. "Way different."

With his free hand, Twilly pulled the vulture-beak necklace from his pocket and tossed it to Marta. "You'll need all the mojo you can get," he said with a tight smile.

Mrs. Starch was obviously in pain, and fading. "Do your best," she told Nick and Marta, and then her eyelids began to flutter.

Twilly pulled Nick aside and said: "I'll be back as soon as I can. Don't get yourselves lost."

"We'll be right here."

Then, without another word, Twilly and Smoke set off grimly across the foggy flatlands. Mrs. Starch was propped limply between them, her feet dragging, an arm around each of their shoulders. Smoke glanced back only once, with an anxious expression, and Nick waved.

Marta put on Twilly's strange necklace and said, "You ready?" The fear was completely gone from her voice.

"Let's do it," said Nick.

The cub was still shaking from the noise of the gunfire when Nick scooped him up.

There was no clawing or biting; little Squirt seemed almost relieved to be held, even by an unknown human.

With the kitten curled against his chest, Nick stood beneath the tall dead pine, trying to visualize the climb. He wanted to put the cub as close as possible to the mother cat, who loomed only as a shadow, high in the gnarled boughs.

"What if it's the wrong panther?" Marta asked.

"No, Smoke said it's her."

"But what if he made a mistake?"

"He wouldn't," Nick said. "And he didn't."

"That's a nasty old tree. Don't break your neck."

"Thanks for the pep talk."

Nick began slowly, using only his right hand to pull himself upward from one bare, brittle branch to the next. Hardly stirring, the kitten was nuzzled in the crook of his other arm.

Purposely Nick didn't look up at the powerful cat who was watching every step of his ascent, but occasionally he glanced downward where Marta stood guard at the base of the tree. Although it was weird seeing his young friend holding Twilly's rifle, Nick felt unaccountably secure. For no

413

particular reason, he was confident that Marta would know how to handle the gun if necessary.

And she did.

He was halfway up the dead pine, at least thirty feet off the ground, when he heard her shout, "Stop, or I'll shoot! Stop right there!"

Alarmed, Nick craned his neck to see what was happening below. As he shifted his weight, the branch beneath him snapped off and he began dropping straight down, feet-first, as if he were in a runaway elevator.

It all happened in a dizzying wisp of a second. Nick's right sleeve snagged on something — another jagged branch — and he heard a sickening crack. A bolt of blinding pain shot from his wrist to the core of his brain, then a wave of frozen blackness crashed over him.

He experienced the sensation of twirling slowly in midair, like a circus acrobat. When he opened his eyes, he realized that he was dangling from a broken arm, and that very soon he would pass out. His chest was on fire from hot stinging needles — it was the panther cub, digging its claws into Nick's skin to hang on.

"He ran away! He's gone!" Marta crowed triumphantly from beneath the tree.

414

"Who?" Nick rasped.

"Some guy wrapped in bandages. I scared him off!"

Then she looked up into the tree and saw Nick swinging by his shirt sleeve. "What in the world are you doing?"

"What does it look like?" he moaned.

"You're gonna fall and kill yourself!"

The possibility had already occurred to Nick. Reaching up with his good arm — the left arm, the same arm he'd been training with and building up for weeks — he grabbed the branch from which he was dangling . . .

And began pulling himself up.

Pulling with all his strength.

Pulling in spite of the worst pain he'd ever felt, or had ever imagined feeling.

Pulling even with a terrified wild panther cub attached like a cactus to his flesh, yowling and spitting in his face.

Pulling and pulling until he'd completed your basic one-handed chin-up, no problem.

Nick suspended himself in this grueling pose long enough to unsnag his sleeve with his teeth. His damaged arm flopped uselessly to his side; the elbow was bent at a very peculiar angle.

An instant later, by some small miracle, his feet found a toehold for support. It was a deserted woodpecker nest, a baseball-sized hole in a weathered knob of the tree.

Marta called, "I'm climbing up!"

"No!" Nick said.

Because the mother panther was climbing down.

Nick could see her silhouetted against the fog, moving closer. The animal easily weighed more than a hundred pounds, yet she darted from limb to limb as if she were light as a sparrow.

There was nothing for Nick to do but catch his breath and wait for the cub's cries to draw the big cat nearer. He supposed he should've been scared, but instead he felt oddly at ease.

The panther was elegant and agile and ghostly, mesmerizing to watch. Although Nick had seen many panther photographs in books and magazines, he found himself in a state of dreamy amazement. The scorching pain in his fractured arm had all but disappeared, causing him to wonder if he was slipping into shock.

Soon the mother cat was only a few yards away, coiled on a heavy Y-shaped branch directly above Nick's head. Her ears flattened, her nose quivered, and her bright eyes fixed with fierce intensity on the noisy bundle that had tacked itself to the front of

Nick's shirt. He knew the panther must be wondering why there was only one cub crying, wondering what had happened to her other one.

Nick heard the deep rolling prelude of a growl that couldn't possibly be coming from the pint-sized kitten, and he knew the time had come.

Even with both shoes wedged in the woodpecker hole, he teetered and swayed as he struggled to unfasten the frightened baby from his chest. The little cat was now squalling loudly and with evident fright; Nick worried that the mother would soon pounce upon him in defense of her offspring.

Marta must have had the same concern, for she'd braced herself against the tree to steady Twilly's rifle, which she was pointing squarely at the adult cat.

Nick raised his eyes to the big panther and very gently said, "It's all right. I'm not gonna hurt your little guy."

The panther blinked, and her ears perked. The cub let go of Nick's shirt, and ever-so-carefully he placed it on the trunk of the tree. Its hooked claws dug into the crispy bark and, with a mighty yelp, the kitten attempted to climb.

Immediately the adult panther raised up, and a distinctly softer rumble came from her throat.

Nick knew what had to be done now. As long as he remained in the tree, the mother cat would likely hold her distance from the baby. It was easy to envision the inexperienced kitten losing its grip and falling before it reached the Y-shaped branch.

So Nick looked down and picked out a landing area.

"Don't do it!" Marta shouted.

"Stand clear," he said, and with his good, strong left arm he pushed himself away from the trunk of the tree. This time, luckily, he struck no branches on the way down.

He landed on his back, in a mound of pine straw. The last thing he saw before blacking out was the panther, outstretched in mid-leap, crossing to another tree.

She was toting her cub by the scruff of its neck.

Drake McBride tried to make up for all the rotten things he'd said about Horace.

"You're a good dog!" he shouted down from the cypress tree.

But Horace didn't budge. Horace continued to bark and howl. Flecks of foamy spittle flew from the bloodhound's large jaws.

Drake McBride was afraid to climb down

because Horace looked positively crazed and ferocious — nothing like the lazy mutt that the dog handler had brought to his hotel suite.

Horace was totally wired. Horace wasn't budging from the base of the cypress tree, up which he had chased the president of the Red Diamond Energy Corporation.

It was the second jarring interruption of Drake McBride's escape. The first had occurred when he'd stumbled into a clearing and come face to face with a skinny Cuban girl holding a seriously large rifle. She had vowed to shoot if he took another step, and she'd seemed serious about it.

So he had turned and fled, and kept on running until the bloodhound caught his scent and treed him like a dumb possum. "Good boy!" hollered Drake McBride for the eighteenth time.

"Ooowwwwwooooooooooo!" replied Horace.

This went on for two hours until, suddenly, the dog wheeled around, fell silent, and began wagging its tail. Momentarily Horace was joined at the foot of the tree by a shirtless man wearing a knit ski beanie, wraparound shades, and an ammunition belt.

Drake McBride figured the man was a

poacher, not that he cared.

"Help me, bro!" he begged.

"Come on down from there," the stranger said.

"What about the dog?"

"Hurry up. I don't have all day."

Timidly, Drake McBride made his way to the ground. He was relieved to see that the bloodhound was now preoccupied with a bag of hamburgers.

"I can't believe I paid five grand for that wacko dog," Drake McBride said to the stranger, " 'cause they said he got eaten by a panther. I wish he had."

"You want him back?"

"After he chased me up a tree? I don't think so."

The man seemed amused. "I guess Horace got bored and chewed through his rope."

Drake McBride was rattled. "How do you know his name?"

"Horace and I go way back. Who are you?"

"I'm Drake W. McBride."

"Well, how about that for luck."

Drake McBride stuck out his right hand. The stranger didn't shake it, though he was smiling broadly.

"You know who I am?" Drake McBride

asked with surprise, and a creeping sense of dread.

The man said, "Yup. You're the boss of the two-bit oil company that's drilling an illegal well in this state wildlife preserve. Or should I say, *was* drilling."

Drake McBride dejectedly wondered how much worse his day could possibly get.

"And who are you?" he asked in a hollow voice.

"I'm the one who called the Fish and Wildlife agents about the panther and glued your man Melton to a tree and sprayed him orange and gutted his truck and ripped off that load of pipes. I'm the one who's gonna shut you down." The stranger took out a cell phone and dialed a number. "The fog's lifting. Get the chopper up and come out here right away," he instructed someone on the other end.

Drake McBride considered making a dash for freedom, but knew he would only get himself more lost than he already was. Besides, it would be easy for the athletic-looking stranger to outrun a chunky, out-of-shape guy with fractured ribs.

"I'll give you five thousand dollars to forget about all this and let me go," Drake McBride said.

The stranger laughed so sharply that Horace looked up from the mulched remains of his Quarter Pounders.

"You remind me of my old man," the man said to Drake McBride.

"That doesn't sound like a compliment."

"It's not."

"Then how about ten thousand?"

The stranger grew serious and swatted a fly on his neck. "Mr. McBride, I'll let you go for free," he said, "but there's not enough money in the world to make me forget what you did here."

"Twenty thousand, if I can hitch a ride back to town on your helicopter. Twenty thousand, cash!"

"Sorry, man. The chopper's full."

"Now, wait —"

"Come on, Horace." The stranger jogged off into the Black Vine Swamp, the blood-hound loping at his heels.

"Hey, where are you going?" Drake McBride shouted after him. "What about me? How do I get out of here?"

EPILOGUE

More than a month after Mrs. Starch vanished, her third-period biology students filed anxiously into the classroom. Their expressions reflected a mix of excitement and uncertainty, for it was rumored that the most feared (and surely the most famous) teacher at the Truman School would be returning for the first time since the fire at the Black Vine Swamp.

By now all the kids knew what had happened — Nick and Marta had told the panther story about a hundred times.

Nick's account of his daring climb to meet the big cat ended with him jumping from the tree and passing out. He also vaguely recalled waking up in a helicopter and seeing a hound dog, of all things, drooling on his shoes.

Marta's necklace of vulture beaks was a big hit at school. Her version of the panther adventure recounted how she'd stood guard with a high-powered rifle, warding off a crazed intruder while Nick was high in the branches, reuniting the cub with its mother. She also provided vivid details of the helicopter rescue, including a hairy landing on the hospital's roof.

It was a good story, no matter who told it.

When the school bell rang, Dr. Dressler walked into the classroom. He looked more crisp and unflappable than usual, with good reason. The board of trustees had just given him a new five-year contract to remain as headmaster of Truman. They had sweetened the deal with a generous raise, based on a wave of positive publicity that the school had recently received.

Bunny Starch and three of her students had saved the life of a rare panther cub, and in the process had helped expose a crooked oil-drilling operation in the Big Cypress Preserve. It was huge news all over Florida, and was even featured by Anderson Cooper on CNN.

As a result, the Truman School was being flooded with enrollment applications and, more importantly, donation checks. While Dr. Dressler had nothing to do with the heroics of Mrs. Starch and her pupils, he was pleased to bask at the edge of the limelight.

"I have two brief announcements," he said to the biology class. "First, the suspension of Duane Scrod Jr. is hereby suspended. I am proud and delighted to welcome him back to Truman."

The headmaster turned toward the open door and motioned with two fingers. As soon as Smoke entered the room, everybody began to applaud except Nick, whose right arm was still encased in plaster from his fingers to his shoulder. Instead of clapping, Nick slapped the palm of his left hand against the top of his desk.

Smoke seemed mortified at the attention, and he hustled to seat himself as fast as possible.

Marta passed a note to Nick: *He looks thinner!*

Nick noticed it, too. Smoke had spent the past fourteen days in the county juvenile hall, which was not famous for serving hearty and nutritious meals.

His classmates had been outraged that Smoke was locked up, after all the good he'd done. Without his keen tracking skills, the missing mother panther might not have been found. And without his muscles, Mrs. Starch might never have made it alive to the emergency room after being shot.

Although the arson case against Smoke

425

was dropped — a Texas oilman named Jimmy Lee Bayliss confessed to the crime — the state prosecutor had insisted on punishing the boy for fleeing from the police. At the time, Smoke had been on probation for the two arsons he'd committed when he was younger.

Even Jason Marshall thought two weeks behind bars was too harsh, considering the circumstances. Libby had persuaded her father to make a call on Duane Jr.'s behalf, but the prosecutor wouldn't budge.

So Smoke had served his time without complaint, a model inmate.

"My second announcement deals with another rumor flying around campus," Dr. Dressler said. "This one happens to be true: Today there will be no substitute biology teacher. Mrs. Starch, do you need some assistance?"

A familiar icy voice from the hallway: "I certainly do *not*."

She clomped briskly and with purpose into the classroom. The crutches didn't make her look frail and wobbly; in fact, she seemed taller and more imposing than ever.

Her bleached hair was piled into an exceptionally steep slope, and the violet shadow on her eyelids appeared to have been applied with an industrial paint roller. The anvil-shaped scar on her chin showed up like a fresh bruise against the hospital paleness of her skin.

Yet the students responded to her arrival in a spontaneous and unexpected way: they all rose from their desks, cheering and whistling and clapping. Dr. Dressler, to his own mild surprise, joined in.

For once, Mrs. Starch was speechless.

She crutched to her desk and fiercely began organizing her teaching materials. It looked to Nick as if she was trying not to cry.

Eventually the students settled down, and Dr. Dressler smoothly excused himself. After an awkward silence, Mrs. Starch cleared her throat and said, "Good morning, people. Please open your books — we have lots of catching up to do."

Graham Carson's arm shot up. Naturally, Mrs. Starch ignored him. Nick smiled and thought: *Some things never change.*

"Who's prepared to tell me about Watson and Crick's model for DNA structure?" Mrs. Starch asked. The usual squirming silence followed. "Anybody bother to read Chapter 11?" she said. "If you're having trouble finding it, try looking between Chapter 10 and Chapter 12."

Graham alone waved his hand. Mrs.

Starch pivoted toward Mickey Maris and said, "Well . . . ?"

Mickey Maris swallowed and began pawing frantically through his textbook. "Watson's crickets?" he asked.

"It's Watson and *Crick*," Mrs. Starch said testily.

"Please?" Graham Carson beseeched from across the room. "Please, Mrs. Starch?"

She turned back and sighed in surrender. "All right, Graham, let's get this over with."

He popped to his feet and composed himself. "Watson and Crick were two scientists who came up with a model of DNA called the double helix. It shows two strands of nucleotides twisting around each other. The outside of the helix is made up of sugar phosphates and the inside is nitrogen bases."

The other students sat stunned and gaping. Mrs. Starch herself rocked back slightly on her crutches.

"Well done, Graham," she managed to say. "This is an historic day."

Nick snuck a peek at Marta, who didn't appear even slightly nauseated, as she often was in Mrs. Starch's class. Marta smiled back and whispered, "I memorized the whole chapter, too."

Having recovered from the shock of Graham's correct answer, Mrs. Starch told him he could sit down.

"But I've got a question. A really important one," Graham said.

"It had better be."

"How are you?"

"What?"

"I mean, are you gonna be okay?" Graham asked. "Everybody's been worried."

Mrs. Starch seemed overwhelmed. Her eyes flickered first to Nick and Marta, and then over to Duane Scrod Jr.

After a moment of fluster, she said, "Thank you for your concern, Graham. I'm going to be fine."

She plucked a yellow Ticonderoga No. 2 pencil from the cup on her desk and tapped the eraser against her left hip.

"The bullet entered right here, below the joint," she said, "and passed all the way through my leg. Luckily, it missed the femoral artery, though barely."

With a skeptical eye she scanned the rapt faces of her students. "I don't suppose anybody besides Libby Marshall can describe the role of the femoral artery in the human circulatory system."

Libby's cheeks flushed. Mrs. Starch said, "Relax, young lady. There's no shame in being smart."

Because of her injury, Mrs. Starch didn't

cover as much territory as when she paced before. However, as always, she stayed in motion.

"Before we discuss the features of the double helix," she said, moving down the center aisle, "I have one small piece of unfinished business."

She stopped at Smoke's desk and handed some papers to him. He examined them closely, his brow knitted.

"That's your acne essay," Mrs. Starch said.

"Right." He brushed a shock of black hair away from his forehead.

She said, "The title is quite clever: 'The Curse of the Persistent Pimple.' A nice touch of alliteration."

"Thanks," Smoke murmured warily.

"I knew you had a sense of humor, Duane. Didn't I tell the whole class? A wicked sense of humor."

He looked up at her. "But it says here I got an A-minus."

Mrs. Starch nodded. "Correct. If you hadn't misspelled 'endocrine,' I would've given you an A."

Marta whistled under her breath. Mrs. Starch was notoriously stingy with A's.

Smoke said, "But Dr. Waxmo gave me a D-plus."

"That's because Dr. Waxmo is hopeless,"

said Mrs. Starch. "A dim bulb, if I may be so frank."

The cruel red slashes from Wendell Waxmo's pen were as vivid as ketchup stains all over Smoke's essay. So, too, was the supersized A– that Mrs. Starch had scrawled on the top page to block out the substitute teacher's grade.

"I never got an A before," Smoke said. "This isn't some kinda joke, is it?"

Nick hoped it wasn't. He hoped Mrs. Starch wasn't messing with the kid, not after he'd helped Twilly lug her out of the boonies and rush her to a hospital so she wouldn't bleed to death.

Balancing on her crutches, Mrs. Starch said, "Duane, I don't joke about academic matters. Not ever."

"Do I still have to read it aloud?"

"Not unless you want to."

"Nope," Smoke said.

"You wrote a solid, well-researched paper. I learned a few things about pimples that I never knew before." Mrs. Starch reached over and waggled the tip of her yellow Ticonderoga at the A– she'd marked on the essay. "You earned this," she told Duane Scrod Jr.

"I guess," he said. Then he casually chomped the pencil in half, chewed up the splinters along with the graphite, and downed the entire mouthful with a crunchy gulp.

The classroom fell quiet as a tomb; nobody could believe what they'd just seen. Nick was vaguely aware that his own jaw was hanging open. From the corner of one eye, he noticed Marta clutching her head in gloom.

Mrs. Starch narrowed her eyes and ominously studied the moist stump of wood in her fingers. Then, slowly, she broke into a rare grin.

"You got me that time, Duane."

"Totally," he said, returning the smile.

That same morning, Jimmy Lee Bayliss posted bail at the Collier County Jail. A female guard named Waters escorted him from his cell to the front desk to collect his belongings.

"Did he turn up yet?" Jimmy Lee Bayliss asked.

He was referring to his ex-boss, Drake McBride, who'd been missing in the Big Cypress since the day he'd run off into the fog. In the meantime, to avoid a long prison hitch, Jimmy Lee Bayliss had agreed to plead guilty to setting the illegal fire in the Black Vine Swamp. He'd also promised to testify against Drake McBride, who faced a pile of serious charges, including the attempted killing of an endangered Florida panther.

"Funny you should ask," Officer Waters said to Jimmy Lee Bayliss. "Mr. McBride turned up yesterday at a fancy hotel in Miami Beach. He'd grown a goatee and shaved his head and was using a fake name."

Jimmy Lee Bayliss was astonished that the moron even made it out of the wilderness, considering his lack of survival skills and lame sense of direction. The jail guard said Drake McBride had lost twenty-two pounds while hiking in circles through the Black Vine Swamp. Eventually he'd stumbled out on Route 29, where a sympathetic trucker had picked him up.

"They busted him while he was getting a massage," Officer Waters said.

"How'd they know where he was hiding out?" Jimmy Lee Bayliss asked.

"His own father turned him in."

"Beautiful."

"Apparently Mr. McBride had called up begging for money. His dad got so ticked off that he phoned the police and gave them the address of the hotel. The room number, too."

Jimmy Lee Bayliss said, "Couldn't happen

to a sweeter guy. Is my lawyer here?"

"He's waiting outside," said Officer Waters.

She handed Jimmy Lee Bayliss a paper bag containing his wristwatch, wallet, cell phone, and a crumpled empty wrapper for Tums stomach tablets. He thanked her and proceeded to the meshed steel door that led to the outside world.

The guard said, "Before you go, Mr. Bayliss, there's something else you should know. My son was one of the students in the swamp that day you started the fire. He was also out there when your pal went ballistic with that rifle."

Jimmy Lee Bayliss realized he was a captive audience, literally. Officer Waters held the keys to the jail door, and she seemed in no rush to open it.

"I'm real sorry, ma'am. I hope your boy wasn't hurt," he said. "But please believe me, Drake McBride was never my 'pal.' "

"Man up, Mr. Bayliss. You guys were in on the oil scam together. Everything that happened out there was your fault as much as his."

She was right, and Jimmy Lee Bayliss didn't have the nerve to argue.

"I'm gonna try to make up for it," he said dismally.

"You were greedy."

"Yes, ma'am, that's true enough."

"And reckless," she added.

"I know." Jimmy Lee Bayliss gazed longingly at the locked exit door. Officer Waters stepped closer and poked him in the chest.

"My son fractured his arm out there," she said.

"Geez, how many different ways can I say I'm sorry?" Jimmy Lee Bayliss felt nervous and trapped. Up until now, the female guard had always treated him decently.

She said, "When you go to court, Mr. Bayliss, you'd better get up on that witness stand and give the truth. That means telling the judge everything you did, and everything you know."

"Sure. Of course."

"You made a deal. Keep it."

"I aim to," Jimmy Lee Bayliss insisted.

"And don't get any clever ideas." Officer Waters produced a stack of glossy travel brochures from Mexico. Jimmy Lee Bayliss paled.

"I found these under the mattress in your cell," she said.

Jimmy Lee Bayliss managed a shrug. "A man can dream, can't he?"

"Not when a judge is holding his passport, he can't. Goodbye, Mr. Bayliss."

Nick Waters' mother unlocked the heavy steel door, and Jimmy Lee Bayliss walked out of jail with no bounce in his step.

The lawyer, whom he'd met only over the phone, was waiting in the lobby. He wore a black double-breasted suit and carried a briefcase made from a dead crocodile. His name was Bernard Beanstoop III.

"But everyone calls me Bernie the Bean," he said brightly.

Jimmy Lee Bayliss shook the lawyer's hand and said, "Pleasure to meet you, Bernie."

But he didn't really mean it.

Millicent Winship banged on the screen door with as much force as she could summon from her seventy-seven-year-old, ninety-two-pound body. She was determined to be heard over the Mahler symphony that was blaring from her son-in-law's house.

Finally she stalked down the steps and picked up a rusty crowbar that was lying in the cluttered yard. Her chauffeur knew better than to interfere as Mrs. Winship calmly walked up to a window and shattered it with one swing.

The music stopped immediately and Duane Scrod Sr. appeared on the porch, the macaw screeching hysterically on his shoulder.

"Millie, you're out of your mind!" he yelled.

"Kindly tell your parrot to hush up."

"Don't you touch Nadine!"

"Help!" cried the bird. *Au secours! Hilfe!*

A brown, floppy-eared head poked sleepily out of the frame of the broken window, startling Mrs. Winship.

"Somebody gave Junior a bloodhound," Duane Scrod Sr. explained unhappily. "His name is Horace."

Mrs. Winship set the crowbar down against the house. She said, "We had a luncheon engagement at noon sharp. It's now half past one."

Duane Scrod Sr. slapped himself on the side of the head and said, "Damn."

Mrs. Winship stroked the hound dog's furrowed forehead. "You know how I feel about rudeness, Duane."

"I got mixed up — I thought our lunch was tomorrow."

"You also know how I feel about carelessness."

"Sorry, Millie."

The macaw squawked and flared its wings as if it were about to make a dive at Mrs. Winship. She glowered at the bird and said,

437

"Don't even *think* about it, Nadine."

Duane Scrod Sr. hustled his noisy pet into its cage. Then he threw on a clean shirt and ran a comb through his hair.

Mrs. Winship had made reservations at a restaurant near the Naples Pier. She chose a table on the patio, where they could see the gulls and listen to the waves on the beach. Duane Scrod Sr. was too nervous to enjoy the sunny setting.

"I'll pay you back," he blurted at his mother-in-law.

"For what?"

"Hiring that lawyer for Junior. I know he didn't come cheap."

Mrs. Winship shook her head and speared a shrimp from her salad. "The man thinks he's Perry Mason, but he sure lost interest in D.J. once the arson charges were dropped. Two whole weeks in juvenile detention? Let's just say Mr. Beanstoop and I have negotiated a steep reduction in his fee."

"Who's Perry Mason?" Duane Sr. asked.

"Oh, never mind."

"I still want to pay you back."

"You take care of the broken window and we'll call it even."

"But I've got a job now, Millie. I'll have money coming in."

Her fork halted in midair, carrying another

438

impaled shrimp. "What kind of a job?" she asked.

"Piano teacher. I already have three kids signed up for weekly lessons."

Mrs. Winship smiled. "That's excellent."

"I won't get rich," Duane Scrod Sr. said, "but it's good work. I'm liking it."

"You've always had talent. That wasn't the problem."

"Guess what else? I got my wheels again — Smithers Chevrolet put a new transmission in the Tahoe! They finally gave up, Millie. I won!"

"Congratulations," Mrs. Winship said.

"They're gonna repaint it, too."

"As they should."

Mrs. Winship didn't mention her recent phone conversation with Randolph Smithers. As she'd suspected, the car dealer had seen the newspaper stories and TV reports about the panther rescue, and he was aware of the important role played by young Duane Scrod Jr.

Mrs. Winship had told Randolph Smithers that her grandson hadn't yet given any press interviews, but that if he did, he would certainly be asked about his father.

The father who had no car, no life, no future — all because the vehicle he'd purchased in good faith from Smithers Chevrolet had blown a transmission.

Randolph Smithers had quickly agreed with Mrs. Winship that it was time to let bygones be bygones, even though Duane Scrod Sr. had burned down the dealership. Smithers said he'd repair the Tahoe on the condition that the Scrods would speak only kindly of his auto business or, better yet, would not mention it at all.

"Junior went back to school today," Duane Sr. said, finally taking a chomp of his fried grouper sandwich.

"How's his attitude?" Mrs. Winship asked.

"Anything beats sitting in jail. I bought him a new book bag."

"I'm impressed, Duane. Seriously."

"And a waterproof tent for his camping trips. I intend to do better by that boy, Millie, I swear."

Mrs. Winship said, "He doesn't need more stuff. He needs a father."

"You're right. That's what I meant."

"Duane, do you really want to pay me back? Then be a dad to your son." Mrs. Winship daintily devoured the last pink shrimp on her plate. She knew what the next topic of conversation would be.

"How's Whitney?" asked Duane Scrod Sr.

"Not happy. The health department shut down her shop after some government minister got sick from spoiled brie that he'd bought there."

"She got busted by the health department in *Paris?*"

"The French take their cheeses very seriously," Mrs. Winship explained.

"So, does that mean Whitney's coming home?"

"No, Duane, she's not."

"Good," he said.

"In fact, she's filing for divorce."

"That's okay with me."

Mrs. Winship blinked. She wasn't sure she'd heard him correctly.

Duane Sr. said, "There's a lady I intend to ask out on a date. She plays folk guitar at the Unitarian church."

"A haircut and a shave wouldn't hurt your chances," Mrs. Winship suggested.

"D.J. said the same thing."

"You might want to clean up the house, too, in case your guitarist also works for the health department."

"Don't worry," said Duane Scrod Sr. sheepishly.

"And you must definitely get rid of that awful parrot."

"Millie, she's not a parrot!"

Mrs. Winship said, "Just think about it, please."

■ ■ ■ ■

In all the media accounts of the panther episode there was no mention of Twilly Spree, which is how he wanted it. Mrs. Starch and the kids had agreed to leave him out of the story, although his role was not small.

After driving Mrs. Starch to the hospital (and leaving Duane Scrod Jr. to stay with her), Twilly had rushed back to get the two other kids. Sprinting through the Black Vine Swamp, he'd encountered first Horace and then Drake McBride, only one of whom would fit in the helicopter along with Nick and Marta. The dog was the obvious choice.

By the time Twilly reached Nick and Marta, the fog had burned away and the woods were bathed in soft sunlight. The boy's right arm was badly broken and he'd passed out from the pain. The girl hovered beside him protectively, the rifle poised and ready. Twilly had no reason to tell her that he'd removed all the bullets before he left.

Using a crude splint made from a branch, he had stabilized Nick's injured arm. Then, with Marta's help, he'd hoisted the boy on his shoulders and carefully made his way toward the clearing where the chopper would land.

It was there Twilly had spotted the panther trotting a hundred yards ahead of them, carrying her cub toward a thicket of palmettos. Before vanishing, the cat had looked back just once. "Keep on moving, momma," Twilly had urged, under his breath.

After the helicopter had landed, Twilly had strapped Nick inside and told Marta to keep an eye on him. He had no intention of riding back to Naples with them — the authorities would have more questions than he cared to answer. His pilot had been briefed on what to say: that he'd been flying from Miami to Fort Myers when he'd spotted the two kids lost in the Glades.

As for Horace the bloodhound, Twilly had instructed Marta to give him to Duane Scrod Jr., who was already at the hospital with Bunny Starch. Since dogs weren't allowed in the emergency room, Twilly had told Marta to tie Horace to the nearest tree and give him some water.

After the chopper had buzzed away, Twilly had returned to camp and quickly packed his gear. He knew the swamp would be bustling in the coming days — news reporters, wildlife officers, and of course the work crews removing Red Diamond's outlaw drilling equipment.

So Twilly Spree had trekked south through the Big Cypress, crossing Alligator Alley in the black of night and, a few days later, the Tamiami Trail. Zigzagging to avoid several small wildfires, Twilly had plenty of time to think about Drake McBride, whose fate he'd left to chance.

There was a time when Twilly would have dealt more harshly with such a brainless greedhead, inflicting some sort of poetic public humiliation. Instead, he'd just walked away and left the man hollering in the wilderness, unharmed and unshamed. Twilly wondered whether he was going soft, or wising up.

He also found himself thinking fondly of Duane Jr., Marta, and Nick, who'd risked their necks for that little panther cub. The kids were tough and brave and determined to do the right thing, qualities that were often lacking among the grown-ups Twilly knew.

Aunt Bunny Starch was right, he'd mused. Hope springs eternal.

Eventually he hooked up with the Turner River and followed it all the way to the mouth of Chokoloskee Bay, where a small blue canoe had been stashed for him in the mangroves.

Twilly stocked up on food and water at

Everglades City, and he also stopped at the post office to mail something to Nick. Then he loaded the canoe and began paddling through the Ten Thousand Islands with no particular destination. It was an easy place to get lost, which was precisely what he had in mind.

Three weeks after returning from the Walter Reed Army Medical Center, Nick's father announced they were going fishing.

They rode to Chokoloskee through heavy fog, which reminded Nick of the day he'd come face to face with the mother panther. The fog made him think about Twilly, too; the man had dropped completely out of sight. A few days earlier, a plain brown package addressed to Nick had arrived by mail. Inside the package was a book: *Hayduke Lives!* by Edward Abbey. An unsigned note said, *"From your favorite monkey wrencher. We'll meet again."* Nick thought it was one of the coolest presents he'd ever received.

The fishing guide, tanned and bearded, was waiting for the Waters family at the marina. The fog was dissolving, and revealed a clear and cloudless morning. Nick and his parents got into the boat and smeared sunblock on their faces.

The guide headed straight for Chatham Bend, zipping across miles of glassy shallows strewn with tree snags and stumps. He said the tide was perfect for snook and redfish.

When they got there, Capt. Gregory Waters moved to the bow, uneasily contemplating his fly rod.

Nick said, "Go for it, Lefty."

Most fly rods are designed to be held and cast with one hand, while the other hand is used to strip in the line. That's what makes the fly scoot like a minnow through the water, and attracts big fish.

Surgeons at Walter Reed had fitted Nick's father with an artificial right arm equipped with an actual bionic hand. The hand, called an i-LIMB, contained a computer chip that transmitted impulses from the nerves in Greg Waters' damaged shoulder. Amazingly, all five fingers of the bionic hand were able to move, almost as nimbly as real ones.

Nick's father had been practicing left-handed casts every afternoon at a pond near the Truman soccer field. He could now shoot a fly seventy feet through the air, true as a bullet.

Stripping back the slick plastic line is what gave him fits. The artificial hand was protected by a special glove made of silicone, which got slippery. In addition, the mechanical fingers weren't quite coordinated enough to keep a firm grip.

"This could get ugly," Nick's father muttered after a few exasperating tries on the skiff.

"Oh, be quiet and catch us a fish," Nick's mother said.

Nick didn't care if they caught anything or not. He was perfectly happy watching his father sweep the slender rod back and forth, the line carving graceful loops in the pale sky. The snook fly, a white sparkled streamer, would settle so lightly in the water that it scarcely caused a ripple.

Nick's father had several hard strikes, but he couldn't set the hook in time; the reflexes of his artificial hand were too slow. Still, it was much better than having no hand at all.

There would be frustrating times, Nick knew, but in the end his dad was going to be fine. Only the day before, they'd staged a backyard pitching contest. Nick's mom, who'd borrowed a radar gun from a friend on the Naples police force, clocked one of Greg Waters' fastballs at eighty-one miles an hour — not too shabby for a rookie southpaw. Nick's fastest lefty pitch was only fifty-nine, and he'd almost beaned a neighbor's Siamese cat.

447

"Your turn, Nicky. I need a coffee break." His father stepped off the bow and passed him the fly rod.

Nick tried over and over to make a decent cast, but his timing was all messed up. The bulky plaster mold on his right arm didn't help; the clockwork motion of stripping the line was virtually impossible if you couldn't bend your elbow. More often than not, Nick wound up thrashing in a comic tangle of knots, and after twenty minutes he good-naturedly surrendered the fly rod. Throwing a baseball, he declared, was a thousand times easier.

Naturally, his mother caught the first and only fish of the morning. It was a husky ten-pound snook that jumped half a dozen times before the guide netted it.

Said Nick's dad: "We'll never hear the end of this."

By noon a westerly wind had kicked up, so the guide moved the boat to Pavilion Key, staking out on the leeward side. For lunch Nick's mom had fixed smoked turkey sandwiches and an avocado salad, which Capt. Gregory Waters pronounced the best meal he'd ever eaten. When Nick asked what sort of food he got on combat duty, he laughed and said, "It didn't matter. Everything tasted like sand."

The island was spangled with birds — herons, egrets, cormorants, terns, gulls, and even a cluster of white pelicans. The fishing guide said that only a week earlier, he'd seen a big bobcat swimming across the shallows.

Intently Nick scanned the shoreline. "Are there any panthers out here?"

The guide shook his head. "They mostly stay up in the Big Cypress and the Faka-hatchee."

"You ever seen one?" Nick's father asked.

"No, sir, and I was born and raised here. Never laid eyes on one in fifty-four years."

"Nick has," said his mother. "A mother and her kitten."

The guide was impressed. "There ain't hardly any of 'em left to see," he said.

"It was on the news," Nick's mother said proudly. Once she'd learned what he'd done that day, high in the dead pine, she had immediately forgiven him for skipping school.

"I'm 'fraid I don't watch much TV," the guide remarked.

Nick's dad chuckled. "You're not missing a darn thing."

"Can I ask what happened to your arm?"

"I was in Iraq," Capt. Gregory Waters said simply.

"My oldest, he's over there now. I wish he wasn't." The guide took a bite of his sandwich and looked at Nick. "What about you?"

"I fell out of a tree. No big deal."

"I'll bet it was."

"You're right," said Nick's mother. "It was a very big deal."

Another skiff came speeding past, closer to the island. The seabirds exploded from the shore, filling the air like a starburst. Nick spotted something blue way up on the beach, and the guide said it appeared to be a small canoe.

Then he said lunch was over and it was time to go fishing again. He said the two lefties had better get with the program.

ABOUT THE AUTHOR

Carl Hiaasen has been writing about Florida since his father gave him a typewriter at age six. Then it was hunt-and-peck stories about neighborhood kickball and softball games, given away to his friends. Now Hiaasen writes a column for the *Miami Herald* and is the author of many bestselling novels for adults, including *Sick Puppy* and *Nature Girl.*

Hoot, Hiaasen's first novel for young readers, was the recipient of numerous awards, including the prestigious Newbery Honor. And *Flush,* his second book for kids, spent more than a year on the *New York Times* bestseller list.

You can read more about Carl Hiaasen's work at *www.carlhiaasen.com.*